Mary Wollstonecraft

Her Life and Times

Mary Wollstonecraft

Her Life and Times

by

EDNA NIXON

London

J. M. Dent & Sons Ltd

First published 1971
© Edna Nixon, 1971

Made in Great Britain
at the
Aldine Press · Letchworth · Herts
for
J. M. DENT & SONS LTD
Aldine House · Bedford Street · London

ISBN 0 460 03975 x

Contents

List of Plates

between pages 114 *and* 115

Mary Wollstonecraft. From the painting by Sir John Opie in the Tate Gallery

Jean Jacques Rousseau, 1712–78, from the painting of 1766 by Allan Ramsay, in the National Gallery of Scotland. The Mansell Collection

Joseph Priestley, 1733–1804, from the painting by Ellen Sharples in the National Portrait Gallery

John Wilkes, 1727–97, from an engraving after Hogarth. The Mansell Collection

Thomas Paine, 1737–1809, from the portrait by Auguste Millière in the National Portrait Gallery

Thomas Holcroft, 1745–1809, from the painting by Sir John Opie in the National Portrait Gallery

William Blake, 1757–1827, from the painting by Thomas Phillips in the National Portrait Gallery

Madame Roland, 1754–93, at the guillotine. The Mansell Collection

Francis Place, 1771–1854, from the painting by Samuel Drummond in the National Portrait Gallery

Henry Fuseli, R.A., 1741–1825, from the painting by Sir John Opie in the National Portrait Gallery

William Godwin, 1756–1836, from the painting by James Northcote in the National Portrait Gallery

Mary Wollstonecraft, 1759–97, shortly before her death, from the painting by Sir John Opie in the National Portrait Gallery

Acknowledgments

Among the many works consulted in the writing of this book I am specially indebted to Professor Ralph M. Wardle's *Mary Wollstonecraft, A Critical Biography*, 1952. This book has been of the greatest assistance and given me a deep insight into her life.

In 1967 Professor Wardle published under the title *Godwin and Mary* a collection of letters which passed between them in the period July 1796 and August 1797, and which throw additional light on Mary's character during the last year of her life. Her letters reveal the fully mature woman, and those of Godwin a devoted husband who was to draw from her dying lips a final tribute, 'He is the kindest best man in the world.'

A third volume which I have found especially helpful is a study in French by Marthe Severn Storr on *Mary Wollstonecraft et le Mouvement Féministe dans la Littérature Anglaise*, 1931. This account of the pioneer of women's rights gives an aspect of Mary Wollstonecraft which is warmly appreciative and places her work in a European context. Messrs James Nisbet and Company Limited kindly allowed me to quote from *Madame Roland* by Una Pope-Hennessy.

I am also most grateful to Lord Abinger for extending to me the permission to quote from the letters in his possession which were made available to Professor Wardle; and to the Directors of the Bibliothèque Universitaire de Genève and of the British Museum, North Library, for their assistance. Finally my thanks go to my husband for reading the manuscript and for many valuable suggestions.

Chronological Table

1792		Returns to London and works for Joseph Johnson
1792		Mary's *Vindication of the Rights of Woman* published by Johnson
1792		Acquaintance with Thomas Paine, William Blake, William Godwin and Henry Fuseli
1792		Attachment to Fuseli
1792		September Massacres in Paris
1792	*Dec.*	Goes to Paris alone
1793	*Jan.*	The Paris Convention votes on the guilt of the King
1793	*Jan.*	Watches Louis XVI pass by her window on his way to execution
1793		Meets members of the Girondin Government
1793		Godwin's *Political Justice* published
1793	*April*	Meets Imlay in Paris
1793		Occupies a cottage in Neuilly
1793		Registered as Imlay's wife
1793	*Oct.*	22 members of the Girondin Government guillotined
1793	*July*	Charlotte Corday assassinates Marat
1793	*Nov.*	Madame Roland guillotined
1793		Mary and Imlay become lovers
1794		Birth of Fanny Imlay
1794		The Treason Trials in London
1794	*Oct.*	Execution of Marie Antoinette
1794		Imlay leaves Paris for London
1794		*An Historical and Moral View of the French Revolution* published by Johnson
1794	*July*	Robespierre guillotined
1795	*April*	Returns to London
1795	*May*	Attempts suicide
1795	*Oct.*	Second attempt at suicide
1796		*Letters written during a short residence in Sweden, Norway and Denmark,* published
1796	*Jan.*	Renews acquaintance with Godwin
1796	*March*	Final break with Imlay
1796	*Aug.*	Godwin and Mary become lovers
1797	*March*	Marries Godwin
1797	*Sept.*	Dies in childbirth

1

Early Struggles for Independence

Mary Wollstonecraft was born, probably in Spitalfields, in 1759—the same year as William Pitt the Younger. There was Irish blood in both parents. Mary's mother had been born Elizabeth Dixon of Ballyshannon; her father, Edward Wollstonecraft, was the son of a prosperous Spitalfields manufacturer of Irish descent. Edward had recently inherited a fortune of £10,000 from his father—a very large capital sum at that time—and he foresaw an agreeable future for himself as a gentleman farmer, apparently oblivious of the fact that his total ignorance of agricultural matters made this a risky choice of career in a period when far-reaching agricultural changes favoured the expert professional and the big landowner. In addition, Edward's character had several fatal flaws. He was moody and ill-tempered to the point of unbalance—this depressive tendency was to be inherited by several of his descendants—and he made no attempt to learn the skills of the career he had chosen for himself. He had little desire for work, and showed complete lack of staying power in any crisis. At about the time of Mary's birth he bought a small farm in Epping Forest. He already had a son, a good omen for a future that was to be devoted to the land, as he thought, but the birth of Mary did not augur so well, for girls were a liability.

The year 1759 was one of great national rejoicing in England. It was the fourth year of the Seven Years War and England had triumphed in many fields of combat—Quiberon Bay, Minden, Quebec.

For the glory of such victories the people accepted the rise in prices inevitable in any war period, and most of them closed their eyes to the other unpleasant aspects of the times. The Industrial Revolution was as yet barely under way, and most of the social evils it brought with it were yet to come. But already many urban centres, London chief among them, were expanding fast, without any corresponding increase in their basic amenities, and the condition of the poor in the cities was often wretched in the extreme. In general, it is true, living standards were slightly higher than in the previous century, but the rootlessness of city life, coupled with bad living conditions, produced a climate of moral degradation and hopelessness among the urban masses which often found outlets in drunkenness and criminal practices on a large scale.

The birth-rate was high in this period, but the infant mortality rate was also high, although the general death-rate was soon to fall significantly, indicating some improvement, however limited, in living standards. The Poor Law was so designed as to allow no one positively to starve, but its application caused intense misery to many brought within its scope by misfortune rather than intentional vagrancy. Society believed that poverty, squalor and ignorance, whether among town or country workers, were the fault of those who were too lazy to learn the rudiments of industry or agriculture, preferring to drown their sorrows in drink. They therefore deserved no better than they got. Until the Act of 1751 gin was dirt cheap because it was so lightly taxed, and drunkenness in England had become a problem of major proportions. When the tax was raised, beer came back into its own. Gin Lane and Beer Street were the haunts of low pleasure. They also helped to dull any revolutionary impulses which might otherwise have been found at these levels. However, a new industrial middle class, which would seek much of its spiritual inspiration from John Wesley, and help to raise the moral atmosphere in many areas of society, was soon to come into being with the onset of the Industrial Revolution, although its political influence would be negligible until well into the next century.

The eighteenth century has been called the century of Enlighten-ment, which indeed it was, for knowledge in a vast field of inquiry was being collected and arranged in a way that would make it available to all intelligent people. The roots of the French Enlightenment were to be found in England, in Locke's famous essay, *Concerning Human Understanding*, and in Hume's treatises. (It was the *philosophes* of France who were responsible for producing the *Encyclopédie*, an immense compendium of all branches of knowledge, Voltaire and Rousseau being the dominating spirits, Diderot and D'Alembert the main editors.)

In England the century of the Enlightenment coincided in its second half with the age of Scandal. Harsh laws, sometimes corruptly administered (though this happened less frequently in England than in most other countries, largely thanks to the English jury system), inadequate education, even among many of the ruling classes, a grossly uneven and archaic system of parliamentary representation, which was open to every sort of manipulation, almost total absence of social conscience by those in power, the brutality of sensual men uncurbed by a sense of moral decency; such was, to a large extent, the nature of society. The Established Church, the Dissenters—even, to some extent, the Quakers—were entangled in a web of conventional values. The poor were poor because they were incompetent and lazy, and the rich rich because they deserved to be; these were considered good grounds for belief in a Higher Order. Poverty was equated with sin and more than 200 offences were theoretically capital ones, although in practice English juries often refused to convict in many of the more trivial capital cases. As in past centuries, however, human life was considered cheap and public executions ranked as one of the mass entertainments of London and the other big cities.

The century has also been named that of Reason. It was the England of Dr Johnson, Hume, Adam Smith, Wesley, Boswell and Gibbon. Great names crowd upon each other, and one, Tom Paine, made Reason the servant of Revolution. It was a period as variegated as a great nursery garden with its percentage of rare blooms and shrubs and ever-widening spread of weeds. Moreover it was to provide more than one turning-point in the European story.

For England in particular this was a century of tremendous expansion, territorially and economically, and, as usually happens during periods of rapid change, traditional institutions and conceptions were being outgrown, and were breaking down. The time was ripe for an intellectual questioning of existing society—of its political machinery, its moral bases, its social codes—and in England there was a radical tradition going back unbroken to the Civil War and beyond which was already beginning to do this, and of which Mary Wollstonecraft was one day to become a part. England's relatively liberal press laws ensured that what social protest there was be heard; and the parliamentary system, imperfect though it might be, with its reliance on uneven and long outdated constituency boundaries and voting qualifications, did from time to time throw up impressive and eloquent champions of political progress and liberty.

In 1759 France and England were at war and England was winning, but that made little difference to people such as the parents of Mary Wollstonecraft. The economic climate of the time favoured the individual who was prepared to utilize his capital wisely, and work hard and long to make it increase. Unfortunately, Edward Wollstonecraft was the reverse of this. Consequently, his family's life became one long struggle against problems which no victory over the French or brotherly co-operation with Prussia could much affect.

Edward Wollstonecraft's farm in Epping Forest did not prosper. How could it? Not only did the master know little about the soil and its products, but he was quite unversed in the current legislation affecting agriculture. Land enclosure, though it varied in effect in different parts of the country, had helped to raise the cost of land available for sale. Had Edward Wollstonecraft possessed the initiative and common sense to employ the new methods of draining, sowing, manuring and the like which would have made his venture profitable even in this highly competitive period—had he even seen fit to engage a manager who would have done so—his schemes would no doubt have prospered, or at least assured him a reasonable livelihood. At the start, he had the means to do this, but he lacked the will; later, he was to lack both. Like a rat in a field of reapers, he tried to escape disaster by moving from farm to farm; after several years of such uprootings he settled for the next four years in Barking, in 1765.

His fortune had by now greatly diminished and his family had increased; two more girls, Elizabeth and Everina, had been added to the family, and later a fifth child, James. Mrs Wollstonecraft was temperamentally unfitted to deal with such a difficult situation. Her character was weak and indecisive, and she had a husband who despised her. He found it easy to reduce her to tearful slavery, and keep her in total submission. It was easy too to destroy not only her freedom of mind but his own material independence.

Mary was still too young to realize fully the impending ruin, but her affectionate nature found an outlet in care for her sisters and young brother. She became at this early age—for she was not yet nine years old—a deputy for her mother, who was by now ever more weakened and reduced by the demands of a drunken and melancholic husband.

Mrs Wollstonecraft's story was to be one of increasing degradation which, to the dismay of her eldest daughter, she accepted apathetically. The fate of Mary's mother, as gradually realized by the intelligent and sensitive child, was at the root of Mary's attitude towards life. She witnessed the total subjection of a decent woman, mother of young children, and a person whom society should have honoured for her contribution to the community, to a brutal master who showered on her blows and indignities beyond any child's understanding. Mary might keep the younger children out of the way of these domestic brawls, but she could not keep her mind from dwelling on them.

Mary's nature was affectionate and idealistic; even at an early age she showed signs of a mystical bent. She loved to walk alone in the country and converse with God, thus representing to herself an ideal by comparison with which all others revealed their inferiority. In later years, while writing her first novel *Mary, a Fiction* she described her heroine's countryside wanderings:

'Sublime ideas filled her young mind. She would gaze on the moon and ramble through the gloomy paths, observing the various shapes the clouds assumed, and listen to the sea that was not far distant. The wandering spirits which she imagined inhabited every part of nature were her constant friends and confidants. She began to consider the Great First Cause, formed just notions of his attributes, and in particular dwelt on his goodness and wisdom. Could she have loved her father or mother, had they returned her affection, she would not, perhaps, so soon have sought out a new world.'[1]

It needed a strong instinct for life, for belief in the possibilities of progress, to enable her, a precocious child, to watch the daily drama enacted before her eyes and not to despair. What Mary found hardest to accept was her mother's helplessness. The girl herself was not submissive; she discovered that passivity was itself a provocation to a brutal nature. Condonation of past cruelty only led to further cruel acts. Once she had realized the lack of defence of women, children, the sick, the poor, the inarticulate, the luckless and the unloved, such knowledge coloured her thoughts to the end of her days. Like a dark cloud it would drift erratically across the sky of her existence, even on the brightest occasions.

In fact nothing could blot out the effect of those early years when crouching outside her parents' bedroom door she heard the cries, the sound of descending blows, the tramp of feet, the utterances of an inflamed drunkard in the presence of his victim. A repellent drama of the married state was being enacted behind that door. One day she burst in on the scene and confronted her parents—a child in stature but a creature of fire, with glowing eyes and a mass of reddish hair falling over a high forehead. A child whose features expressed horror and from whose lips fell such hot words that the man shrank from her, and from then on began to fear his eldest daughter.

Soon it became obvious that the Barking farm, like that in Epping Forest, would never support the family, and Edward Wollstonecraft, having heard of a property in Yorkshire near Beverley, decided to sell out and try his luck in the north. They moved at Michaelmas 1768 and stayed in Yorkshire for the next six years. For Mary it was a long stationary period which allowed for developments and opportunities of happiness hitherto unknown. Here she was to discover that she could create her own world. Although she attended the local school she was in fact her own educator and began to read avidly. Soon her awakened spirit became dissatisfied with the limited sources of knowledge and the poverty of her human contacts. But for one enlightened soul, a Miss Massey, known to Mary through her school, she had no guide along the ways of learning. She wrote frequently to this lady and treasured the replies she received. She discovered that writing was in itself an important means of self-knowledge, and now began to exploit this gift for setting out the tumultuous mass of ideas and aspirations that were accumulating in her mind.

Beverley was an old town with an ancient church and market-place, set in beautiful countryside. The children loved to ramble over the hills accompanied by their eldest sister, who preferred to pass her time thus rather than play with dolls. But soon she had to give up her rambles to help with the new baby, a third son, Charles, who was to be a charge upon her for many years to come. The new arrival did nothing to reconcile her parents to their lot. The father grew increasingly brutal and Mary spent whole nights sleeping by her parents' bedroom door, ready to intervene in the event of violence. The blows intended for her mother then fell on her, but with different effect. Mary understood life as a struggle in which the weak faced the strong and by some miracle survived. What was that miracle? She could give no clear answer, but for her one fact stood out above all the rest: the imperative need for independence.

As things were then, independence of mind was the sole form open to her, as for most women. Independence of mind, the ability to face life unaided but for the power of understanding, became for her very early on one of the basic principles of existence. Her father was not necessarily cruel by nature, nor her mother stupid, but they had failed to understand, let alone control, the forces that governed their lives. Lacking understanding and lacking education, they were like hard-driven brutes butting their way forward, heads down with unseeing eyes.

She could not love her parents, and at the age of fifteen resolved never to allow herself to fall into the abject position of her mother. Never to marry, for marriage meant servitude, unrelieved and hopeless. She must attain to independence and keep her freedom; this was her first goal in life. But, she reflected, freedom for what? She could not yet formulate the answer, but the protective care she gave her young brothers and sisters, the determination with which she defended her mother, the spirit in which she stood up fearlessly to the family tyrant, exemplified the principles that were going to rule her life. Freedom was the word that dominated her thoughts. To be herself without hindrance, to follow the way of her own understanding, to ask protection of no one, to depend only on the law for her rights. But the law was a most faulty instrument of defence as far as women of the eighteenth century were concerned; their legal rights were almost non-existent. A tremendous campaign lay before her.

When Mary was fifteen the family left Beverley with its moors and natural charms for Hoxton, then a suburb on the outskirts of London, no place for a farmer. But Edward Wollstonecraft had decided to abandon farming for a business venture, which proved to be even less within his competence.

Outwardly, Hoxton had little to recommend it. A commonplace residential area ungraced by any fine architecture, it contained a couple of lunatic asylums, a workhouse, a hospital, an academy for dissenters and rows of unlovely houses. The academy housed one exceptional student, by name William Godwin. But the moment had not yet come for William's and Mary's paths to cross, and what indeed could bring an earnest young student of theology to cast his eyes upon an untidy-looking girl with abundant auburn hair and little else to recommend her, surrounded by a troop of young brothers and sisters?

Although viewed from one angle Hoxton was a mere wilderness of brick and mortar, the fact of its nearness to the capital redeemed its lack of interest. It was the place of residence of a small number of cultured intellectuals without the means to live in the capital but accustomed to some of its amenities. Such were the Clares, an elderly couple occupying a house in the same street as the Wollstonecrafts.

Mr Clare, a retired clergyman, was a cripple who seldom left the house and gave most of his time to study. Mrs Clare was devoted to her husband and more ready than he to take an interest in the neighbours. Yet soon both husband and wife were captivated by the lively Wollstonecraft children, and in particular by the eldest daughter. She could romp as well as any of the others, but her expression betrayed a maturity beyond her years.

Mr Clare recognized in her an eager mind deprived of the substance necessary for its development; inevitably Mary became the recipient of his store of knowledge and affection. In fact Mary became the adopted daughter of the couple, spending whole days and even whole weeks with them. They supplied the sort of parents she had never known, the kindly father endowed with learning, the tender and encouraging mother for whom she longed. It was the beginning of what she understood by the home life that she desired so ardently. The Clares limited their interest to the eldest of the troop, who lost no time in taking advantage to the utmost of Mr Clare's teaching; in fact it was only now that her formal education really began. Under her master's guidance she read widely and cultivated a critical faculty. From the same source, in all probability, she got her grounding in French and German. More important still, she was introduced to an informed selection of French literature and thought, at a most crucial period in that country's history.

Much as life had changed for the better, Mary still lacked companionship of her own kind. She was happy now as never before, since she had at last entered into her own domain, that of the intellect; yet she realized that to advance alone, without means of comparison with someone of like talents similarly situated, deprived her judgment of much of its value. How far her appreciation of the masters of literature, both English and French, was the mere echo of her teacher's views she could not be sure.

It was at this moment that occurred one of the most fruitful contacts of her life. She was now rising sixteen years of age; without vanity, without much that could truly be called education, and without love. Her mother had no conception of her daughter's need. She made use of her to ease her own lot but had no idea of making a relationship of the spirit. They were mother and daughter and Mary owed her unlimited respect and obedience. As for the rest of the family, Mrs Wollstonecraft gathered up all her maternal affection for her eldest son. But Mary understood how unjust to the other children her mother was and already foresaw the family role she would be called upon to play.

One day Mrs Clare invited Mary to accompany her on a visit to friends who lived in Newington Butts, a Mr and Mrs Blood. Mrs Blood and Mrs Wollstonecraft had this in common: both had to nourish and clothe a big family on inadequate means, since both were burdened by drunkards for husbands. And both women had exceptional eldest daughters, outstanding in intelligence and heart.

Fanny Blood was two years older than Mary. She was a gifted girl who could sing, play the spinet, write and draw. Her family responsibilities were even greater than Mary's; for she it was who directed the family in nearly every respect. In her Mary witnessed the first instance of a cultivated young woman exercising her powers, although not in a field that gave them much scope for development. None the less it was Fanny who commanded the household and saw that all its affairs proceeded in the best manner open to them.

All this produced its effect on Mary; for the first time in her short life she was awakened to the meaning of love. Love and admiration for Fanny revealed the depths of her own heart. Fanny became the symbol of growth and advancement. Loving Fanny meant an introduction to rare pleasures beyond Mr Clare's power to bestow: the pleasure of a relationship on her own level; the joys of discovery and sharing; a companionship where heart and mind played equal parts. Introduction to Mr Clare had meant the beginning of Mary's formal education, introduction to Fanny meant the significant start of her personal history of passionate attachments. Into love for Fanny went the first fresh vigour of her ardent nature. To others later on in life she might seem to make a more complete surrender, but never again would she be so wholehearted in devotion, gratitude and hope. It was for her a crisis reached at a very young age. Such a love, untouched by sex, was the beginning of a long discipline of the heart which ended only with her death.

She began to learn from Fanny. Although they could not meet often, they corresponded frequently. Fanny's letters faithfully conveyed her own spirit and Mary studied Fanny's style, tried to copy it but found it difficult to fit her own ideas into this framework. There was one significant difference between the two girls. Fanny's sense of right and wrong did not go far beyond family experience, whereas Mary had already glimpsed a wider field. Her reading, guided by Mr Clare, had shewn her facets of society where inherited wealth and manipulations of the law played a discreditable part.

Mary asked her friend to correct the style and substance of her own writing. Fanny complied, and with these links the two friends were drawn even more closely together.

Mary now desired advantages similar to those enjoyed by her friend. She too must have her own room, a place where she could supplement Mr Clare's teaching by her own efforts. Her parents were outraged by such extravagant demands, but Mary insisted and even threatened to leave home if her wishes were not granted. It was a tribute to her innate qualities of character that the parents recognized in their eldest daughter one superior to themselves. Indeed both were slightly afraid of her, for she had a command of language far surpassing their own and would no longer accept their authority. All this astonished a man in whose idea of domestic order women enjoyed no privileges whatsoever. It was obvious that Mary was soon going to dominate the family, but the parents decided she should pay fully for it. More and more responsibilities were placed on her shoulders. She foresaw that unless she could escape and strengthen her position by pursuing studies which would eventually lead to independence, she would be overwhelmed, much as the brilliant but fragile Fanny was, by carrying burdens far beyond her strength.

After eighteen months at Hoxton Mr Wollstonecraft, reflecting that, unsuccessful though he was, farming was at least a matter in which he had some experience, returned to this means of livelihood. The family left London for a farm in Laugharne, a seaport in Carmarthenshire, in the spring of 1776. At first the change seemed for the better because of the attractive character of the place. There were cliffs and caves, and tales of haunting and romantic adventures which thrilled the children as they explored the beautiful country-side, accompanied at times by their eldest sister, who better than any other member of the family responded to the charms of nature and legend.

But Mary was not happy. Having tasted the delights of intellectual companionship she could not be content with solitary studies; more-over in this new home she was deprived of her own private room.

The farm, alas, did not prosper and Mary, feeling profoundly depressed, decided she must get away and earn her own living, otherwise her life would follow the course of those of her mother and Fanny's mother, doomed to domestic slavery with no hope of the least independence, no possibility of self-education, and, as it happened in her instance, no recognition of her services; no love, no gratitude, only a melancholy acceptance of an irremediable state of affairs. She could not bear it and told her mother she was going to take a situation in a family where at least she would receive some monetary reward.

Mrs Wollstonecraft was appalled at the prospect of losing her main support and persuaded Mary to stay on, since they were on the point of moving again. The farm was to be let to a capable manager and the family would return to England where Mr Wollstone- craft proposed to live on what remained of his capital. Mary, having consented, suggested to her father that he should take a house in Walworth where she would be within easy visiting distance of Fanny.

Again a family upheaval took place without much benefit to anyone. In fact the unrest at home was increased and became quite intolerable to a highly strung girl of nineteen years frustrated in every prospect she cherished. Idealistic and strong-minded as she was she realized her family responsibilities, but could not be blind to her own nature and its urgent desire for expansion.

Mr Wollstonecraft, having given up farming, was at home all day, unoccupied and bored. Drink was his only solace. The children quarrelled more than ever and the mother blamed Mary for the general misery. There was no one else to take the blame, but now Mary repudiated it, knowing full well that as long as she stayed by her mother's side she would be the recipient of endless reproach. She could not stand between husband and wife, and could do noth- ing to eradicate the root cause of the ill. It was useless to incite her mother to rebellion: the blows would only fall the thicker. Mary saw no way out of a situation which was none of her making. It held a terrible lesson: never would she allow herself to become a victim of domestic tyranny. Marriage was an evil trap for women, for the law favoured the convenience of men and gave rein to brutal natures. Every advantage went to the stronger side. The legal bulwark against injustice was faulty, the social angle utterly biased, and the women themselves, if of the upper class, too ignorant, illeducated and comfortable to care; if of the lower, too oppressed, poor and timid to fight a losing battle. Altogether the situation looked hopeless, yet she was convinced she could never fit herself into the present conventional framework of society. The first step was to win her independence.

2

The Horizon Broadens

In Walworth the Wollstonecrafts were within visiting distance of the Bloods, which was a great satisfaction for both Mary and Fanny. The two girls carried like burdens, except that Mr Blood had a far more pleasant character than Mr Wollstonecraft. None the less he also drank away a considerable portion of the family income, which Fanny tried to remedy by selling her paintings and helping her mother with outside laundry work. Mary often helped Fanny in this task and in other ways the tie between the friends was becoming closer. In fact Mary seemed to get on better with the Bloods than with her own family, and one of Fanny's brothers, George, took Mary as his confidante and adviser.

Mary, however, was far from satisfied with the conditions of her life. She knew that it was essential that she should become independent of her family and earn sufficient money for her efforts at self-education to continue. Mrs Wollstonecraft was not sympathetic. She thought Mary owed her first duty to her family and was quite uninterested in ideas concerning the liberation of her sex. She had never been free; she had never known happiness. Her life with a brutal husband had obscured any light of understanding there might have been. As far as the affections went she loved, if what she felt could be termed love and not self-indulgence, only her eldest son Edward, upon whom she poured the whole contents of her heart. Certainly there was none left over for her eldest daughter, whom she reproached for lack of filial duty. But Mary was determined to get free.

She heard of a position as companion to a rich widow living in Bath. Although she knew this meant putting up with the humiliations which were the lot of an upper servant, at least it would give her time for study. It was against the opposition of all her family that she left home for Bath in 1778 and arrived when the season was at its height.

The scenes she witnessed in the streets, the public assembly rooms, the pleasure grounds, the concert halls and theatres were in themselves an education. Here was a display of the pleasures of high society where women dominated the scene, the unmarried seeming to have but one care, to ensnare a rich husband. Here was England's fashionable marriage market. It was a way of life so artificial that she could not witness it without wonder and revolt. Where lay the possibilities of happiness in such a system, she asked herself, at least for any woman with a mind of her own? She herself had had little education and lacked any means of buying her freedom. What chance had she of sharing in the life of the intellect which she thought was the only one worth while?

Her companionship with Mrs Dawson had started well but soon it deteriorated. In truth the rich widow was a bad-tempered old woman, who to revenge herself for the disappointments she had met with in life made her companion's existence unendurable. Mary described her lot in her first book *Thoughts on the Education of Daughters*:

'To live with Strangers who are so intolerably tyrannical that none of their relations can bear to live with them. [She was] above the servants yet considered by them a spy and ever reminded of her inferiority when in conversation with superiors. If she cannot condescend to a mean flattery she had not a chance of being a favourite, and should any of the visitors take notice of her and she for a moment forget her subordinate state, she is sure to be reminded of it.'

Mary's resentment was all the more acute since she knew that mingling in this butterfly society were women of high culture and independence such as she aspired to be. How had they arrived at this enviable position? There was Mrs Elizabeth Montagu, Queen of the Blue Stockings, greatly admired by Dr Johnson; there was Fanny Burney, who had just published her novel *Evelina*, which was everywhere being discussed; and above all there was the historian, Mrs Catherine Macaulay, the friend of Dr Johnson, Walpole, Hume and Pitt. Pope's dictum, 'A perfect woman is but a softer man', was often heard in the drawing-rooms. In the theatre Mrs Siddons, later to become one of Mary's closest friends, was having a season of enormous success.

Yet even among these eminent successful women were those who held views quite divergent from Mary's. For instance, Mrs Chapone, friend of Dr Johnson and Samuel Richardson, expressed the following opinions in a letter to a newly married lady published at about this time:

> 'I believe that a husband has a divine right to the absolute obedience of his wife in all cases where the first duties do not interfere; and that as her appointed ruler and head, he is un-doubtedly her superior.
>
> 'I believe it expedient that every woman should choose for her husband one whom she can heartily and willingly acknowledge her superior and whose judgment and understanding she can prefer to her own.
>
> 'Notwithstanding this acknowledged superiority of right of command, I believe it mightily conducive and to delicate minds absolutely necessary to conjugal happiness, that the husband have such an opinion of his wife's understanding, principles and integrity of heart as would induce him to exalt her to the rank of his first and dearest friend.'

Mary remembered the sound of blows raining down on her mother's back; herself intervening between a cowed woman and a cruel man; her mother's utterly dreary life, lacking all means of defence, justice or hope; and asked herself how could any woman accept submission to a superior being, 'one whose judgment and understanding she can prefer to her own'. It was nonsense, written by someone who had no experience of the true nature of men and women. People read it and believed these were ideals to be blindly followed. Mary's mind seethed with the desire to reveal the full extent of women's subjection, and force a remedy upon society. She knew of course that there existed happily married women who were protected by decent, generous-minded men, good husbands, good fathers to their children; and how enviable were the women married to such paragons! But even their power rested where it should not rest, on one alone of the two contracting parties. This she considered was one root of the trouble. Although the matter was of importance to women throughout the world, for the time being she would concentrate her studies upon her sisters in England and France.

Mary had wished to put a distance between herself and her family temporarily, but she was far from shirking responsibility towards various members of it, the most important of whom was her mother, now seriously ailing. She wrote to her sister Eliza from Windsor whither she had accompanied Mrs Dawson on a short visit. Her younger sister Everina was also ill. Obviously the family had not prospered in her absence. Moreover the feckless father had again changed the place of residence to Enfield. Mary's letter was in reply to one Eliza had written accusing her sister of indifference and condescension.

'There is an air of irony through your whole epistle that hurts me exceedingly. . . . I hate formalities and compliments, one affectionate word would give me more pleasure than all the pretty things that come from the head but have nothing to say to the heart. . . . As to Everina's illness, my Father only mentioned it in a careless manner to me and I did not imagine it had been so bad. . . . You don't do me justice in supposing I seldom think of you, and the happiness of my family is nearer my heart than you imagine—perhaps too near for my own health and peace. For my anxiety preys on me and is of no use to you. You don't say a word of my mother. I take it for granted she is well—tho' of late she has not even desired to be remembered to me.'

Mary's state of mind is revealed in this letter. She longed for affection and at the same time feared the ties it entailed. Her mother had never loved her, and her sisters were highly critical without understanding her. To none of them could she confide the turn of her thoughts and her ambition to escape into the world of larger issues. She decided to visit her family but to keep an avenue of escape open. 'Pray make my love and duty acceptable to every part of the family—and beg them all to receive me with smiling faces—for I cannot bear frowns or sneers.'[1]

However, very soon the position became beyond frowns or sneers, for her mother was dying and insisted upon being nursed by none other than her eldest daughter. It was to Mary, to whom she had shown so little motherly affection, that the unhappy woman now appealed, knowing well that her cry would not go unheard. Mary had written in a letter to a friend, 'I think I love most people best when they are in adversity: for pity is one of my prevailing passions';[2] and pity it was that now sent her rushing back to Enfield and her mother's bedside.

Mrs Wollstonecraft's last illness was long and most trying for the one who nursed her. The husband did nothing to help; he was constantly in the way and resented his wife's condition when it came between him and his pleasure. As before, Mary tried to pacify her father, and was banished from the room; as before, she waited outside the door and intervened when she considered her mother could bear no more. It was a time of inexpressible misery, but at least Mrs Wollstonecraft became aware of the daughter's devotion and showed a late appreciation of the one being who had brought some light into the gloom of her married life. 'A little patience and all will be over,' she murmured when dying, words that never faded from Mary's memory. The sadness of her mother's life and death added force to the ideas that were simmering in the mind of the young student of social conditions, whose work had been abruptly disturbed by this event.

As soon as the funeral was over the family dispersed. Edward the eldest boy was a lawyer, married and living in London; Charles, a third son, who was articled to him, shared his home. Everina the youngest girl also joined Edward and took upon herself most of the housekeeping. James had become a sailor and proposed to go on a voyage to the New World, where he hoped to prosper and restore the family fortunes. Eliza made a bid for happiness by marrying a Mr Bishop.

Mary, worn out by nursing her mother, could not face life with Mrs Dawson at Bath any more. Temporarily she took refuge with the Bloods at Walham Green. The two friends still rivalled each other in their efforts at self-education, but Mary had acquired the wider experience of life. She had lived in lonely villages, in big cities and in fashionable resorts; she had observed the people who lived there and studied their ways of life; she had reflected on their situation in the social pyramid; all of which gave her much food for thought. Having excelled Fanny in experience her character had grown in breadth and resolution. Both girls had suffered set-backs, but whereas Mary refused to give in, Fanny, the more fragile both physically and mentally, was beginning to show signs of exhaustion. Mary now took the lead in the Blood family as once she had taken it in her own home.

All this time she had continued to read French and German and had acquired a good working knowledge of the first. Rousseau was among those French authors who most impressed her. He had died in 1778 and now, two years later, his renown had grown even greater. He was known personally to radical circles in London, for Hume had offered him a refuge in England from persecution for his subversive ideas. Two of his books, *Julie, ou la Nouvelle Héloïse* and *Le Contrat Social*, written at about the time of Mary's birth, were widely read by educated people of liberal views. The two friends, who themselves aspired to be so classed, found much there to stimulate their minds, certain ideas of which they strongly approved and others as strongly disapproved. Rousseau professed little respect for women in any sphere but the maternal. His ideas about female education could scarcely have differed more widely from Mary's.

Societies and clubs advocating political and economic reform were multiplying in England at this time and Mary was beginning to discover along which paths she must go forward. She decided that the crux of the problem, her own and that of society at large, was education: its nature, organization and availability to both poor and rich, and above all to that half of the population—the female— hitherto deprived of its benefits.

Mary was receiving from life a preparation which surpassed that of most young people of her time.

'Fatigued,' she wrote many years later, 'during my youth by the most arduous struggles, not only to obtain independence but to render myself useful, not merely pleasure, for which I had the most lively taste—I mean the simple pleasures that flow from passion and affection,—escaped me, but the most melancholy views of life were impressed by a disappointed heart on my mind.'[3]

True as this was she was none the less steeling herself for a future of strife, exercising, by the writing of many letters, her chief weapon, the pen. She urgently needed the companionship of her own kind, of those liberal writers whose outpourings in the press and in pamphlets were the echoes of her own thoughts.

During the two years Mary spent with the Bloods at Walham Green she participated fully in the bitter struggle of a decent family to keep its head above water. In 1780 the cost of living had risen again considerably as one consequence of the Seven Years War and the American War of Independence. High taxation particularly afflicted the poor; rural and urban labourers had no redress against miserable pay and conditions of work. Parliamentary representation was open to corruption and manipulation. Ten years previously John Wilkes had fought a stubborn battle to be admitted to a seat in Parliament to which he had been elected four times. Economic reform, which radicals were beginning to consider essential, depended upon a strong and incorruptible administration. Thomas Paine, a writer after Mary's own heart, had recently published a republican pamphlet of great force called *Common Sense*. Burke's parliamentary efforts for economic reform and the Duke of Richmond's for manhood suffrage were of this date. The spirit of democracy was active in England and it found an echo in the heart and mind of Mary Wollstonecraft.

The Blood family found it impossible to keep out of debt. Mrs Blood, assisted by her daughter, was a pathetic slave to her needle. Fanny described their labours in a letter she wrote to one of Mary's sisters. 'My mother used to sit at work in summer from four in the morning till she could not see at night, which with the assistance of one of her daughters did not bring her more than half a guinea a week and often not quite that.'[4] Needless to say Mary was not idle during these interminable hours. Fanny describes her as being blinded and sick to death on one occasion of protracted work. Even so the family was insolvent and Mary had to borrow £20 from Eliza's husband without which it would have collapsed. The head of the family, finding himself incapable of meeting the situation, took increased refuge in drink. He was not a cruel tyrant in the manner of Mary's father, but he lacked energy and saw no outcome to the unequal struggle. Alcohol was the only answer.

Mary's long stay with the Bloods gave her a deeper insight into Fanny's character, which was not as perfect as she had at first understood it. Fanny was irresolute; she could not share Mary's schemes of rebellion; in fact she was no fighter. As this was borne in on Mary she realized that henceforth she must take the lead. A little later she discovered the main reason for Fanny's irresolution. She was in love and hoped to be asked in marriage. Marriage! that dangerous state of subjection, that trap for ignorant young women who could not apparently believe the evidence of their eyes! Yet, in her heart, Mary understood. She herself ardently desired a partner in life, someone to love even more than to be loved by, yet for women with no dowry that was hardly to be hoped for. It was useless to go over the old arguments with Fanny, and for the moment there was no need, since the man in question, a Mr Hugh Skeys, was reluctant to come to a decision. Fanny, whose affections were deeply engaged, began to languish. Unless Mr Skeys soon made up his mind it seemed she might go into a decline.

This matrimonial problem was accompanied by another nearer home. Eliza's marriage to Mr Bishop had reached a serious crisis. She had given birth to a daughter and now her mind had become unhinged. Possibly this was a basic post-natal depression made abnormal by a naturally neurotic nature—part of the Wollstonecraft inheritance. Time and affectionate care might well have brought a solution. However, Eliza succeeded in convincing Mary that she had been so unhappy during this first year of marriage that she had taken a profound dislike to her husband, an unimaginative but not deliberately cruel man; his mere presence destroyed her self-control. If she was ever to recover her balance of mind it was imperative to find another home for her.

Mary was overburdened by these domestic tragedies in the lives of people so near to her. She felt they could have been avoided if these young women had possessed greater understanding. Fanny, for instance, had never realized where to place her confidence. 'In everything,' she wrote, describing her friend, 'it was not the great but the beautiful or the pretty that caught her attention. In composition the polish of style interested her much more than the flight of genius or abstracted speculation.' Fanny, more artist than philosopher, could not understand why her friend spent so much valuable time in study of authors 'whose words were addressed to the understanding'. In Fanny's opinion it was not understanding that counted but feelings.

Eliza's troubles were more fundamental; moreover she lacked all power of self-analysis. The one thing she was sure about was the necessity to get out of the reach of her husband, who had become positively abhorrent to her. Even if it meant abandoning her baby, she must get away. Mary described her condition in a letter to Everina. 'Her ideas are all disjointed and a number of wild whims float in her imagination and unconnected fall from her—something like strange dreams when judgment sleeps and fancy sports at a fine rate.'

In these somewhat stilted lines Mary seems to be experimenting with her powers of expression. Deeply concerned as she was with all this misery, she was as much concerned to record it in the appropriate words. Writing to Everina she expressed herself thus: 'May my habitation never be fixed among the tribe that ... draw fixed conclusions from general rules—that attend to the literal meaning only, and because a thing ought to be, expect that it will come to pass.'[5] In the instance of Eliza's unhappy marriage—of any unhappy marriage—it was not sufficient to apply the general rules of domestic peace. General rules could never ensure justice; each case called for individual attention. Eliza was being driven out of her mind by her husband, therefore Eliza must break the general rule whatever the verdict of society. The fault lay in the conjunction of many circumstances, chief among which was women's ignorance of the world, of men and of themselves. The whole structure of society was responsible for unhappy marriages. To witness in Eliza's ruined life another such as her mother's had been was more than Mary could contemplate and she therefore felt bound to intervene.

Eliza wrote to her brother Edward begging for hospitality, but he refused to be associated with the revolt of a woman leaving her husband. As a lawyer it would damage his reputation; it was altogether out of the question. Mary was now staying with the Bishops and running the household. Apart from all else she was not in Bishop's good books since she had repaid only five out of the twenty pounds she had borrowed. The situation was becoming increasingly difficult and Eliza's condition worsened accordingly.

Mary was at her wits' end when she received a visit from Fanny; they were able to discuss at length what could be done to prevent Eliza from falling into complete insanity. Finally they decided to abduct her, but first they must find a refuge. Money of course was lacking; the capital possessed by the two sisters was no more than three guineas. However, the plotters were not deterred. On a day when they knew Mr Bishop was going to be absent Fanny came and took away the sisters' belongings in a conveyance to deposit them at the house of a brushmaker in the Strand. Then Mary, having found lodgings in Hackney, departed with Eliza in another conveyance. On the journey Eliza bit her wedding ring to pieces in terror and they arrived at their destination in a state of mingled triumph and despair; none the less they inhaled the breath of freedom from which Mary at least drew her strength. She wrote hopefully to Everina: 'All these disorders will give way in time, and the thought of having assisted to bring about so desirable an event will ever give me pleasure to think of.' For a while her mood stayed on this hopeful level and she wrote again: 'The mind of man is formed to admire perfection and perhaps our longing after it and the pleasure we take in observing a shadow of it is a faint line of that Image that was first stamped on the soul.'

The adverse opinion of friends and Eliza's longing for her baby began to lower the moral temperature. Mr Bishop called on Edward /

23

Wollstonecraft and asked him to compel his sister to return home. Edward refused to intervene; much as he disapproved of Mary's bold action, he had no wish to be involved in a contest for Eliza's possession, for he knew his eldest sister was immovable once convinced she was following a right course. To persuade and aid a woman to leave her rightful lord was a serious action which might have grave consequences. Mary should have thought things out much more carefully before acting. But this was not Mary's way. Her instinct for what she considered right was so strong that no further consideration seemed necessary. Everything was against women who found themselves in the position of Mary's mother and sister: the law, the Church, public opinion and women's morbid sense of duty and guilt. All these would condemn her action in rescuing Eliza, but she persisted. Women, though treated as slaves, were *not* slaves and must struggle for their freedom, as other submerged members of society were preparing to do.

To be sure there were some women writers who showed concern about this matter; the Blue Stockings, for instance. Mrs Elizabeth Montagu, the 'Queen of the Blues', was considered by Dr Johnson as the most learned woman in England. She had suggested to Mrs Barbauld, author of the successful novel *A Simple Life*, the foundation of a College for Young Girls with Mrs Barbauld as Directress, but the latter refused the honour. She considered that women needed only as much education as would make them agreeable companions to cultivated men; too much education would not contribute to women's happiness. There was Mrs Catherine Macaulay, who ten years later was to write her famous *Letters on Education*. She urged parents to give their daughters the same education as they gave their sons. There were Fanny Burney and Hannah More, both outstanding women. But all of them lived on a much higher social level than the Wollstonecraft sisters and Fanny Blood. Fanny Burney, when she published her novel *Camilla* in 1796, received £2,000 for it and in 1814 £7,000 for *The Wanderer*. Such sums were unheard of by less fortunate sisters of the pen, who had great difficulty in reaching the first rung of the ladder. Like most of the Blue Stockings, Fanny Burney was uninterested in the economic condition of women. She failed to appreciate the root cause of feminine insecurity. It was argued that a woman lacking a husband could always get occupation as a governess; that she was ill paid and ill prepared for the work by lack of education did not enter into the question.

Hannah More had strong opinions on women as long as they did not interfere in politics and were guided by religion. She promoted the Charity Schools, encouraged by her friend the philanthropist Wilberforce. The instruction given at these institutions was along traditional lines and did little to elevate the feminine position. She supplemented this work by the organization of Benefit Societies which gave financial assistance to poor women during sickness and pregnancies. Without doubt she was an enlightened thinker but she did not touch upon the fundamental cause of much feminine misery.

And so it was with all the emancipated women of that time. In Mary's opinion they had small claim to the title and she considered that most women in society were 'great fools'. They lacked a valuable asset which she possessed: first-hand experience of the unfair circumstances that shackled women, married or single, in the struggle of life. This had been vouchsafed to her in plenty and had served to stimulate her exceptional powers of expression, which she continued to cultivate by daily practice.

Some old friends made an attempt to influence the sisters. Mrs Clare of Hoxton offered money and cautious advice. Hugh Skeys, the man whom Fanny Blood loved, got in touch with Bishop and tried to bring about a reconciliation between husband and wife. But in this he got no encouragement from Mary, who was convinced the marriage could come to no good. She wrote in self-righteous vein to Everina:

> 'Though we declare in general terms that there is no such thing as happiness on Earth yet it requires severe disappointments to make us forebear to seek it and be contented with endeavouring to prepare for a better state. . . . The cant of weak enthusiasts has made the consolations of Religion and the assistance of the Holy Spirit appear to be inconsiderate and ridiculous . . . but it is the only solid foundation of comfort that the weak

efforts of reason will be assisted and our hearts and minds corrected and improved till the time arrives when we shall not only see perfection but see every creature about us happy.'

It is hard to believe that Mary in this bland, imperceptive mood could bring much comfort to the distracted Eliza, bereft of her child, penniless and prevented from taking advantage of Hugh Skeys's proposals for a reconciliation with her husband.

Bishop now gave up hope of regaining his wife. He restored her baby to her and accepted the break-up of his marriage, without making any offer of financial help. This was Mary's responsibility, for she it was who had finally dissolved the little family. But Mary had no misgivings. She was twenty-four years of age and convinced that she had acted for the best for all concerned. As for the burdens she had taken upon herself, they seemed well within her capacity to carry. It was a matter of seeing straight, then getting to work.

Her first idea was to set up a haberdashery with the help of Eliza and perhaps Fanny, who was still awaiting a proposal of marriage from Hugh Skeys. But the idea of a shop did not appeal to Fanny, who was in ill health; one way or another Mary was forced to the conclusion that her friend lacked fortitude. Finally the idea of a shop gave way to one of opening a school in North London.

A legal separation for the unhappy Eliza having been arranged, Mary, Fanny and Eliza were now at liberty to work out their salvation. At first they rented a house in Islington where the Bloods lived, but the scheme did not prosper and soon they moved to Newington Green, a more agreeable and progressive area. Almost immediately they acquired about twenty pupils and in addition took in lodgers.

At first all went well. Mary was a brilliant teacher, with a far wider background of experience and book knowledge than most of her kind. She was immediately recognized as a valuable adjunct to the neighbourhood, not only by the parents of the children but by many other residents. She grew in spiritual stature. The children became devoted to her; she was so patient, so understanding of their difficulties, so ready to put all her gifts at their disposal. With success her appearance improved and one way or another she acquired local renown, making interesting friends right and left.

Among the most important of these was Dr Richard Price, a Dissenting minister of remarkable gifts, a friend of Joseph Priestley, the famous natural philosopher. For Mary to have made such contacts at this stage of her development was an education in itself. Dr Price attracted an enlightened congregation at his chapel by virtue of his powerful mind and imagination. He was a Fellow of the Royal Society and was recognized as an authority on financial and scientific matters. His pamphlets on the American War of Independence made him famous. He was a man of conscience, much concerned with religious and political problems. At the time Mary moved to Newington Green he was sixty years old and at the height of his powers. A few years previously he had published *Observations on the Nature of Civil Liberty*, and *Justice and Policy of the War with America*, which sold 60,000 copies and brought him great renown. He was one of the first authorities in England on finance, and had contacts with the leading thinkers of the day, among whom were Hume, Priestley, Franklin and Condorcet.

He preached in a modest little chapel on Newington Green and most of what he uttered found an echo in Mary's mind. After chapel she would at times walk back to the minister's home and keep company for a while with his invalid wife. Talk with the Prices had a wide range; literature, politics, ethics were closely examined. He introduced her to the instruments in his laboratory: the telescope, microscope and electrical inventions of recent date. The tone of discussion was detached and tolerant—truly scientific, although at that time the term was held to be vulgar. From him Mary learnt a necessary lesson in intellectual humility and some of her overweening self-confidence evaporated. Brilliant as Dr Price was he did nothing to discourage his followers by forcing the contrast with his own eminence. As Mary observed in a letter, he was 'heavenly minded' and formed her spirit in a way that endured for life.

Joseph Priestley, Fellow of the Royal Society, was a Unitarian; that is to say he denied the divinity of Christ, and repudiated dogma; he attacked ignorance and prejudice where he found them. He lacked enthusiasm, believing it to be a state of mind which favoured

side-tracking the truth. Reason was to be the only light leading to
the heights of wisdom. He believed in a humanity which is reasonable, a Nature which is reasonable and God who is reasonable. None
of this made him popular and he was accused of robbing the poor
of the consolations of religion. A few years later he was to express
strong approval of the French Revolution, which provoked such
angry opposition that his chapel and house were burnt down. Mary
was to meet Joseph Priestley when he came to live in London; at
the moment she felt the force of his mind and personality through
the contact she had with Dr Price.

Another member of Price's circle to affect Mary's existence was
the Anglican, the Reverend Joshua Waterhouse, a resident of St
Catharine's College, Cambridge. He was young, handsome and well
dressed, without doubt the most attractive member of his sex that
Mary had so far encountered. She fell in love with him and soon
they were exchanging long letters. They both knew Bath, although
he viewed the society there from a very different angle from hers;
he had been one of that fashionable sophisticated crowd which she
had castigated in her letters. For the time being, however, she was
strongly attracted by this elegant man of quality who for a while
reciprocated her feeling. Although he had little else beyond his
agreeable appearance and genial manners to recommend him this
was exactly what she needed to sweeten her recent sad experiences
of life. But all too soon the incompatibility of their natures began to
make itself felt.

This cheerful period in Newington Green did not last. The first
break in it was brought about by the reawakening of Hugh Skeys
to the charms of Fanny Blood, who had so patiently awaited his
proposal. It came now just when the friends were doing well and
needed time to stabilize their position. Mary distrusted Hugh Skeys,
who had dallied for three years before making up his mind, years of
tortured hopes for Fanny which had not improved her delicate
health—by now she appeared to be in the early stages of tuber-
culosis.

Although Mary feared this union for her dearest friend, she could
not discourage it, knowing as she did how long and hopefully Fanny
had awaited it; to turn away now was more than anybody could

expect of her, especially as Skeys was still hesitant and more than once postponed the date of marriage. He had business in Portugal and it was to this country he proposed to take his bride; the two friends were going to be widely separated. Mary, by now increasingly apprehensive, wrote to Fanny's brother George: 'I have lost all relish for life and my almost broken heart is only cheered by the prospect of death.' There was more than Fanny's departure and doubts about Mr Waterhouse's sincerity to reduce her to such a state of misery. The school did not prosper as well as it had promised at first; pupils fell off, some omitted to pay the fees, the paying guests departed, Eliza's help was insufficient and Mary was seriously overworked. She swayed in her moods from one extreme to another and when she wrote of being 'cheered by the prospect of death' she meant it at the time of writing. But then these depressions would give way to a more hopeful frame of mind and she would struggle on.

A few months later news came that Fanny was expecting her first child. She was still far from well and longed for Mary to be with her at the time of the birth. So Mary began to make the necessary arrangements. She was able to put the school in the charge of a Mrs Burgh (wife of the liberal writer James Burgh), another kind friend in Newington Green, who moreover undertook to lend her money.

Mary's devotion to Fanny was rooted in a love greater than she felt for any member of her own family. They were more than sisters in blood, they were sisters in experience and hope. What made one of them happy made the other equally so, and the same was true of unhappiness. 'Without someone to love,' Mary wrote to George, 'this world is a desart [sic] to me.'[6] Now that the friends were separated by many miles of sea and land the desire to be together was stronger than ever before.

Mary sailed for Portugal in the autumn of 1785. The voyage was extremely rough; luckily she was a good sailor and could help less fortunate passengers. As she wrote to her sisters: 'The water came in at the cabin windows and the ship rolled about in such a manner it was dangerous to stir.'[7] She went without sleep to nurse a man who appeared to be dying. 'I have supported him hours together gasping for breath. I never expected he would live to see Lisbon.'

It was a very weary Mary who arrived at her friend's house just at the time of Fanny's labour. Four hours later a son was born, but the mother was desperately weak and Mary almost lost hope of her recovery. Yet she survived the night and next day there was a small improvement. Mary rejoiced with trembling lips, but later the exhausted woman collapsed and died in her friend's arms.

This was for Mary the cruellest blow of her life. Fanny had been closer to her heart than any other being in the world. They were fellow pilgrims making their way forward over rough ground, at first Fanny leading, then Mary. They had always been faithful to each other. The uncertain nature of Hugh Skeys's love for his wife, if love it could be called, made a poor contrast with the long years of devoted friendship. Fanny would never be dead as far as Mary was concerned; they were too intimately linked from the earliest years. Fanny had been the living symbol of Mary's aspiration. The gentle, clever Fanny, who with but a modicum of assistance from society might have graced the ranks of the artists and scholars of the day! The Blue Stockings' Clubs knew nothing of her existence, but it was the life and death of Fanny Blood, standing for many others of her kind, which drove home to Mary the injustice of the system under which women were obliged to exist. It was merely a matter of luck whether they ever survived with honour.

3

In Ireland. Contact with the Nobility

During her three weeks' stay in Portugal Mary was very much impressed by the contrast in the conditions of the rich and the poor, which surpassed anything she had experienced in England. The ruins of the great earthquake of 1755 still cluttered the streets, rank with the filth of daily living. Clouds of flies hovered over everything, spreading disease. Yet Lisbon viewed from the ship on entering the port had seemed, with its clustering white buildings, to be a vision of delight. Delight there was but it was limited to the very few; the majority of people lived a debased existence. She put the blame largely on the influence of the Roman Catholic Church, which was in a corrupt state in Portugal at this time, with its stress on obedience to a clergy almost as ignorant as the flocks they led.

She described what she saw in her first novel *Mary*:

'The Portuguese are certainly the most uncivilized nation in Europe. . . . The gross ritual of Romish ceremonies is all they can comprehend: they can do penance but not conquer their revenge or lust. . . . Taste is unknown. Gothic finery and unnatural decorations which they term ornaments are conspicuous in their churches and dress. Reverence for mental excellence is only to be found in a polished nation.'

She could hardly bear to witness the misery of the poor, and the attitude of women of all classes of society towards the lascivious

31

advances of men shocked and astonished her. It was, she thought, a survival of the *mores* of the Middle Ages, when well-bred women not only did not resent the assaults upon their virtue but seemed offended if they did not have the opportunity to fend them off. What did all this mean? How did it fit in with her standards of male and female behaviour in an ideal society such as she cherished: equality of treatment, reform of the law, economic freedom and general decency? England, she perceived, was in the vanguard, much as she might be lacking in social justice. The world across the seas presented a more disturbing spectacle to her eyes than she could ever have believed.

Soon after Fanny was buried the baby died. There was little to keep Mary in Portugal and she prepared herself to face the long journey back. The voyage took a month and was even more stormy than the previous one. An exciting incident broke the monotony. They encountered a French vessel in difficulties, and the captain of the ship in which they travelled refused to take on extra passengers because of the shortage of food. Mary intervened and pointed out it was impossible to let these people perish. Unless the captain relented and took them on board she would report him. The passengers were rescued. Doubtless Mary became most unpopular on the bridge but that meant nothing to her. Desperate people had to be succoured; the world had been squeezed like a hard orange and yielded a few drops of sweet juice.

At the end of her voyage nothing but further cares awaited her. Some of the lodgers had departed without paying their bills. Everina, her sister who had left the shelter of her brother's home to help run the school, had proved unequal to the task. A large payment for rent was due, and now that Fanny was dead her parents looked to Mary to shoulder some of their financial responsibilities. The load was almost too heavy for her to carry.

Back again in Newington Green she found the school in even greater straits than she had supposed. George Blood suggested she should not attempt to meet the situation but escape to Ireland and join him there, leaving her sisters and his parents to fend for themselves. This way out she would never consent to take, but she was prepared to unload George's parents onto his shoulders.

'Nothing would induce me to fly from England,' she wrote.

'My creditors have a right to do what they please with the school. I am not able to satisfy their demands. ... Your father and mother have been a continual weight on my spirits. You have removed part of the load, for now I hope you would be able to keep them from perishing should my affairs grow desperate.'

Mary decided that she and her sisters could no longer make their living by running a school. She looked around for other ideas and received help from another good friend at Newington Green, the Reverend John Hewlett. An acquaintance of the well-known publisher and bookseller, Joseph Johnson, of St Paul's Churchyard, publisher of some of the most outstanding authors of the time, including Coleridge, he strongly advised her to try and make money by writing, and promised to send her manuscript to Joseph Johnson.

With this encouragement she began to work on her first book to be called *Thoughts on the Education of Daughters*, a series of short essays with headings such as *Moral Discipline, Artificial Manners, Fashionably Educated and left without a Fortune, On the Misfortune of Fluctuating Principles*. The author's intention was to awaken parents to the dangers of the low grade of education they were prepared to give their daughters and the consequences of such a skinflint policy.

The little work in which she expressed ideas won from her own experience of life earned the good opinion of Joseph Johnson, who was to become one of her most faithful friends. That she so frequently attached to her men of outstanding qualities of heart and mind, although she stood in some danger of being labelled an enemy of the strong sex, gives proof of the sincerity of her nature and power of attraction. She possessed that rare quality, personal magnetism, which drew to her men who might otherwise have resented her outspoken criticism of alleged masculine superiority. At twenty-seven years she was becoming beautiful. Time was adding to her charms, the habit of thought having given a noble cast to her features. The mobile lips expressed courage and imagination, the broad forehead high intelligence.

The book does small justice to the truth of her nature. At this point she was much exercised in her mind about the effects of passion. 'I think,' she wrote, 'there is not a subject that admits so little of reasoning as love.'[1] Perhaps the fact that she herself had failed to master her strong feelings in this respect made her over-puritanical on the subject. 'The main business of our lives is to learn to be virtuous,' she wrote. Yet she had never forgotten handsome young Waterhouse:

> 'A young mind looks round for love and friendship but love and friendship fly from poverty; expect them not if you are poor. The mind must then sink into meanness and accommodate itself to its new state, or dare to be unhappy. Yet I think no reflecting person would give up the experience and improvement they have gained to have avoided the misfortunes; on the contrary they are thankfully ranked among the choicest blessings of life, when we are not under their immediate pressure.'[2]

Mr Johnson bought the manuscript for £10, which she promptly presented to the Blood parents to pay their fare to Ireland, where their son George offered hospitality. *Thoughts on the Education of Daughters* was published in 1787, sold well, and was eventually translated into several languages.

It was now urgent to find a means of livelihood. The choice was miserably restricted; inevitably she decided upon being a governess, but on a higher level than her sisters. Through all the perturbations of recent years she had persisted with her study of the French language, and the reading of radical and progressive writers of the day, both English and French. First of these was Rousseau, whose *Émile* greatly impressed her. Of him she wrote: 'He was a strange, inconsistent, unhappy, clever creature yet he possessed an uncommon portion of sensibility and penetration', words which to a certain measure she could have applied to herself. But there was an aspect of his teaching she was later to repudiate with all the power of her pen. '*Les femmes,*' he wrote, '*doivent avoir du goût sans études, des talents sans art, du jugement sans connaissances ... et leur éducation ne doit être ni brillante ni négligée.*'

She was always positive in her views and had no qualms about the unapproachable heights of genius. All heights could be scaled, she thought, with the help of Reason. 'I am sick of hearing of the sublimity of Milton, the elegance and harmony of Pope, and the original untaught genius of Shakespeare,' she wrote. It was Reason and Reason alone that could light the way forward. In this she was at one with Tom Paine, whom she had not yet met but who was going to have, along with Rousseau, the same vitalizing effect. Rousseau and Paine were new men and Mary was a new woman. Paine was conscious of the prison of class and ignorance in which the poor were confined, and dedicated himself to their liberation, just as Mary was to dedicate herself with equal vigour and passion to the freeing of women. At this moment Paine was in America, where he had recently published a collection of essays on such subjects as *Slavery, Duellings, The Treatment of Animals* and *Marriage and Divorce*. The last comprised many of the arguments that were then foremost in Mary's mind.

The school having been disbanded, Mary was living in lodgings and doing her best to discharge her debts, making a little money by coaching the few scholars who had remained faithful to her. Her rigid economies imposed a restricted life and her spirits fell. 'I am sick of everything under the sun,' she wrote in a moment of depression which did not last or prevent her active mind from making efforts to improve matters.

One of her friends, a Mrs Prior, was the wife of a master at Eton, and through him Mary heard of a position in Ireland where she would receive a salary on which she could save to pay her debts. The proposal was to be governess to the children of Lord Kingsborough of Mitchelstown, County Cork. She was to have £40 a year, for those days a not ungenerous salary.

Mrs Burgh, the friend who had financed the journey to Portugal, now found a new situation for Eliza at a boarding-school at Market Harborough. Everina returned to her brother's house, where she was most unhappy. 'If you possibly can, try and exert yourself,' Mary wrote to her. 'Those you are with· are the merest earth worms.' So much for Mary's opinion of her eldest brother! It is not surprising she was not popular in that quarter, but she could take that in her stride. As for her creditors, once she could promise to give them sums of money at regular intervals she would no longer have to endure 'insults which my unprotected situation naturally produces' and could think of higher matters.

Before leaving for Ireland she met her new pupils by arrangement with Mrs Prior at a house in London, and plans were made for all of them to travel together to Ireland. But the Misses King (the daughters of Lord Kingsborough) were not yet ready to depart and Mary filled the interval by staying with the Priors at Eton.

The weeks she spent at this famous school exasperated her as a tedious delay, but at least she could get an insight into the working of a great English institution. By this time educational matters of whatever nature were of the greatest interest to her and she was eager to receive as much information as she could absorb. Unfortunately the headmaster at that time was in difficulties with some of the pupils, who in revolt against his strict rule were damaging the premises. Mary's impressions therefore were not particularly good from the point of view of discipline; nor for that matter, of learning, for she considered natural history afforded a much more useful preparation to life than the prolonged study of the classics which was the rule. Also the quality of the masters left her dissatisfied. They seemed to be young men of fashion rather than of scholarship. How could boys acquire knowledge from such frivolous sources? In fact she found herself out of sympathy with most of the company she met there, with the exception of a group of boys gathered round a highly gifted pupil, George Canning, the future Prime Minister, who with some brilliant friends was preparing the first issue of a school magazine, the *Microcosm*. This small enclave struck her as an oasis in a desert. She was unfair in many of her observations and in one way or another lacked perception in evaluating the spirit of the place. Censorious and humourless, she saw everything from an angle which was less favourable than she imagined. Addressing herself to Everina she wrote:

'I could not live the life they live at Eton—nothing but dress and ridicule going forward—for I really believe their fondness for ridicule tends to make them affected, the women in their manners, the men in their conversation—for witlings abound and puns fly about like crackers, tho' you would scarcely guess they had any meaning in them if you did not hear the noise they create.'[3]

Such observations reveal how far her understanding lagged behind her knowledge. Biased by her painful experience of life she had not grasped how happier circumstances might have affected her judgment. At this early age she considered herself in a position to make sweeping generalizations. What she felt went so passionately deep that it seemed out of the question there could be doubt about its truth. She was dogmatic to a degree.

While awaiting the Misses King she spent some time making some clothes for herself. She was not a brilliant dressmaker but she managed to produce a gown and an overcoat, and a friend presented her with a pretty blue hat. She was worried about Everina stranded again with an unwilling host, her brother Edward, and continued to search for a means of escape. Would the three sisters ever be satisfactorily settled? Some of her creditors called at the house and were most rude, putting her to shame. Whatever happened she must get rid of her debts. 'I owe near eighty or ninety pounds,' she wrote to George Blood, 'and it harasses me beyond measure. Some of the debts I would give the world to pay.'

It was not till October 1786 that she took the boat for Ireland. She was alone, the King girls being still detained in London, but it was a blessing for her to have a short period of solitude for reflection. There was little comfort to be found but for one happy thought, the success of her book and the hope it raised that she could make a career as an author. Here was a chance of real independence: to sell her writings, pay her debts and be free to live according to her principles.

She had a pleasant voyage and made friends with a young clergyman travelling for the same purpose as herself—not only frustrated and talented young women had to take thankless tasks for lack of more opportunity. Women's difficulties were in reality but a portion of the great burden carried by underprivileged people the world over. This was a wider angle from which to survey the position, a common cause for which to battle. Mary's thoughts took a new turn, but for the moment she could not afford the time to divert her efforts from the main attack.

She stayed a few days in Dublin with the Blood family to satisfy herself that their affairs were in good shape, then was conducted to Mitchelstown in Cork by a Kingsborough servant, a kindly thought on the part of her employer which should have predisposed her to him. Indeed she could have fared much worse, for her new masters were in some respects far more considerate than was usual, but she had fallen into a complaining mood. Too much had been demanded of her; her blood had become thin and she fell a prey to self-pity. 'I entered the great gate of the castle with the same kind of feeling as I should have if I was going to the Bastille.'[4] A little later she wrote to Everina that there was 'such a solemn kind of stupidity about this place as froze my very blood ... I hear a fiddle below; the servants are dancing and the rest of the family diverting themselves. I only am melancholy and alone.'

Robert King, Viscount Kingsborough, owned some hundred square miles of territory. He was a pleasant and benevolent man who believed in progressive forms of agriculture and, generally speaking, in progressive views of life, even for governesses. Mary was surely prejudiced when she found that his countenance 'does not promise much more than good humour and a little fun not refined'. It cannot be denied that in her overwrought state, consequent upon the death of Fanny and the collapse of her relationship with Joshua Waterhouse (about whom she did not care to speak), she was becoming priggish. The world for her was a cold, unfriendly place, hardly worth her attention. Even the beauties of nature failed to touch her heart; which was strange, for she had never been housed in a more romantic place than the castle set on a cliff overlooking a river with a prospect of distant mountains.

Her mistress, Lady Kingsborough, was even less successful in pleasing Mary, who acknowledged that she was 'well-meaning but not of the order of being that I could love'. Temporary manager of Lord Kingsborough's estate was Arthur Young, the great authority on agriculture. He was also a social economist, historian and novelist, author of many varied works and a man of much experience. His presence might have been thought to have compensated Mary for much she disliked in the routine at Kingsborough Castle, but such was not the case.

Lady Kingsborough and Arthur Young used to play chess together after dinner, observed by Mary's sad eyes. There were other eyes far from sad to watch, for Lady Kingsborough was sociable by nature and surrounded herself with female relatives, three sisters and a stepmother, none of whom, unfortunately, made a good impression on Mary. They put on rouge without any *mauvaise honte* and spent as much as five hours over dressing.

> 'You cannot conceive, my dear girl,' she wrote to Everina, 'the dissipated lives the women of quality live. . . . They labour to be civil to me but we move in so different a sphere, I feel grateful for their attention, but not amused. . . . I am treated like a gentlewoman but I cannot easily forget my inferior station.'[5]

The Kingsboroughs were quick to recognize that Mary was not of the stuff of which governesses are usually made, and treated her with far greater respect than any previous occupant of the position. It was impossible to do otherwise, for her whole being expressed high quality, due mostly to an unconscious distinction in appearance and behaviour, but also to the fact that she could not open her lips without revealing the extent of her culture. She was more widely read and possibly more widely travelled than any other woman present. She had known and conversed with famous men; she had thought about universal problems, and on one subject at least was passionately convinced. Latent genius could be detected by those who had discerning eyes, such as Dr Johnson on the one occasion he met her, and invited her to visit him as often as she pleased. Unfortunately he died soon afterwards.

In one respect alone Mary felt she was not losing her time and that was her management of the Kingsborough children, hitherto in her opinion much neglected as far as essentials went. Her pupils consisted of three girls, who at first disliked her for the sufficient reason in their eyes of being English. But soon she won them over, she was such good company, her talk so lively and varied, her manner so affectionate. With children the petals of Mary's true nature unfolded like a flower in sunshine. She was her best self, helpful, gay, imaginative and encouraging; a child too in her enthusiasm and enjoyment of simple things. The Kingsborough girls responded fully; in particular the eldest, Margaret, who eventually took such a strong liking to her governess that her mother had to take second place, which did not at all please Lady Kingsborough.

The children, far from being ill educated, were if anything over educated as far as the acquisition of factual knowledge went, for they knew several languages and 'cartloads of history'. But this was not what Mary understood by 'education' which for her was a 'holy cult' of the entire personality—positive living in which the teacher and the taught collaborated. She thought with Locke that education is largely a matter of observation, a matter of example and visual illustration.

Her favourite pupil was Margaret, later to become Lady Mount-cashel, who as a woman of the world was as much attached to the famous writer as the child was to her governess. 'My sweet little girl is now playing and singing to me,' Mary wrote to Eliza.

> 'She has a good ear and some taste and feeling. She has a wonderful capacity . . . but such a multiplicity of employments it has not room to expand itself—and in all probability will be lost in a heap of rubbish miscalled accomplishments. I am grieved at being obliged to continue so wrong a system.'[6]

Mary left indelible marks on these impressionable children, whose parents were beginning to realize the hold she exercised over their minds. Lady Kingsborough in particular resented her authority being replaced by that of a governess who was turning out to be quite different from what they desired. There was no denying that the children were happy in her charge, for she taught a way of living and learning quite new to them and immensely appealing to their youth. Moreover she insisted upon employing her own methods of control, which had little or nothing to do with punishments and everything to do with the affections. Mary, aware of disapproval on high and realizing how impossible it was to undo the work of years, fell frequently into moods of despondency. Genteel company at the Castle did not compare in interest with the stimulating personalities she had had the good fortune to meet in Newington Green. 'I am confined to the society of a set of silly females,'[7] she complained in a letter. This was not wholly true, but her critical attitude and scorn of social graces tended to isolate her from the genial if shallow gathering at the Kingsboroughs and it is small wonder that they lost patience with her in the end. 'Shall I try to remember the titles of all the Lords and Viscounts I am in company with,' she wrote to Eliza, 'not forgetting the clever things they say? I would sooner tell you the tale of some humbler creatures. I intend visiting the poor cabins as Miss King is allowed to assist the poor.'

The 'poor cabins' shocked her beyond measure, perhaps because of the contrast with the idle, luxurious existence at the Castle. Hitherto she had measured poverty by the yardstick of her own and her friends' existence, which had not shown such a huge discrepancy in conditions of life. Now she found it well-nigh unbelievable that people such as the Irish peasants could live as they did, be exploited so mercilessly without raising their hands against a government that permitted such injustice. There was a shift in her protest. Women were indeed victims of an unfair social system, but the injustice went far wider than she had realized hitherto. There in those Irish cabins she saw such deplorable poverty, life reduced to a bare struggle for survival, that even the misery she had seen in Lisbon did not quite equal it, if only for the reason that there a kinder climate made hunger and cold more bearable. As she and Margaret King went among the wretched families, distributing a few comforts by way of soup and warm garments, it was brought home to her how inadequate was private charity. She held that it did more harm than good, for it soothed the conscience of the rich without bringing lasting relief to the poor. No! Private charity was not the answer. There was something radically wrong with the world, and she could hardly tolerate the company of those who saw no reason to complain. She felt herself to be a 'sojourner in a strange land', but what was strange land to her seemed to be familiar country to most people. Most people were deaf and blind and unaware of their spiritual mutilation. She was not of their kind. The social structure of England might be rotten, but the entire universe now seemed almost as bad.

What could she do about it? At the moment nothing more direct than to apply herself more earnestly to her studies. She had a suspicion the Kingsboroughs were not satisfied with her teaching of

French, which she had claimed as being more solidly founded than it was. She must work harder in her spare time. She must strive to become more familiar with other foreign languages, and with French in particular, because in France a great movement of liberation was in its first phase. One day she would go there and meet enlightened rebels, but that was not for now. Now she must stay where she was, although she was in such low spirits that she wrote to Everina: 'I think anything like pleasure will never visit me.'

She fell ill and was treated by being fed on asses' milk. But asses' milk was no panacea for her debts, her unhappy sick Everina, the poverty of the peasants, the problems of social justice, the lonely heart. None the less, she tried to become a better mixer in the drawing-room, 'to talk of getting husbands for the Ladies—and the dogs—and [to be] wonderfully entertaining.'[8] Soon, however, she was back in her own apartment, brooding alone, listening to the wind and bowing her head beneath a wave of self-pity, now becoming a major indulgence.

She considered the root cause of her unhappiness to be her dependent position in the household. She had been at the Castle three months, but although treated as one of the family she was very much a subordinate. She thought longingly of her school, of herself as the sole director of her affairs. Independence! Nothing, it seemed, could compensate for loss of it. 'I have plenty of books,' she wrote to Everina.

> 'I am now reading some philosophical lectures and metaphysical sermons, for my own private improvement. . . . Books are my only relaxation. Yet I do not read much—I think and think, and these reveries do not tend to fit me for enjoying the common pleasures of the world. What does it signify? I am going home! I am only alive to *attendrissement*. Certainly I must be in love—for I am grown thin and lean, pale and wan.'[9]

In the early spring of 1787 the Kingsborough family moved to Dublin, which meant for her a much needed change of scene. Dublin, the world of fashion, offered distraction and pleasure and for once she welcomed them: visits to the theatre, concerts, parties and balls, a Handel festival, and receptions where she met people of note. One lady, impressed by Mary's conversation, was astonished to discover she was conversing with a governess. Other ladies having made a similar mistake showed a most unflattering resentment. Mary turned the occasion into satire and found relief. Satire became her best defence and the better to express it she developed a false gaiety.

'That vivacity,' she wrote to Everina, 'which increases with age is not far from madness, says Rochefoucauld. I then am mad—deprived of the only comfort I can relish, I give way to whim. And yet when the most sprightly sallies burst from me, the tear frequently trembles in my eye, and the long-drawn sigh eases my full heart—so my eyes roll in the wild way you have seen them. A deadly paleness overspreads my countenance —and yet so weak am I a sudden thought or any recollected emotion of tenderness will occasion the most painful suffusion. You know not, my dear Girl, of what material this strange in- consistent heart of mine is formed, and how alive it is to tenderness and misery. Since I have been here I have turned over several pages in the vast volume of human nature and what is the amount? Vanity and vexation of spirit, and yet I am *tied* to my fellow-creatures by partaking of their weaknesses. I rail at a fault, sicken at the sight—and find it stirring within me.' [10]

The style and the sentiments do not do justice to her true quality. She had reached an unrewarding stage in her development; self-pity and self-dramatization were not proper to her. The passages read like an exercise in rhetoric at which she was trying her hand. Relieved of the worst aspects of poverty and for the time being secure, she was suffering a reaction from the years of struggle. It was a period of *accidie*, of loss of faith; her whole being cried out for warmth. Although she did not acknowledge the demands of the senses, it cannot be doubted that in one so affectionate, so wide in imagination, so gifted in the qualities that unite human beings, sexual desire was strong. Her disappointment over the affair with young Waterhouse went deep. At the time in which she lived sex was a strictly private matter, in no sense open to debate. Women were objects of desire; that they are subjects in the same sense that men are never entered the question. Mary knew her own nature. She was beginning to understand that although an attitude of universal benevolence brought satisfaction to the spirit it did little to comfort the heart. 'I cannot live without love,' she wrote in her novel *Mary*, 'and love leads to madness.'

Love leads to madness, but from such madness sanity may emerge. Her madness was due to spiritual undernourishment; for years she had been pouring the riches of her nature on her mother, her sisters, Fanny and the Blood family, and now she found herself drained of strength and those qualities of the spirit which sustain the mind during struggle.

Her love for Fanny, a mutual enrichment, had sublimated her sexual longings. This went hand in hand with love for humanity. It sweetened her feelings for her ungracious and ungrateful family. Now that Fanny was dead she had lost the only source of reciprocal tenderness. Fanny was dead, and a man who might have replaced her in Mary's heart had turned aside. 'There is no cure for a broken heart,' she wrote.

> 'It is true it may languidly perform its animal functions but it can no longer be inflated with hope. I want a tender nurse— I want—but it matters not.'

Lady Kingsborough was becoming increasingly dissatisfied with her governess who, though treated as one of the family, seemed hardly aware of the great condescension this implied. Also, the 'higher servant' had become the children's friend, even their champion against their mother, whose disciplinary methods were wholly at odds with the liberal ideas their governess had inculcated. The mistress of the Castle was torn between satisfaction at having such a remarkable woman at her service and envy of her intellectual distinction. She could not conceal her mixed feelings, and Mary thought best to withdraw as much as possible from participating in the social life of the family. But Lady Kingsborough missed the stimulus of Mary's presence in her drawing-room; it led to a general heightening of the tone of the conversation, which for all its unfashionable course proved nevertheless an attraction. Lady Kingsborough envied Mary's superior powers and discovered to her own surprise that she began to fear her.

This was not the first time Mary had roused fear in her immediate *entourage*. At home her father had been intimidated when she came between him and his victim, his wretched wife; the captain of the vessel from Lisbon, who until she intervened had not wanted to succour a ship in distress, obeyed her; and now her employer found to her surprise that her underling possessed unsuspected power. The children had already experienced it, but since it was exercised in their favour they made no complaint. Lady Kingsborough tried to conquer her feelings and for a time succeeded. 'Lady Kingsborough and I are on much better terms than ever we were,' Mary wrote to Everina. 'To tell the truth she is afraid of me ... [She] keeps in temper surprisingly before me and really labours to be civil.'[11]

It was obvious that a crisis was approaching, but a lucky event postponed it. She unexpectedly received the offer of a considerable loan from a friend whose name, she wrote in a letter to Eliza, she was not permitted to mention; this would enable her to pay her debts, and also make it possible for her to join her sisters for a winter vacation. This temporary relief somewhat restored her faith in humanity. 'Let me tell you, dear Girl,' she wrote to Eliza, 'the manner in which this favour has been conferred on me greatly enhanced the obligation. I could have no scruple—and I rejoiced to meet with a fellow creature whom I could admire for doing a disinterested act of kindness.'

Although some of the gloom was dissipated she knew her days with the Kingsboroughs were coming to an end. The family was about to move again; at first there was talk of Bath and Bristol Hot Wells, then of a trip to the Continent. Change was in the air and Mary felt the moment had come to plan her own future in a way that offered better prospects. No more teaching of children whether in her own school or away from home. Not because she felt herself unfitted for the task; on the contrary, in Godwin's opinion, expressed in his *Memoirs*, there was no one better gifted in this respect. But the time had come for her to aim at a truly independent existence, to become her own mistress, responsible to herself alone for her opinions and acts. She knew that the type of female education she advocated would meet with fierce opposition. Rousseau had proclaimed that '*toute l'éducation des femmes doit être relative aux hommes. Il faut qu'elle étudie à fond l'esprit des hommes auxquels elle est assujettie, soit par la loi, soit par l'opinion'.*[12] This expressed the general view of men on the subject, and of many women who had for so long borrowed masculine ideas that they could no longer function as independent thinkers.

Mary, well versed in Rousseau's *Émile*, had also read John Locke's *Reflections on Education*, which so nearly expressed her own thoughts. 'Genteel women,' she protested later in her *Vindication of the Rights of Woman*, 'are literally speaking slaves to their bodies and glory in their subjection.' She shared Dr Johnson's view that 'most vices may be committed very genteelly', and she knew only too well that 'genteel' was the qualification which best described the feminine approach to the question of women's emancipation.

She scorned the ideas of a few educated well-born females who knew little about the lives of their less fortunate sisters, wives of drunken spendthrift husbands such as Edward Wollstonecraft; or sisters of tyrannical brothers spoilt by having the lion's share of the family fortune, and educated to maintain their independence; or of single women such as Everina, and Mary herself, struggling with poverty and debts while she provided her own education after a day of tedious work in some ill-paid inferior position as companion or governess. There were many more women so situated than there were those who enjoyed 'genteel' conditions. It was a bitter thought to Mary that a gifted woman such as Mrs Barbauld could be so eloquent on the subject of men's rights yet so lukewarm on women's. This talented writer feared she had stepped outside the bounds of respectability by becoming an author, just as Lady Mary Wortley Montagu, who had translated Epictetus, felt it necessary to apologize for her 'unnatural' act.

Mary, in reviewing the efforts of women writers of her time, and getting little encouragement from the narrowness of their standpoint, decided to join their ranks and add a wiser and more positive element to what they had contributed. Apart from a general shallowness of thought, they gave no hint of the political, legal and economic difficulties which lay at the heart of the women's question. It was like treating a cancer with a soothing ointment. She considered that now her proper place of residence was London, in the company of those men and women of vision whose articles appeared in serious periodicals or in books published by Mr Joseph Johnson of St Paul's Churchyard.

4

'A Pack of Dirty Jacobins'

It was the year 1787, two years before discontent in France blazed up in a first act of revolt, the destruction of the Bastille. In England it was a time of renewed hope centred on the figure of the younger Pitt. He had been in office several years now and had done much to restore confidence after the lamentable Peace of Paris, which brought to an end the Seven Years War and drew from the elder Pitt the cry 'We retain nothing although we have conquered everything'.

France had lost that war, but thanks to the political ineptitude of George III and his ministers almost the same could be said of Britain. She handed back to France the best of her conquests: Guadeloupe, Martinique and, worst of all, the fishing rights off Newfoundland. The national debt had nearly doubled and taxation was running at a very high rate. The American War of Independence, which had lasted over seven years, was concluded in 1783 by the Peace of Versailles, which gave the colonists their liberty and thereby deprived the United Kingdom of the benefit of their revenues. Only the enormous ability of William Pitt saved Britain from financial disaster: he and the genius of those gifted men whose inventions were revolutionizing industry and already laying the foundations of a new industrial prosperity. The average Englishman was happy to discover that Britain was solvent again and let matters rest there, but the dissenting academies, where economics, history and natural science were studied, were turning out a new type of middle-class intellectual, barred from the traditional avenues to power and fame but more ready to question the established order of things.

A few fruits of prosperity, such as new pavements and street lighting, began to appear in the cities. In London in particular there was much rebuilding and street-widening. About the middle of the century Blackfriars and Westminster Bridge were built. Acts of Parliament provided for sewage disposal and scavenging. But Mary, writing in her novel *Mary*, saw only the seamy side of the metropolis:

'As she passed through the streets in a hackney-coach, disgust and horror alternately filled her mind. She met some women drunk; and the manners of those who attacked the sailors made her shrink into herself and exclaim are these my fellow creatures? She saw vulgarity, dirt and vice—her soul sickened; this was the first time such complicated misery had obtruded on her sight.'

In fact, London at this time was a safer and more salubrious capital than most. The Prince of Monaco, invited to London by George III, arrived in the evening and believed the magnificently lit streets had been specially illuminated in his honour; he was seeing only the ordinary street-lighting, but it was lavish by continental standards.

The poor and unemployed were, as always in the past, largely abandoned to their own devices. There was a Poor Law, but the relief it gave was deliberately minimal. Any person likely to become a burden on the parish was liable to be driven away; those who were cared for in the almhouses and asylums of the day led a humiliating existence. Such institutions were the last refuge of the desperate.

At the top of the scale wealth and leisure were increasing. The loss of the American colonies had little effect upon the lives of ordinary people; as for the ruling classes, so far as material matters went, they had never seen better days. There was much heavy drinking, sport, gambling, travelling abroad; and at home, an easy-going society where literary, sporting, fashionable and political sets inter-mingled. The arts flourished, the theatre had its Garrick and Mrs Siddons to bolster its fame. The modern newspaper was in the making, also a modern appreciation of the pleasures of the table. The rich dined on many courses of meat, game and fish accompanied by French and Portuguese wines. The poor lived for the most part on bread, cheese and vegetables; meat was a luxury and the staple drink was beer. Their standard of living was, however, vastly superior to that of the French and, indeed, to that of the European peasantry in general. In years of national prosperity, the majority of Englishmen could make what to them was a tolerable living. It was rare to find a radical agitator of really humble origins in England: revolutionary thinking was almost totally the preserve of the bourgeois intelligentsia, of whom Mary was one.

This intelligentsia, with many of its roots in Puritan Dissent, and with all the moral fervour that this implied, saw much in the existing order that was fundamentally rotten and unjust. The most extreme considered that a reformation of the entire political and adminis-trative system was the best hope of those who loved their country. While Government was corrupt and Parliament unrepresentative, little could be achieved: therefore political reform was a paramount necessity, social and economic reform following from it. When the radical reformers introduced through their writings their earliest proposals for social improvement, the names of Richard Price and Joseph Priestley came to the fore. They preached redemption through knowledge on the widest possible scale; this was the correc-tive to social prejudice and injustice. Intellectual sloth was the prime cause of the people's misery, but Reason could right most wrongs. There was a wave of intellectual optimism, based on Reason, which swiftly became the panacea for all ills, and which was elevated to the status of a religion by its most fanatical advocates. The exercise of rational thinking, cultivated in the schools, colleges and progressive societies, was the way of true wisdom. Few people, however, appeared to realize the fact—a situation which never failed to astound the radical philosophers; but they insisted on regarding this state as only a temporary aberration. 'But what are we doing?' cried Richard Price in his work *On Civil Liberty*.

'We are running wild after pleasure and forgetting everything serious and decent in Masquerades—We are gambling in gaming houses: trafficking in boroughs: perjuring ourselves at elections: selling ourselves for places.'

This was in brief the world that Mary surveyed as her last period of servitude was drawing to a close. Lady Kingsborough, unable to accept a state of affairs where the governess was preferred by the children to the mother, finally dismissed Mary, who was ready to go. She had been enriched by her contact with wealth and fashion, but her experience in these fields had now to be integrated with what she had known of hardship and poverty.

The ready acceptance for publication by Joseph Johnson of her little work *Thoughts on the Education of Daughters*, and the £10 he paid her so promptly, had encouraged her to think that salvation lay with the pen. She would write for her living, join the ranks of her friends in Newington Green and become like them, independent-minded architects of society. But realizing her lack of any formal education, her scanty knowledge of history, of the rudiments of political science, of the new idealism in religious and scientific thought, she passed through moments of lacerating doubt. How could she find her way alone in that maze of conflicting possibilities?

She would write to Johnson and describe her difficulties and her attitude towards the ills she could discern in the social fabric. There was one ill that had received small attention from writers who were sensitive to far less injurious conditions; this was the incredible injustice of women's position in society. Women deprived of legal rights, uneducated, poor (since if married they had no control over their own property, or if single they came under the rule of some form of masculine authority), deprived even of proprietorship in their own children, exploited in almost every aspect of their existence, there was barely a voice raised in their defence. One half of the community was being abused by the other half; this to Mary was wholly unacceptable. The plain lack of humanity, the brutality of material and physical dominance over the female half which was the cradle of the race roused an anguished revolt in her heart.

She was not blinded by her partisanship of women to other social wrongs. She wholly approved of efforts to bring greater equality of conditions for workers, and had become a friend of several men whose thoughts and activities turned in this direction. She followed closely developments in France where it seemed the 'labouring poor' were far more dangerously alert than in England. She agreed with Dr Price when he wrote in a letter to Burke: 'In order that liberty should have a firm foundation it must be laid either by poor men or philosophers.' Any organization of workers which fostered plans and projects of betterment among the lower income groups had her support.

There were contemporary writers who had kindled a blaze that would not be extinguished for years. In France first among these was Rousseau; in England John Wilkes and Thomas Paine brandished a torch for Liberty and Reform. Wilkes, speaking in the House of Commons, declared: 'The meanest mechanic, the poorest peasant and day labourer has important rights respecting his personal liberty, that of his wife and his children, however inconsiderable his wages, his earnings, the very price and value of each day's hard labour.'[1] At the same time Thomas Paine, who had been one of the leading spirits of the American rebels, was completing his survey of the conditions of the English working man, the faults and failings of an hereditary system of government, the inequitable system of taxation, the impressment of sailors and soldiers in wars about which they had no voice but had to take the consequences in terms of poverty and mutilation without compensatory measures of relief.

People of this rebellious nature were described in a letter written by Lady Hester Stanhope as a 'pack of dirty Jacobins', and it was to this 'pack' that Mary aspired to belong. She sent the MS. of her novel *Mary*, which she had been writing for the last couple of years, to Johnson, accompanied by a letter describing the state of her mind after service with a rich and, on the whole, kindly family entirely unaffected by the new progressive spirit.

'I long for a little peace and independence. Every obligation we receive from our fellow creatures is a new shackle, takes from our freedom, and debases the mind, makes us mere earth worms. I am not fond of grovelling.'

She followed up her communication by paying a visit to the

publishing house at 72 St Paul's Churchyard, where she was received with much sympathy and appreciation. Greatly encouraged she voiced her relief and her hopes for the future in a long letter to Everina.

'Mr Johnson, whose uncommon kindness, I believe, has saved me from the despair and vexation I shrink back from ... assures me that if I exert my talents in writing I may support myself in a comfortable way. I am then going to be the first of a new genus. I tremble at the attempt, yet if I fail I shall only suffer, and should I succeed my dear girls will even in sickness have a home and a refuge where for a few months in the year they may forget the cares that disturb the rest. I shall strain every nerve to obtain a situation for Eliza nearer town; in short I am once more involved in schemes, heaven only knows whether they will answer! Yet while they are pursued life slips away. I could not on any account inform my father and Edward of my designs—you and Eliza are the only part of the family I am interested about. I wish to be a mother to you both. ... This project has long floated in my mind. You know I am not born to tread on the beaten track, the peculiar bent of my nature pushes me on.'

Johnson not only accepted the MS. of *Mary* but also offered hospitality to the author in his home for two or three weeks while she searched for suitable lodgings. Before taking advantage of this she visited Everina in the Henley school where she was now employed and strengthened her nerves by long walks in the countryside. From Henley she wrote to Johnson:

'I often think of my new plan of life; and, lest my sister [Eliza] should try to prevail on me to alter it, I have avoided mentioning it to her. I am determined! Your sex generally laugh at female determinations; but let me tell you, I never yet resolved to do anything of consequence, that I did not adhere resolutely to it, till I had accomplished my purpose, improbable as it might have appeared to a more timid mind.'[2]

Meanwhile Johnson had found lodgings for her at 49 George Street, Blackfriars. Feeling certain that he could provide her with sufficient work to ensure her financial independence he encouraged her to come to London. She would, he calculated, be an asset, socially and intellectually, in the circle of friends who gathered almost nightly at his house.

George Street was a part of London inhabited by writers, actors, publishers and people who liked to be conveniently situated for Covent Garden, the eating-houses of the Strand and the coffee-houses of Fleet Street, where Dr Johnson was wont to preside. The Sheridans lived in Henrietta Street, David Garrick in the Strand and Sir Joshua Reynolds in Leicester Fields.* This was the heart of literary and artistic London, though it did not impress foreigners as much as the fashionable quarters round St James's Street, where the new pavements and street lighting made Frenchmen exclaim at the contrast with their own dirty capital (although even in these fashionable streets footpads and highwaymen were not unknown). None the less slums such as the tenements in the parish of St Giles, Black Boy Alley and other unsalubrious parts were all too evident.

Although the sedan chair was still in use, the invention of the umbrella, together with the improved street lighting and pavements, made foot travel less hazardous. Fashions were losing much of their inconvenient luxuriousness. For males, suits of velvet and brocade were giving place to those tailored of good English cloth. With lower head-dresses women were no longer obliged to sit on low stools in their coaches. There was a feeling for hygiene arising out of the new knowledge about public health and the raising of private standards of cleanliness.

Constant exchange of distinguished visitors between the French and English capitals was normal. David Hume, Tobias Smollett, Horace Walpole and others of their kind were as much at home in Paris as were the Rolands and members of the future Girondin Party in London. Any Englishman who aspired to be considered a person of culture had to be familiar with the French language and literature and the customs of the country. Much the same was true for enlightened Frenchmen, who were usually able to read English books and were conversant with English history and literature. Brissot, future leader of the Girondins, lived for two years in

* Now known as Leicester Square.

Brompton, Danton stayed in Wimpole Street, Marat studied in Edinburgh, Oxford and Dublin.

Mary now moved into the lodging in George Street with the hope she was to be allowed time for herself, time in which to complete her education in view of her future responsibilities. But both her sisters considered this an opportunity for a little break in their monotonous lives. Everina resigned her position at the school where she had been teaching for the last year. Fortunately Eliza retained hers at a similar establishment in Market Harborough, but she too decided to pay a visit to her sister. The Bloods had a wayward daughter, Caroline, who had ended up in the workhouse, and a sum of half a crown a week had to be paid for her keep. As usual appeals were made to Mary, who wrote to George Blood:

'What is to be done, my dear boy? I cannot allow them again to turn her out—nor will I see her. If she knew where I lived she would come to me and be a burden I could *not* bear.'

Mary nurtured ambitious hopes for Everina. She would arrange to send her to a position in Paris for a few months to 'catch the French accent'. But for a short while George Street became the refuge of all three sisters while Mary gave her attention to the problem of providing for their keep. 'I have done with the delusions of fancy. I live only to be useful. Benevolence must fill every void in my heart,' she wrote.

Since Johnson had consented to publish her sentimental novel *Mary* she felt encouraged to write a semi-fictional book of the sort made popular by Thomas Day's *Sandford and Merton*, called *Original Stories from Real Life*, a work dedicated to the enlightenment of young people with a view to forming good citizens of a brave new world. This work too is highly sentimental, based on her own hard experiences in life, which so far she had met by nursing wounded feelings without making sufficient effort to understand their cause. Johnson was doubtful about the book's prospects, because of the author's unflattering observations about parents pursuing their own pleasures rather than furthering their children's usefulness in society. But Johnson was wrong, for the book sold well and went into a second edition with engravings by William Blake. Its popularity lasted into the nineteenth century, which was surprising since, illustrated, it cost as much as half a crown. It was not yet imbued with Mary's mature spirit. Few of her liberal ideas on the brotherhood of man and the equality of the two sexes were ventilated. Perhaps it was for this reason that the work turned out to be so successful and brought her the assurance that she could make her living by her pen, provided she remained guarded about her true opinions.

She was able forthwith to carry out her plans for Everina and send her to Paris to 'catch the French accent' and take account of the people.

> 'Pray enquire,' she wrote to her sister once she was established in the French capital, 'of the literary men about some particulars relative to M. Necker, the late Minister, which I shall mention. He has written a book entitled *De l'importance des Opinions Religieuses*. It pleases me, and I want to know the character of the man in domestic life and public estimation, etc., and the opinion the French have of his literary abilities.'[3]

Mary considered that she could make a contribution to her income by undertaking translations from the French. She had placed her hopes on a new magazine, the *Analytical Review*, brought out in 1788 by Joseph Johnson and Thomas Christie. She not only translated for it Necker's *Of the Importance of Religious Opinions*, but made an abridgment of Lavater's *Physiognomy*, and took in her stride studies in the German and Italian languages.

The *Analytical Review* was clearly going to make extensive demands upon her capacities, and since it was furthering her intellectual development and material independence she could not be too grateful for its appearance. Translations and adaptations and articles for the *Review*, together with the compiling of a *Female Reader*, filled her time almost to the exclusion of all else.

She wrote cheerfully to George Blood:

> 'I have lately been very busy translating a work of importance, and have made a very advantageous contract for another. Besides, I have had a variety of other employments. In short,

my dear Boy, I succeed beyond my most sanguine hopes and really believe I shall clear above two hundred pounds this year, which will supply amply all *my* wants and enable me to defray the expenses of Everina's journey and let her remain in Paris longer than I first intended. I am thankful to Heaven for enabling me to be useful and this consideration sweetens my toil, for I have been very diligent. . . . I have had some difficulties at the outset which imperceptibly melt away as I encounter them—and I daily earn more money with less trouble.' [4]

In this flowering of her talents Johnson played a major role. Nothing could exceed his kindness and understanding. Friendship with him was one of the rare strokes of good fortune she was to receive in her short life. She wrote to Everina: 'I am sure you would love him did you know with what tenderness and humanity he has behaved to me.'

As she grew happier she blossomed into generous femininity. But her cup was not entirely full. The wound left by Joshua Waterhouse had not yet healed. She was aware of a gap in her life, for which no literary success could compensate.

5

Her Reply to Burke's 'Reflections'

Mary had scaled the first peak of her mountain range. She was an independent woman, living on the fruits of her intellect and imagination. No one had claims upon her, other than her family. She could write and act at the prompting of her own understanding and strong sympathies.

Her lodging in George Street was not far from that of her best friend, Johnson the publisher, where she went most evenings to join the group of free-thinkers, writers, artists and radicals who met there to discuss, for the most part, the outbreak of the revolution in France and the works of those who had inspired it, Rousseau and Voltaire. Among this 'pack of dirty Jacobins' were John Wilkes, Tom Paine, William Godwin, Thomas Holcroft, William Blake and Henry Fuseli.

Mary, who had only recently been an obscure governess barely tolerated in polite society, an upper servant with a difference, was now meeting some of the most powerful intellects of the day. She was certainly not overcome by modesty. The discipline of having to state her opinions in writing, the many pages of analysis she had turned out at top speed during the last year, had added greatly to her intellectual capacity. She was accustomed to think swiftly and stand firmly by her conclusions. Having great faith in her powers of understanding she would seldom go back on any judgment she had made and wore an air of authority which contrasted curiously with her claim of being a mere tiro. Although she was always ready to admit the disadvantages of her self-acquired mental development it was chiefly to give point to her main contention: women's unfair lack of education and training. She was a bold neophyte who liked to hear her own voice. It was pleasant to find that her vocabulary would expand to the demands she made upon it; without doubt her translations from French and German authors had greatly helped in this.

She had, for example, wrestled for many months with the translation of Necker's *De l'Importance des Opinions Religieuses*, a work which on the whole pleased her, although Necker's special mixture of rational argument and wordy flights of intuition left her doubtful. Moreover she found the complexity and length of his paragraphs tiring, so she met the situation by omitting repetitive passages and ornate rhetoric that did nothing to make the argument clear. Having taken such liberties with the text in the interests of lucidity she produced a result which was not wholly a success and Johnson never reissued the book. Nevertheless it ran into two American editions, one in Philadelphia in 1791 and another in Boston in 1796. Johnson realized that the fault lay more with the author than with the translator and continued to pass on to her other works of translation, both from French and German, all presenting problems to Mary who in German at least was on very unsure ground.

One of her German translations was Salzmann's *Moralisches Elementarbuch*, a book of stories for children. *Elements of Morality* as she called it was one of her lasting successes, far more encouraging than the Necker translation. She could not, however, resist the temptation to improve it and introduce matter of her own construction, going so far as to change the nationality of the protagonists from German to English, so that Herr Herman and his wife Sophie became Mr and Mrs Jones. The work, in three volumes, was illustrated by Blake. Two editions appeared in London and several in America; later it was reissued in Baltimore and Edinburgh, and finally in Boston as late as 1850.

In July 1789 French revolutionaries stormed the Bastille, released the prisoners, executed the governor and proclaimed the start of the French Revolution. The effect of this on the band of English radicals with whom Mary now associated, and in particular on Mary herself, was tremendous. Almost overnight matters which had been discussed as purely intellectual speculation became facts—and moreover facts spattered with blood. Abstract rights put on flesh. Men holding the ideas of Voltaire and Rousseau were striding the streets of Paris armed with pikes and hatchets. This was the end of bloodless debate. The emancipation of mankind in France, and it was to be hoped in England and in every country where the French *philosophes* and the *Encyclopédistes* had made their impact, was about to be realized.

That same year, Mary's old friend Dr Price delivered a sermon *On the Love of our Country* to the Society for Commemorating the Glorious Revolution of 1688. When published it roused the whole radical movement in support of its call to revolt. 'I see the ardour for liberty catching and spreading; a general amendment beginning in human affairs; the dominion of kings changed for the dominion of laws, and the dominion of priests giving way to the dominion of reason and conscience,'[1] Price declaimed, rousing his audience to such a degree that it was impelled to compose on the spot a congratulatory address to the French National Assembly.

All this set fire to Mary's smouldering dissatisfaction with the state of society. Her championship of the women's cause was now engulfed in the greater cause of the citizen and his relationship to the State. Women were indeed slaves to men, but men themselves were equally enslaved and there was no chance of betterment for women until men had shaken off some of their bonds. And now in France she was witnessing the first movements of a general emancipation. Price's sermon provoked Burke's celebrated *Reflections on the Revolution in France* which in turn provoked Mary to write in reply *A Vindication of the Rights of Men*.

It seemed to Mary that the world of the underprivileged was rising to her challenge, the challenge of one whose experiences were the epitome of man's struggle for freedom unaided by privilege or training. She had for years listened to the opinions of learned men on this question; of those, for example, at Newington Green where she had first met Dr Price and, at second-hand, had absorbed the ideas of David Hume and Joseph Priestley. Then came her en-

counter with John Hewlett, who took her to visit the great Dr Johnson, and James Burgh, whose *Political Disquisitions* recently published went beyond even her democratic sympathies.

Mr Johnson did not give her much time for reflection on her own development, however. Work was showered on her, good, bad and indifferent. One can sympathize with her curt dispatch of one mediocre novelist, 'Pray, Miss, write no more', and recognize the change in her attitude towards fellow-writers. They no longer represented a company of the elect to which she aspired to belong. She now considered that their numbers should be reduced to allow those authors who were governed by Reason and Understanding the better to be heard.

Among the books that influenced her was Catherine Macaulay's *Letters on Education*. Education for Mary was the panacea for most social ills; not only education for under-privileged women but for all who desired it. Recently she had read *Sandford and Merton*, whose author, Thomas Day, was a disciple of Rousseau and a firm believer in the ideal state of nature. He was a light in the gloom of prejudice and tradition that obscured so much in the field of learning.

Mary sat with a volume of Burke's *Reflections* open before her and wrestled with her anger at this breach in the democratic front by one who had once been a friend of the American rebels and should have been foremost in the ranks of those who fought for freedom and equality. On the contrary, he now surpassed himself in an attack on Jacobinism, whether French or English, in all its forms, and had become an implacable enemy of the French revolutionaries. They were, he said, the destroyers of the national institutions set up by experienced and informed men. (Few men were fit to govern themselves, let alone their neighbours.) They were guilty of frauds, burnings, murders, confiscations, tyranny and cruelty. Such means could never achieve liberty, and England with her experience of the Bloodless Revolution knew this all too well. But England would never copy her neighbour. She believed a country should be run by professional statesmen and not by a murderous rabble. The treatment of Marie Antoinette was an appalling disgrace to a cultured nation, and indeed an outrage upon the entire

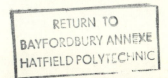

civilized world. That beauty and high birth could be so used meant the end of chivalry and the refinement of centuries.

It was perhaps when Mary came to the passage on Marie Antoinette that she veered most abruptly away from Burke. In this piece of fine writing he is elevating a woman for reasons of which Mary strongly disapproved, reasons that would lead only to woman's lasting enslavement. It was woman as a symbol of man's need for a feminine ideal, not woman for herself and in herself, that had stirred his eloquence. Woman's significance for man was his real theme. And indeed the whole passage is redolent of those values which Mary's new insight into the ills of society had taught her to eschew; more than that, to expose for their inherent dangers.

Burke began by recalling his first sight of Marie Antoinette when she had become Queen sixteen years before.

'I saw her just above the horizon, decorating and cheering the elevated sphere she just began to move in—glittering like the morning star, full of life, and splendour, and joy. Oh! what a revolution, and what a heart I must have to contemplate without emotion that elevation and that fall. Little did I dream when she added titles of veneration to those of enthusiastic, distant respectful love that she should ever be obliged to carry the sharp antidote against disgrace concealed in that bosom, little did I dream that I should have lived to see such disasters fallen upon her in a nation of gallant men, in a nation of men of honour, and of cavaliers. I thought ten thousand swords must have leaped from their scabbards to avenge even a look that threatened with insult. But the age of chivalry is gone. That of sophisters, economists and calculators has succeeded; and the glory of Europe is extinguished for ever. Never, never more shall we behold that generous loyalty to rank and sex, that proud submission, that dignified obedience, that subordination of the heart which kept alive, even in servitude itself the spirit of an exalted freedom. The unbought grace of life, the cheap defence of nations, the nurse of manly sentiment and heroic enterprise is gone. It is gone, that sensibility of principle, that chastity of honour which felt a stain like a wound, which inspired courage whilst it mitigated ferocity, which ennobled whatever it touched and under which vice itself lost half its evil by losing all its grossness.'[2]

Such a passage sickened Mary. How much suffering was smothered beneath those fine phrases 'proud submission, dignified obedience, subordination of the heart'. Was it not exactly those so-called virtues that blinded men and women to realities; such realities as those of a child lying all night outside her parents' bedroom door ready to intervene should the sound of blows from the hand of a brutal husband on his wife become too terrible for her to bear? 'The unbought grace of life, the age of chivalry, the ten thousand swords that must have leapt from their scabbards to avenge even a look that threatened her with insult'—how splendid it sounded when uttered by a famous orator in defence of a queen. But hundreds and thousands of women, poor, ignorant, unjustly used and without defence inspired no eloquence. As for 'that distant respectful love' which should have stirred a nation of 'gallant men, men of honour and cavaliers', were there not numberless exploited workers, toilers of the soil and in the cities, labouring long hours for a pittance, subject to cruel laws, forfeiting their lives for small unlawful acts such as pilfering and disrespectful speech? Who wrote fine phrases in their defence? Why was Burke's eloquence so bounded in its range? That sensibility of principle which he so rightly admired, why did it cease to operate as soon as the subject was lowly and unwashed?

Doubts of a different order also assailed Mary. Was she not in the ardour of her feeling for justice going beyond her powers? In her *Vindication of the Rights of Men* she was attacking a statesman of top rank, highly educated, armed with all the weapons of his station in life and experience of office, leader of a powerful party in Parliament. It was unheard of that a woman so recently promoted to intellectual ranks should challenge such eminence. Also she knew how little versed she was in matters of government and how unprepared to criticize Burke's analysis of the new French constitution. She was more at home in attacking the common failings of politicians and their fashionable wives, accusing Burke of his partiality for 'gentlemen' as against the poor man with only his native dignity to recommend him. In general terms she declared that the rights of men were 'such a degree of liberty, civil and religious, as is compatible with the liberty of the other individuals whom he is united with in a social compact'. But she could bring no background of long study and knowledge of comparative systems in support of her views. It was her strong feeling for social justice that fired her words and gave them depth.

'Man preys on man', she wrote, 'and you mourn for the idle tapestry that decorated a gothic pile and the droning bell that summoned that fat priest to prayer. You mourn for the empty pageant of a name when slavery flaps her wing and the sick heart retires to die in lonely wilds far from the abodes of man. ... Hell stalks abroad—the lash resounds on the slave's naked sides, and the sick wretch who can no longer earn the sour bread of unremitting labour steals to a ditch to bid the world a long good night—or neglected in some ostentatious hospital breathes his last amidst the laughs of mercenary attendants. Such misery demands more than tears—I pause to recollect myself and smother the contempt I feel rising from your rhetorical flourishes and infantile sensibility.'[3]

Mary's book was not the only answer to Burke's *Reflections*; nor in truth was it a particularly worthy response to that eloquent, forceful work. She could not give a worthy response and she knew it. She could only express in her own words her 'indignation roused by the sophistical argument'. To her it seemed he had betrayed the cause of humanity by upholding principles based on tyranny which had already been repudiated in America. He was not the great humanist she had supposed, but a man of strong prejudices, and as far as women were concerned, the blandly indifferent superior of the mass of the feminine world. No, Burke must be shewn for what he was, a brilliant and misleading relic of the past. But someone better qualified than herself must repudiate his argument, and in fact when the first part of Thomas Paine's *Rights of Man* was published in 1791 this was magnificently carried out. Paine's work supplied the comprehensive answer Mary would have liked to be able to write. Paine summed up in a single sentence the falsity of

Burke's special pleading: 'He pitied the plumage but forgot the dying bird.'

His book was highly inflammatory and, as Pitt remarked, 'true as it was, if acted upon would lead to bloody revolution in England'. Paine was indicted for treason in 1792 but, warned in time by Blake, managed to escape to France where he was immediately elected by the Departement of Calais to the French Convention. Considered the arch-revolutionary in England, he was soon to fall under suspicion in France on account of the moderation of his views, as compared with those of the Jacobins.

The composing of Mary's book gave her considerable trouble and, worse than that, filled her with doubts about her rights to such authorship. Also she was beginning to lose interest in Burke's long, involved sentences. Johnson, who had first encouraged her to the task and had already seen the part she had written through the press, was not in the least disheartened by her lapse of courage. When she confessed to him her misgivings he consoled her and offered to destroy what was already printed. This was enough for her to muster her forces again. If he had abused her she would have accepted defeat and fallen into despair, but his unexpected sympathy and kindness restored her faith in herself and her lack of faith in Burke. She set about writing once more and worked so rapidly that in less than two months after Burke's *Reflections* appeared Mary's *Rights of Men* was on sale in Johnson's shop.

Her book might be inadequate but it had a force of passion which impressed readers, and personal attack has a much greater popular appeal than abstract reasoning. The book sold well and brought her renown not only in radical circles but also in the literary world at large. She had become a powerful propagandist of the democratic principles to which she had been converted. New converts are given to over-emphasis and certainly Mary had this fault. Also rhetoric came naturally to her, and once the flame was lit it would burn fiercely without much further effort.

The first edition, anonymous, was soon exhausted, but the second edition, appearing in December 1790, bore her name and placed her on the list of *avant-garde* political authors. Now she felt she could face her fellow writers as an equal. Her position was most agreeable. This is what she had set out to achieve in those days of exile and humiliation in Ireland. This was the reward of lonely hours of study and reflection during which she could hardly bear to contemplate her goal, so remote and unattainable it had seemed.

For the first time in her life she enjoyed a period of affluence. True, both her sisters and at least one brother still called upon her generosity; none the less she felt she owed it to her promotion in learned society to be better housed than in the dingy precincts of Blackfriars. She moved to superior lodgings in Store Street, near Bedford Square, an improvement which called for similar efforts on behalf of her personal appearance. During those years when she had neglected herself, she had almost forgotten what it was to look in a mirror; for there seemed no point in viewing her uncared for condition, her abundant hair hanging untidily to her shoulders, her lack of cosmetics, her coarse clothes. Now she resolved to correct her slovenliness. The mirror reminded her that she had claims to beauty which needed but a little attention to become evident. It was amusing for one who had dared to scold a great orator as though he were a schoolboy, to be seen as a coquettish young woman who took an interest in elegant attire as much as any other female member of the polite world. Soon she was acknowledged to be an ornament to the masculine company Mr Johnson entertained. In short, she blossomed as a beauty, and as such changed the direction of her efforts, or rather, new inspiration was added to her zest for living. Life was not all work and no play; life was fulfilment of every facet of the human personality.

In the meantime her sisters were not enjoying the contrast between Mary's position and their own dreary existence. Why was this reprehensible eldest sister who broke all the rules in such a superior situation? And what was she doing to extend her prosperity to her family, who surely had first claim? The Blood family still clung to the friend of their unfortunate daughter and seemed to think they had a right to her assistance. Moreover Mary had adopted a little girl, Ann, a niece of Fanny Blood's husband. She called the child her daughter and lavished love on her, and money that she could ill afford.

Eliza was employed at a school in Putney owned by a Mrs Bregantz, and Everina was still in France at Mary's expense, yet they gave their sister no rest, so that in exasperation she wrote:

> 'Respecting you, I should have a little peace. ... If I had not cared for my sisters, who certainly do not adore me, the last two years of my life might have passed tranquilly, not embittered by pecuniary cares.'

This straight speaking did not draw the sisters together and from that time the distances that divided them grew.

Not only the sisters but also her brother Charles and her father considered they had claims upon her. Charles, the youngest brother, had been articled to the eldest, Edward, a successful attorney, but the two men fell out and Mary had the task of finding another master for Charles. This too failed and Charles escaped to Ireland. Mary lost patience and wrote to George Blood:

> 'He has wounded a heart that was full of anxiety on his account, and disappointed hope. ... Let me now request you to have an eye on his conduct, and if you can get him into any employment you will relieve me from a heavy weight.'

Eventually Charles turned out not too badly, thanks to Mary's efforts. After trying unsuccessfully to get him settled in India she managed to apprentice him to a farmer in America and he left England in 1792. Farming being his true vocation, he was at last off her hands and she could give her attention to James, who was a sailor. She sent him to study mathematics at Woolwich and within a few months he was able to join the fleet of Lord Hood and rose to be a lieutenant. One way or another Mary had launched her brothers and sisters, and found herself the poorer by £200. But there was still her father to be considered. Almost destitute by now, with a new wife, he depended on Mary to bring some order into his existence. Eliza, who had recently left Mrs Bregantz's school to fill a position as governess at Upton Castle in Wales, took the opportunity to visit her parent at Laugharne and drew this picture of him for Mary's benefit:

> 'The sight of my father's ghostly visage haunts me night and

day; for he is really worn to a mere skeleton and has a dreadful cough that makes my blood run cold whenever I listen to it; and that is the greater part of the night, or else he groans most dreadfully; yet he declares he has good nights. There cannot be a more melancholy sight to see him not able to walk ten yards without panting for breath; and continually falling —still he is able to ride ten miles every day; and eat and drink very hearty. . . . When I beg him to be more careful on money matters he declares he will go to London and force Ned, or when I tell him how Mary has been distressed in order to make him save on trifles, he is in a passion and exhausts himself.'[4]

There was little comfort for Mary in this. As she said in a letter to George Blood,

'I live in continual fear of having him thrown upon me for his whole support; for though Edward is once more in business and even in a flourishing way, I am told yet he is going on in the old track, and it does not require great foresight to see what must be the consequence. However I do not disturb myself by anticipating an evil which no forethought can ward off.'[5]

George Blood, always a faithful friend, had lent her money when what she had was exhausted; Johnson had been so generous in the matter of advance payments that she felt she could not appeal further to him. 'Excepting Mr Johnson I do not owe twenty pounds,' she wrote to George. 'This winter I shall try hard to lessen the pounds that stand against me in his books.' There was no remedy for her troubles but persistent hard work. Three of her books were bringing in a steady return: *A Vindication of the Rights of Men*, *Original Stories* and her translation of Salzmann's *Elements of Morality*. Together with her own *Original Stories* this last was the most rewarding of her ventures, due partly to the fact that Blake had illustrated both works.

6

Fuseli and Other Company

Few of the men who assembled in Johnson's upper room had yet the reputation they were to acquire posthumously. A number of them were engaged on work that has immortalized their names, but at this epoch they represented a new class, a generation of educated men (many of them religious dissenters) who were determined to challenge the abuses of the law and the constitution common in the eighteenth century, and who were therefore looked upon with distrust by the majority, and, by the 1790s, with active hostility. They formed clubs and societies, were generally prosperous in trade and the professions, and they had the means for leisure. Such were the new middle classes, looked down on by the upper classes who sat in Parliament and ruled the country. As reformers they had little respect for tradition and the conventions, but were motivated by what Godwin qualified as a 'strong benevolence of soul'. They thought the French Revolution ushered in the New Age and as such merited their whole-hearted and largely uncritical support. Some of them had travelled to Paris to see for themselves what was happening there and in their turn they welcomed in London any French rebel who crossed the Channel.

Tom Paine was perhaps the most remarkable of Johnson's friends; his outward appearance was not such as to inspire confidence. He was far from handsome, his coarse skin, eyes that had a 'strange ideotish [sic] obliquity' and frizzy hair carelessly tied behind, did nothing to improve his looks which were those of a rough working-man, though he was, in fact, the son of a small Thetford farmer, and a former excise officer. Yet Tom Paine had an influence, in English-speaking countries, comparable with that of Rousseau, with his powerful mind, his perceptiveness, his wide generosity of soul, his command of language, and his feeling for the as yet undeveloped potentialities and aspirations of the masses.

While in Philadelphia in 1775 he had written a forceful essay on *Slavery* in which he assembled facts and ideas that came in useful later when he was dealing with the cause of Feminism. (John Stuart Mill in his essay on *The Subjection of Women* was to maintain that the slavery of women was more degrading, cruel and hopeless than that of the black man in the cotton fields.) He wrote on marriage and divorce, with emphasis on the feminine aspect of the question, on international arbitration, on pacifism, on duelling, on cruelty to animals and other issues upon which he thought men should exercise their reason rather than indulge their passions. His book entitled *Common Sense* was the voice of the New Man pointing the way to freedom and to what came to be called democracy. A hundred years ahead of the times he wrote a clear, unencumbered language easy for all classes to understand. Once his book was published he joined the American army and fought in the ranks through the war.

Tom Paine was a brother in thought to William Godwin, and in vision to William Blake, the outstanding artist of the group. Blake was self-taught, had read widely and was a visionary of amazing power; eventually he became an ardent revolutionary and he alone of the English Jacobins had the courage to wear the *bonnet rouge* of the French revolutionaries. Yet he considered himself wholly an artist and was primarily a mystical, not a political, thinker. He maintained that he acted 'by command'. The spirit had said to him: 'Blake, be an artist and nothing else.' He concurred, replying: 'I should be sorry if I had any earthly fame . . . I wish to do nothing for profit. I wish to live for art.' Yet his compassion for suffering, an empathy of feeling, converted him to the cause of Liberty. His *Songs of Innocence* had been published in 1789, but his *Songs of Experience* and prophetic books were still in the making. He was not yet established as a notable man of letters and in fact was far from looking the part; short and corpulent with a round smiling face, it was difficult to see in him a prophet of the future.

Mary herself was not impressed and was even condescending to this strange, gifted man who at times seemed a little lost in the company of hard-headed philosophers; particularly that of Godwin, who had little understanding of unseen realities.

Blake was a friend of Sir Joshua Reynolds and the two artists sometimes met to exchange views on the fundamentals of their work. 'Art,' said Reynolds, 'is intrinsically imitation. Genius is not inspiration but the effect of close observation and expression.' 'Damned fool,' answered Blake. 'In the midst of the highest flights of fancy and imagination, reason ought to preside from first to last,' said Reynolds. 'If this is true,' said Blake, 'it is a devilish foolish thing to be an artist.' 'Mere enthusiasm will carry you a little way,' said Reynolds. 'Mere enthusiasm,' Blake answered, 'is the all in all.'[1]

In this judgment Mary was of the same mind. For her too enthusiasm was the all in all, and she also had to be careful of her quick tongue and over-eager participation in the argument. Like the poet, she was uncertain of Godwin, who regarded her as an intruder and one who took more than her fair share of the talk.

Mary first met William Godwin at a friend's dinner party. Tom Paine was also there and Godwin wanted nothing better than to exchange ideas with this much experienced revolutionary. But Paine was not loquacious and required to be drawn out, which Godwin was prepared to do had not Mary frustrated him, airing her own views and coming between the two men. Godwin was optimistic and constructive by nature. Mary was pessimistic and full of condemnation of those writers who did not share her opinions. This annoyed Godwin, and when they got onto the subject of religion and he discovered how closely she still adhered to the accepted code, he mentally dismissed her as an unoriginal thinker. Later on, however, discussing Voltaire their opinions coincided, which did a great deal to improve his first unfavourable reaction to her.

Godwin was the son of a Unitarian minister whose example he was expected to follow. With this idea he attended Hoxton Academy

and was in fact in residence when the Wollstonecraft family moved
to that place. But there was no meeting, no knowledge of this turn
of destiny. Feeling he had not a true vocation for the Church, he
turned to writing. At the time when he first met Mary he was writing
his masterpiece *Political Justice* which was to place him foremost
among writers on political science. His ideas were anathema to
most people, for he disapproved of so much: of the monarchy, of
marriage, and of all forms of government which he thought were
inevitably corrupt; and in any case, according to Godwin, all control
of man by man was to be deplored. He was against punishment as
it was productive of further evil. The acquisition of property was
an outrage against equality. Man, he said, has no innate vice in
him and needs only to be left to himself to achieve happiness. The
one true guide to right living is pure reason. Once this lesson has been
learnt all will be well.

Although he was a propagandist of universal benevolence something was lacking in his approach. His passionate belief in the working
of logic was not calculated to warm the hearts of his followers. He
had no common touch; he had no creative imagination. As one
critic remarked, 'his great head was full of cold brains'.

Such was Godwin when Mary first knew him. He was soon to be
engaged on his novel, *Things as They Are: or, the Adventures of
Caleb Williams*. It is a book with a purpose, social justice, and
contains psychological matter far in advance of contemporary
writing on the subject. In this respect it may be reckoned a modern
work with a theme that still challenges the psychologist.

Caleb Williams reveals the Godwin who was eventually to rouse
Mary's love, but for the time being, on the few occasions they met,
these two did not draw out the best in each other. Godwin was
reserved, cold and obstinate. Both his parents had been Unitarian
Calvinists and he had inherited from them a disciplined habit of
mind which was alien to impulsive Mary, who had found the discipline of hard experience sufficient in itself. Her desire now was to test
her growing power, to spread her wings, to fly with the high flyers.

There were other notable visitors to Johnson's room who were
endeared to her by the support they gave to her opinions. Among
them were Thomas Christie (and his wife) co-founder with Johnson

of the *Analytical Review*, and Joel and Ruth Barlow, American idealists, who saw the French Revolution as the great release from tyranny and not the unleashed ruthless struggle for power that it was fast becoming. And there was the eminent Dr Priestley, now resident in London after the destruction of his home and chapel in Birmingham. Priestley was a scientist in the modern sense, who spoke French, Italian and German and was much travelled. His interests were wide: politics, philosophy, religion, science or the systematic knowledge of nature. While in Paris he knew Lavoisier and other French researchers in the field of Natural Philosophy, with whom he shared his discoveries. For Mary such a person represented a one-man university, and although there is no record of their having met, it cannot be doubted that the writings of this master of new developments in several departments of knowledge who at the same time did not lose sight of men's happiness in its everyday aspect, had its influence on her. Her experience of life, of men's ways of thought and action, was deepening with every day she spent in London.

There was another remarkable man who had for a short period more influence on Mary's life than any other she had met hitherto. This was Henry Fuseli, friend of William Blake, an artist with dramatic powers of expression, who never underestimated himself however tempted he might be to render this service for others. 'He was,' Godwin wrote, 'the most frankly disingenuous and conceited man I ever knew. He could not bear to be eclipsed or put in the background for a moment.'[2] This was true, but at the same time there was much to respect in Fuseli, and as Goethe pointed out, 'not only to respect but to contemplate with awe'.

Henry Fuseli, born in Zürich in 1741, was the son of a painter of mediocre talent, who was the father of eighteen children, Henry being the second. Like his father he became an artist and considered from the first that he was one of those who would 'conquer immortality'. His nature was proud, self-opinionated and harsh. He had great gifts although not of the magnitude he imagined. Michelangelo was the painter he most admired and the model that inspired him.

Zürich at that time was a European intellectual centre, harbouring famous men. Here Fuseli met J. K. Lavater—'the incomparable

Lavater'—the physiognomist who was the recipient of Goethe's warm affection; also J. J. Bodmer, the eminent Professor of Helvetian History, who had translated *Paradise Lost* and edited an edition of the *Nibelungenlied*. The intellectual atmosphere in the Swiss city owed much to English influence, and Fuseli decided to seek inspiration in the land of Shakespeare. At the age of twenty-two he came to London, where he stayed several years—supporting himself by writing until persuaded by Sir Joshua Reynolds to devote himself to art. Next he visited Rome, Venice and Naples and came under the influence of Michelangelo. 'When anyone speaks the word "Rome",' he wrote, 'my heart swells, my eyes are inflamed and I am seized with frenzy.' Eventually he returned to England, which then became his permanent home.

Nature did not inspire Fuseli; he found his chief stimuli in museums and libraries. He was a literary painter, a weakness which cut him off from fresh sources of inspiration and filled his vision with dramatic figures, with grimacing devils and demons, or with beautiful females who in the extremes of suffering maintain a smooth statuesque appearance. His creatures are those that haunt dreams and furnish fantastic reveries. When he painted he was possessed by a frenzied impatience and worked to deliver himself.

He could be vindictive. At his first, unsuccessful, application for admission to the Royal Academy, two of his friends, Opie and Northcote, voted against him and later called to explain their attitude. He brushed them aside saying:

> 'I regret you have taken the trouble to come and see me. My reputation with my neighbours will suffer. They will take one of you for a petty Jewish creditor and the other for a clerk.'[3]

As one of Johnson's oldest friends and a co-founder of the *Analytical Review* he used to frequent the room above the shop at 72 St Paul's Churchyard, mixing with the radical group. Here he met Mary Wollstonecraft, who shared some of his tastes, in particular his admiration for Rousseau.

> 'Rousseau,' she wrote, 'speaks to the heart, and whoever reading his works could doubt whether he wrote from it had

better take up some other book. . . . It is impossible to peruse his simple descriptions without loving the man in spite of the weakness of character that he himself depicts which never appears to have risen from depravity of heart.'[4]

It may be imagined that Fuseli's devotion to Rousseau derived from qualities other than these, nevertheless Mary's appreciation of this genius did much to predispose Fuseli towards her. In 1778 he had visited Rousseau in Paris, had met the great man face to face. It had been one of the climacterics of his life.

Fuseli's conversation was brilliant and the force of his personality overwhelming. He was fifty years of age and Mary was approaching thirty-three. She had never been loved and longed for this, and in her turn to love. The force and originality of the Swiss artist were more than she could meet with calm. Her imagination took fire and soon she was profoundly in love, without at first realizing the fact. They were most stimulating to each other; they conversed chiefly on the virtues of painting, and from that subject were led on to discuss literature, in particular Homer. Rousseau was their chief point of contact. Fuseli agreed with Rousseau's condemnation of civilization and with his advocacy of the noble savage; he even went further than Mary was prepared to follow; fortunately his caustic mind supplied its own corrective.

Fuseli had married Sophia Rawlins in 1788. His marriage was one hurdle she had to surmount in her passionate desire to get nearer to him; another was his time-consuming work for the Shakespeare Plan, with which Mary much sympathized. It was two years previous to his marriage that he became engaged on this work, which was to make him famous. It consisted of nine illustrations on Shakespearian subjects which he contributed to Boydell's Shakespearian Exhibition in Pall Mall. Referring to the Plan, Mary writes:

'We consider the Plan of Messrs Boydell as a nursery of Historic painting, as a hint towards the true method of calling forth the grandeur of art in a country whose religion, climate and fashions have hitherto repressed it.'

Mary was in a dangerous state of exultation alternating with moods of despair. 'I am a strange compound of weakness and resolution. There is certainly a great defect in my mind, my wayward heart creates its own misery,' she wrote to Johnson, who was always her faithful ally. 'You are my only friend,' she wrote on another occasion, 'the only person I am intimate with ... we must each of us wear a cap and bells but mine has lost its bells. Too often should I have been out of patience with my fellow creatures whom I wish to love.'

The heart of her trouble lay in her passion for Fuseli, which he did not reciprocate. He had already too much to express in his general philosophy. Sophia Rawlins, a forthright woman, had little sympathy with views of marriage deriving from Godwin's anarchical approach to the subject. For Sophia marriage was marriage, an indissoluble bond; whereas Mary, with her knowledge of how cruel a prison marriage could prove, had little respect for the institution. Her respect was for the quality of the people who were involved. She saw Fuseli, Sophia and herself as superior beings who could ignore conventional standards of conduct. Jealousy was unthinkable to creatures of their superior cast. Her ardent longings blinded her not only to characteristics in Fuseli which were far from being ideal from her point of view, but also to the humiliations she was inviting. She began to bombard him with letters, which he did not always read but tied up in neat packets and kept in a drawer.

What did Mary really hope for in courting this extremely fastidious painter who considered he had every reason to be difficult in his choice of companion? A member of the *élite* of Zürich upon whom the glory of Goethe had been reflected, dear friend of 'incomparable' Lavater and J. J. Bodmer, one who had 'seen Rousseau plain', one upon whom the mantle of Michelangelo had fallen? Twenty years her senior in age he regarded this importunate young woman with impatience, if not disdain. Although he could approve her republicanism, her insistence upon the 'woman question' struck him as having little relevance to the infinitely more important issues of the day. It is true that Mary was now physically an extremely attractive woman, who could hold her own in brilliant talk, and was much admired by the men whom Fuseli respected. Southey writing of her said:

'She is a first-rate woman, sensible of her own worth, but without arrogance or affectation.'[5]

A contemporary, writing of her charm, was particularly struck by a countenance that betrayed years of trial.

'Her face was striking. The unutterable sadness of her expression combined with her other charms made strangers turn to look a second time. Few could resist the influence of her personality. She talked cleverly and even brilliantly, although at times her conversation was acrid and gloomy . . . she was recognized as a woman of more than ordinary talents.'

Fuseli was too egocentric to be accessible to the appeal of a talented woman interested in a field that did not attract him. Although he was plunged in dreams and reveries to which he gave feverish expression in his paintings, he was not indifferent to the opinion of the world on his personality and genius. His appearance was not particularly impressive. Short of stature and thickly built, he felt he needed rich apparel to compensate for what nature had denied him. He wanted clothing that would do justice to his genius, and he had tailored a flame-coloured coat which he wore with great satisfaction, until the jeers of his friends, who considered the garment too fantastic to honour fashion, robbed him of his pleasure in it.

He habitually stated his age as four years less than it was. This, like the flame-coloured coat, did not enhance his reputation; moreover his merit as a painter was sufficient without these doubtful props. One of his pupils was the artist Haydon, who closely watched his master at work.

'He painted with impatience, in a sort of fury, improvising in a way which was evident in the result. He would take his brush and transfer to the canvas a thick layer of blue, or red or white, and suddenly he had created a head, a shoulder, a movement.'

Few painters equalled him in the power of interior vision. But the pictures were often terrifying, as though he had been long haunted by them and had to be delivered of their hold upon his imagination. In all this he could not have differed more than from the serenity of Blake's mystical works. Both artists drew upon strong sexual fancies, but whereas Blake gave them a spiritual interpretation, Fuseli emphasized the physical aspect: males with bulging muscles and heroic stances, females whose flesh was either like foam dashed against rock, or statuesque and deathly. Michelangelo's influence was evident but, lacking his spiritual quality, the tone of Fuseli's work was romantic eroticism. For the most part all was fury and movement, every inch of the canvas inhabited by fantastic creatures. The paintings made a tremendous impact upon the viewer, who might at first turn away in unbelief but usually came back to look once more upon those curious, violent statements.

Mary with her ardent nature and an unsatisfied longing for full-blooded happiness fell into the trap nature had laid for her. However much she preferred the company of males to females, she had no lover and had come to a point when masculine company was essential to her happiness. She did not allow herself to look too closely into Fuseli's character. His gifts spoke for him, and they were enormous.

She had been a friend of Fuseli's wife Sophia before her marriage; together with Johnson, the four companions passed many pleasant evenings at the theatre or the coffee-house. The more Mary saw of Fuseli the more she was convinced that she had found the ideal partner to satisfy the calls of her intellect and the needs of her temperament. Without the possibility of seeing Fuseli every day, life would lose all its savour; she addressed passionate letters to him and remained unaware how impossibly exacting she was. 'If I thought my passion criminal I would conquer it or die in the attempt,' she wrote to him. She agreed that Mrs Fuseli had a prior right to the person of her husband, but she, Mary, might claim to hold a place in his heart and in his intellectual life. Also, since they had so much in common it was only natural that they should be allowed full intimacy of their persons.

She wrote to Mrs Fuseli describing 'the sincere affection which I have for your husband, for I find that I cannot live without the satisfaction of seeing and conversing with him daily'. Why, she asked, should she not join their household and all three of them profit by mutual enrichment? As she dwelt on this picture of triangular bliss it appeared to solve her worst problems, her solitude, her unsatisfied nature, her longing for stable day-to-day happiness, so necessary for the writer and artist to produce his best work. She was contemplating a new book and Fuseli was engaged on his Shakespearian portraits. Both of them had work that claimed the major part of their time and attention; but Mary was starving for an intimate relationship and could not wait for what she considered were her rights as a human being.

Had not Godwin written that 'marriage is an affair of property, the worst of all properties'?[6] And as she herself pronounced in one of her writings, 'to be married is to be bestilled for life'; and in another passage, 'Gain experience—ah! gain it while experience is worth having and acquire sufficient fortitude to pursue your own happiness; it includes your utility by a direct path.'[7]

Her opinion of marriage based on her memories of her mother's and Eliza's servitude, and on observation of the married state at all levels of society, brought her to the conclusion that 'marriage as at present constituted leads to immorality' and 'the laws respecting women make an absurd unit of a man and his wife'. There was little on her conscience to restrain her from proposing to share another woman's husband. Why should her old friend Sophia object to extend her happiness to a less fortunate sister? All situations yield to reason. Man left to himself, uninhibited by law and custom, was full of virtue. It was governments and legal injunctions that corrupted him. She had not read Rousseau and Godwin to no purpose.

Mrs Fuseli was probably less well read, and nothing in her nature or in her situation encouraged her to think along these lines. Her marriage was of recent date and probably she had not yet realized that Fuseli was not the ideal husband she supposed him to be. She knew that although he thought well of Mary's intelligence and literary achievements he had no liking for women who claimed to exist in their own right and not as adjuncts of man. He had argued this point with Mary and had been shocked by her vigorous dissent.

Her admiration of his work was flattering but it was only what he had expected.

Mary continued to send him letters assuring him that her love was inspired by his intellect and that her feelings were 'unalloyed by passion'. She had never before known a man with 'those noble qualities, that grandeur of soul, that quickness of comprehension and lively sympathy' such as he possessed. He made no reply and allowed things to take their course.

When Lavater visited Fuseli in London she was invited to go out with them, to theatres and on excursions, none of which helped to calm her passion. She was excellent company if only she could govern her wayward feelings. Unfortunately she grew increasingly blind to the reality of the situation in spite of plain speaking from Sophia.

Although Mary still insisted that her feelings were platonic and was hurt by Sophia's suspicion, nevertheless her mind was split. She needed to convince herself that she was innocent of harm. She was honest and did not pretend that her interest was wholly centred in Fuseli's intellect. No, it was in his heart that she wanted to be welcomed. And her imagination tortured her with visions of what might be if only he were free, if only their union could be complete. It was difficult to believe that all the advances came from her side, for it seemed to her impossible that his feelings did not match hers; that 'First as last I have not quickened his pulse one beat, Fixed a moment's fancy bitter or sweet,' as Browning put it in later years.

Her great work, *A Vindication of the Rights of Woman*, published in 1792, was written in six weeks in a rush of strong feeling, and under the pressure of a vast accumulation of facts on the situation of women: domestic, political, financial, and especially in education. That same year she received a visit from Talleyrand, a former ambassador at the Court of St James, and discussed with him his *Rapport sur l'Instruction Publique*. They had not seen eye to eye on all points and after much argument, in which it was obvious that he was not much interested in the liberation of women, she offered him wine in a teacup, and probably took the opportunity to remind him that Condorcet in his *Rapport sur l'Organisation Générale de l'Instruction Publique* had insisted that all citizens irrespective of sex or rank should benefit by free state instruction. Co-education on a footing of total equality was entirely in accordance with her views. Both Talleyrand and Condorcet, like herself, owed much to Locke's *Thoughts Concerning Education* and *Essay Concerning Human Understanding*; also they subscribed, with reserves from Talleyrand, to the English philosopher's concept of 'indefinite perfectibility' for both men and women, given the means, that is, the training of the mind, in the cause of human progress.

Among French writers who considered women's education a matter of primary importance was Olympe de Gouges. She had founded women's clubs and supported the Fraternal Societies of Patriots for the two sexes, which were complementary to the salons of the accomplished hostesses of the *Encyclopédistes*. Olympe de Gouges published in 1791 a *Déclaration des droits de la femme et de la citoyenne*. Taking the seventeen articles of the *Déclaration des Droits de l'Homme* and replacing wherever she found it the word man by woman, she demanded that women should have exactly the same political and social rights as men. One of her convictions was that marriage as an institution had failed and should be substituted by '*une sorte d'union libre*' within the context of '*le contrat social*', where the interests of the children are safeguarded in the event of infidelity of one partner or the other. But Olympe de Gouges met with little sympathy from members of the Convention Nationale, which suppressed the women's clubs and effectively put an end to hopes of equal political freedom for women of the Revolution.

All this lit a flame in Mary. The attack on marriage as an institution, if indeed she read it, would have supplied further justification for her passion for Fuseli, and blinded her to the wrong she was doing his partner. Yet deep in her conscience she must have been aware she was offending against long-established principles and was earning Fuseli's scorn. But much else of what she advocated offended against long-established principles and was not to be condemned for that. It was difficult to be entirely fair to oneself, to distinguish between ardent desire and objective truths. Politics, religion and morals were interdependent disciplines. It was a person's attitude of mind that determined his actions. She had sought experience and had not shrunk from mental strife, but so far happiness had eluded her. Surely she should be allowed to conquer a little for herself.

In England other women were writing about these problems. Mrs Barbauld, for one, held that an immoderate love of study rendered women unhappy, and young girls should have just sufficient education to make them agreeable companions to men. Also a poet, she dedicated one of her works *To a Lady with Some Painted Flowers*. 'Your best, your Sweetest Empire is to please,' she informed the recipient.

In opposition to these sentiments Lady Mary Wortley Montagu considered that 'learning is necessary to the happiness of women, and ignorance the common foundation of their errors'. Yet she advised that a woman should conceal her learning 'with as much solicitude as she would hide crookedness or lameness'.[8] Mary remembered that her friend, Dr George Fordyce, one of the habitués of Johnson's upper room, had a brother, Dr James Fordyce, who had written *Sermons to Young Women* in which he recommended 'the retiring graces'. Women should be meek, timid, yielding, complacent, sweet, benign and tender, with 'a propensity to melt into affectionate sorrow'.[9]

With the exception of Lady Mary Wortley Montagu who, writing under the pseudonym 'Sophia', had already in 1740 made a plea for better education for women and published a paper entitled *Woman's Superior Excellence to Man*, and Catherine Macaulay with her *Letters on Education*, there was little comfort in present or past publications. And no writer dealt with Mary's particular aspect of the problem, woman's right to contrive her own happiness without the restraints imposed by false modesty and female docility. 'It would seem,' she wrote, 'that one reason why men have superior judgment, and more fortitude than women, is undoubtedly this, that they give a freer scope to the grand passions, and by more frequently going astray enlarge their minds.'[10] Docility had been the cause of women's lack of development and limited nature; it must be obliterated from the list of feminine virtues. The same could be said of false modesty.

Human beings must be active in their own creation. The contrast of her present station in life with that of her 'docile' sisters amply proved her point. '[A man]', she wrote, 'may avoid gross vices because honesty is the best policy, but he will never aim at attaining great virtues.' Then 'he should walk alone, only dependent on heaven for that emulous panting after perfection which ever glows in a noble mind'. Surveying recent perturbations in her life she regretted nothing. 'If in the dawn of life we could soberly survey the scenes before as in perspective, and see everything in its true colours, how could the passions gain sufficient strength to unfold the faculties?'[11] It was passion that nurtured intellect. She echoed Blake's words, 'Enthusiasm is the all in all.' Had she not given full rein to her 'enthusiasm' for Fuseli? 'The habit of reflection and the knowledge attained by fostering any passion might be shewn to be equally useful, though the object proved equally fallacious.'

7

'A Vindication of the Rights of Woman'

'Contending for the rights of woman, my main argument is built
on this simple principle, that if she be not prepared by education
to become the companion of man, she will stop the progress of
knowledge and virtue; for truth must be common to all, or it will
be inefficacious with respect to its influence on general practice.'

In this passage taken from her Dedication to M. Talleyrand-
Périgord is to be found the kernel not only of Mary's masterpiece,
A Vindication of the Rights of Woman, but of all her treasured
thoughts gathered from the stony soil of her life. The acquiring of
knowledge and truth, and the ability through education to give
them the greatest possible development, summed up the whole of
her philosophy.

By the year 1792, in the early part of which she wrote her book,
she had experienced many sides of life, most of them painful. And
now she had arrived at the fulfilment of her first obsessive ambition:
she was economically free, able to support herself by her pen, and
confident that she would always have this means at her disposal.
This, however, was but a beginning. She considered that her situation entailed responsibilities. She had not striven against almost
unsurmountable obstacles in order simply to triumph over opposing
forces. That was not her purpose, that alone would never have given
her the strength to endure what she had endured. It is true that her
personal victory gave her moments of profound satisfaction, a time

in which to inhale the breath of happiness arising out of a sense of achievement. It was legitimate to inhale this exhilarating air for a while, to draw new courage into her lungs.

As she looked back on her life, the impressions that came to her mind were so vivid, violent and many-sided that she felt she risked being submerged by them. Her sanity demanded a reckoning-up, a confrontation with the powers that had worked upon her, the good and the evil. She told herself it was not for her personal edification that all this had happened to her. The joys and sorrows of love (for Fanny in the first instance); the experience of cruelty such as she had witnessed in her mother's and sister's marriages, and her own involvement in them; the experience of living among a class of highly privileged and in the main irresponsible people such as the Kingsboroughs; the glimpses into the miseries of hopeless poverty as in Portugal and Ireland; the challenge of the contact with men of outstanding quality such as those she met in Johnson's house; the long solitary hours of study; the mastery of her own tongue and foreign languages necessitated by her work for the *Analytical Review*; and, last but not least, the impact upon her mind of the tremendous upheaval in France, the struggle for social justice going on there. All these had assailed her, changing the nature of her convictions, until she became convinced she must work for the betterment of humanity at large and not concentrate just on her own sex. So her vindication was that of women, but women in relation to men, in relation to the human race, in relation to the entire human experience. As she saw it, one half of humanity was being dragged in chains, a dead weight retarding the advance of the other half.

This was senseless; the liberation of women was intrinsic in that of men. Look where she might she saw men plunging forward in blindness and confusion, unaware of what it was that made the way ahead so hard, and what it was that so often turned the sweets of success into bitterness.

She chose, in ignorance of his true opinions, to dedicate her great effort to a man in whom lack of perception of the inner quality of the other sex was paramount. His interest in education had led her to believe he had understood that 'truth must be common to all' and not the perquisite of a select class and of one sex. Nor, it must

85

be acknowledged, did she at first realize that the new constitution of France did nothing to remove the gross inequalities in the treatment of women.

For Mary, education was the crux of the question. Education meant access to knowledge which was the key to thought, to creativeness, to the good life. Knowledge was meant to be used and its right use was consequent upon understanding. Understanding came through experience, for which economic freedom was essential. The mind must be liberated from the shackles of prejudice, greed and financial uncertainty: only then could the human spirit achieve its fullest expression.

The status of women in the eighteenth century—and for many centuries previously—was so low that the modern historian is tempted to ask how men who were most fierce in their struggle for social justice could at the same time condemn one half of humankind to conditions which were comparable to and even lower than those of the Negro slave in the fields of America. How came it that women were treated by men with such cruel partiality for the stronger and less handicapped sex? The fact of muscular superiority had determined the situation for so long that little sense of the enormous injustice to women had pierced the understanding of the great majority of men. It was enough that it was in their power to enforce their advantage, and they were doing this even in an epoch in history when the ideal of the equality of all mankind was being written in blood.

At the time Mary wrote her book she had sufficient first-hand experience of the callousness of the law and the general attitude of mind about women then prevailing to fire her pen. It was ironic that the man whose writings did most to set in motion that great upheaval for social justice, the French Revolution, was at the same time the most ruthless opponent of any improvement in the lot of women. Part of Mary's book could almost be described as a dialogue with Rousseau, as she comments on the opinions he sets out in *Émile*; for Rousseau she had in other respects much admiration, but his notion of what should be women's place not only in society but in the whole human drama was to her so false to the values that spell civilization that she centred her book on meeting his challenge.

She began by dealing with legal and educational aspects of the question which were consequent on a long-established attitude of mind. Accustomed over generations to a certain way of looking at the question, men envisaged that way with reverence as though it had been bestowed from on high by a superior intelligence which relieved them of their responsibility in the matter. Thus Mary attacks the poetical cosmogony of the Bible and the account of the fall of man, stoutly doubting at the same time the theory that women were created solely for men's convenience, 'though the cry of irreligion, or even atheism be raised against me'.

> '"Women [says Rousseau] have, or ought to have, but little liberty; they are apt to indulge themselves excessively in what is allowed them. . . . There results from this habitual restraint a tractableness which women have occasion for during their whole lives, as they constantly remain either under subjection to the men, or to the opinions of mankind. . . . The first and most important qualification in a woman is good nature . . . ; formed to obey a being so imperfect as man . . . she ought to learn betimes even to suffer injustice, and to bear the insults of a husband without complaint."' [1]

Mary, roused to indignation by such advice, retorts: 'The being who patiently endures injustice, and silently bears insults, will soon become unjust; . . . of what materials can that heart be composed which can melt when insulted, and instead of revolting at injustice, kiss the rod? . . .' [2]
'"Woman [continues Rousseau] has everything against her, as well our faults as her own timidity and weakness; she has nothing in her favour, but her subtility and her beauty.[3] Is it not very reasonable, therefore, she should cultivate both?"' Mary protests:

> 'Greatness of mind can never dwell with cunning or address; for I shall not boggle about words . . . but content myself with observing that if any class of mankind be so created that it must necessarily be educated by rules not strictly deducible from truth, virtue is an affair of convention. . . . Men have superior strength of body; but were it not for mistaken notions

87

of beauty, women would acquire sufficient to enable them to earn their own subsistence, the true definition of independence; and to bear those bodily inconveniences and exertions that are requisite to strengthen the mind. Let us then, by being allowed to take the same exercise as boys, not only during infancy, but youth, arrive at perfection of body, that we may know how far the natural superiority of man extends. For what reason or virtue can be expected from a creature when the seed-time of life is neglected?'[4]

'"The tongues of women [Rousseau asserts] are very voluble. . . . A man speaks of what he knows, a woman of what pleases her; the principal object of a man's discourse should be what is useful, that of a woman's what is agreeable. . . . We ought not, therefore, to restrain the prattle of girls . . . with that severe question, *To what purpose are you talking?* but by . . . *How will your discourse be received?*"'[5]

To which argument Mary objects: 'To govern the tongue in this manner . . . is too much practised both by men and women. Out of the abundance of the heart how few speak! So few that I . . . would gladly give up politeness for a quarter of the virtue that has been sacrificed to an equivocal quality which at best should only be the polish of virtue.'[6]

The 'dialogue' continues with Mary doing her best not to abandon politeness. But it was particularly hard when her clear-sighted eyes detected the real motive behind his plea for women's chastity. 'Rousseau insinuates that he should not blame those, who contend for leaving woman in a state of the most profound ignorance, if it were not necessary in order to preserve her chastity . . . to give her a little knowledge of men, and the customs produced by human passions: else she might propagate at home without being rendered less voluptuous and innocent by the exercise of her understanding. . . .' During the first year of her marriage, he suggested that she might dress like the heroine of *Émile*:

'Her dress is extremely modest in appearance and yet very coquettish in fact; she does not make a display of her charms, she conceals them; but in concealing them she knows how to affect your imagination. Everyone who sees her will say, There is a modest and discreet girl; but while you are near her your eyes and affections wander all over her person, so that you cannot withdraw them; and you would conclude that every part of her dress, simple as it seems, was only put in its proper order to be taken to pieces by the imagination.'[7]

'Is this modesty? Is this a preparation for immortality?' demands Mary. . . . 'Will it be allowed that the surest way to make a wife chaste is to teach her to practise the wanton arts of a mistress, termed virtuous coquetry, by the sensualist?'[8]

Her final verdict on Rousseau in this respect is that he had debauched his imagination; by keeping women from the tree of knowledge in order to render them an object of desire for a short time he was prepared to debase one half of mankind, with little thought for the effect upon future generations. In conclusion she points out that his life was divided between ecstasy and misery, produced by the effervescence of his imagination. But 'Peace to his *manes*!' she cries. 'I war not with his ashes, but his opinions. I war only with the sensibility that led him to degrade woman by making her the slave of love.'[9]

After Rousseau, lesser social philosophers came under her scrutiny. Dr James Fordyce's *Sermons* were often put into the hands of a young woman as a guide to good conduct. 'But,' states Mary categorically, 'I should instantly dismiss them from my pupil's attention if I wished to strengthen her understanding.'[10] Indeed Mary was so hostile to this cleric's influence that she said she would like to withdraw his *Sermons* from all libraries. In her judgment he did little more than sentimentalize the teaching of Rousseau. He was highly considered by the society of his time and his *Sermons* were upheld as exemplary of the best edifying literature available. Mary cunningly observes while reviewing his work, 'He shall speak for himself, for thus he makes Nature address man:

'"Behold these smiling innocents, whom I have graced with my fairest gifts, and committed to your protection. . . . They are

89

timid and want to be defended. They are frail; oh, do not take advantage of their weakness! Let their fears and blushes endear them. Let their confidence in you never be abused. But is it possible, that any of you can be such barbarians, so supremely wicked as to abuse it? Can you find it in your hearts to despoil the gentle, trusting creatures of their treasure, or do anything to strip them of their native robe of virtue? Curst be the impious hand that would dare to violate the unblemished form of chastity! Thou wretch! thou ruffian! forbear; nor venture to provoke Heaven's fiercest vengeance.'''[11]

Such idle empty phrases, Mary says, do no more than give her a sickly qualm. She asks: 'Why should a grave preacher interlard his discourse with such fooleries? Surely he must have little acquaintance with the human heart.'[12] With this observation, supported by a short scathing commentary upon other aspects of his work, she dismisses him.

With Dr Gregory, author of *Legacy to his Daughters*, she has more sympathy. His book, written while he mourned the death of a beloved wife, was dedicated to his daughters. But the advice he gives them with the intent of making them amiable is vitiated by the fear of instilling sentiments that might draw them out of the track of common life without enabling them to act with consonant independence and dignity. Most of his observations on behaviour appear to her to begin at the wrong end. She thinks the starched rules of decorum he lays down should not supplant the promptings of nature. 'A cultivated understanding, and an affectionate heart' would make such rules superfluous. 'There would be no end to rules for behaviour if it be proper always to adopt the tone of the company; for thus, forever varying the key, a *flat* would often pass for a *natural* note.'

She then expresses an opinion which predates the findings of modern psychology: 'This desire of being always women, is the very consciousness that degrades the sex.'[13] This section of Chapter V, one of the most interesting in the whole work, closes with the words, 'Wisdom is the principal thing: *therefore* get wisdom; and with all thy getting get understanding.'

One of the most discouraging discoveries she makes is that some women 'argue in the same track as men, and adopt the sentiments that brutalize them'.[14] Such a one was Mrs Piozzi, a friend of Dr Johnson and Fanny Burney, who often repeated by rote what she did not understand. 'Dread a refinement of wisdom as a deviation into folly,' she writes. 'All our attainments, all our arts, are employed to gain and keep the heart of man.' These opinions outrage Mary. 'Thus is the understanding of the whole sex affronted,' she replies, 'and their virtue deprived of the common basis of virtue.'[15] Madame de Staël, dynamic in nature and generous in most respects, is even more discouraging. Rousseau denied woman reason, shut her out from knowledge and turned her aside from truth. 'What signifies it to women', Madame de Staël asks, 'that his reason disputes with them the empire, when his heart is devotedly theirs?'[16]

All this turns Mary's heart to stone and she seeks comfort in writers whose vision has more of her own quality, such as Madame Genlis, Mrs Chapone, and above all Mrs Macaulay, who she thinks is 'the woman of the greatest abilities, undoubtedly, this country has ever produced'.

She admits that Lord Chesterfield's *Letters* must not be silently passed over, but finding his system 'unmanly and immoral' she dismisses him as an educationist who makes 'the vain attempt to bring forth the fruit of experience, before the sapling has out-thrown its leaves.'[17]

After her severe criticism of the masculine influence on women in their own (men's) interest she feels a more constructive approach on her part is necessary. The one answer to all condemnation from left or right, male or female, is education. Education, not instruction, not precepts heaped upon precepts; but education through learning, through knowledge, through experience of life. She points out that one reason why men have a more solid basis to their virtue is that they have more opportunities for experience. Their freer lives give them the chance to prove for themselves the reality of good and evil.

'The world cannot be seen by an unmoved spectator: we must mix in the throng, and feel as men feel, before we can judge of their feelings. If we mean, in short, to live in the world, to grow wiser and better, and not merely to enjoy the good things of life, we must attain a knowledge of others at the same time that we become acquainted with ourselves. . . . [No] knowledge can be attained without labour and sorrow; and those who wish to spare their children both should not complain if they are neither wise nor virtuous.'[18]

This approach to the education of the young was not calculated to win the approval of most parents. Youth should *act*, she persists, even if the knowledge thus acquired is purchased at a dear rate. Prudence in early life is 'the cautious craft of ignorant self-love'. She gives warning against prejudice, the poison that insidiously enters the mind while the mind is gathering knowledge; 'moss-covered opinions . . . indolently adopted only because age has given them a venerable aspect, though the reason upon which they were built ceases to be a reason, or cannot be traced'.[19] Prejudice that usurps the throne of reason and distorts judgment must be overthrown. 'Go back,' she advises, 'to the simple principles that were antecedent to the prejudices broached by power; and it is ten to one but you are stopped by the philosophical assertion that certain principles are as practically false as they are abstractly true.'[20] 'The fact is,' she maintains, 'that men expect from education what education cannot give. . . . The honey must be the reward of the individual's own industry. . . . The business of education . . . is only to conduct the shooting tendrils to a proper pole; yet after laying precept upon precept, without allowing a child to acquire judgment itself, parents expect them [children] to act in the same manner by this borrowed fallacious light as if they had illumined it themselves; and be when they enter life what their parents are at the close.'[21]

These ideas were far from being in accord with current thought, which as far as the young were concerned could be summed up in the admonition 'Obey your elders' and 'Keep to the paths already laid down'. But Mary wanted morality to 'rest on a rock against which the storms of passion vainly beat', and that rock was truth, and knowledge of the truth in all things.

Her ideas on education, such as the encouragement of observation in children and their commentary on what they have observed, resembled those advanced by Pestalozzi and later on by Froebel.

'The great Principle and Foundation of all Virtue is placed in this:' she wrote, 'that a man is able to follow what reason directs as best.' The object of education is to make men virtuous and through virtue happy. Women should acquire human virtues by the same means as men, instead of being educated 'like a fanciful kind of half being. Genteel women are literally-speaking slaves to their bodies and glory in their subjection. . . . The power of generalizing ideas, of drawing comprehensive conclusions from individual observations is the only acquirement for an immortal being that really deserves the name of knowledge. Merely to observe without endeavouring to account for anything may serve as the common-sense of life, but where is the store laid up that is to clothe the soul when it leaves the body?'

Like Talleyrand, she was in favour of co-education. She believed that bad habits were generated when females (likewise males) were shut up together.

'Marriage will never be held sacred till women by being brought up with men are prepared to be their companions rather than their mistresses. I venture to predict that virtue will never prevail in society till the virtues of both sexes are founded on reason, and till the affections common to both are allowed to gain their due strength by the discharge of natural duties. Lessons of politeness which tread on the heels of falsehood would be rendered useless by habitual propriety of behaviour. A taste for the fine arts requires great cultivation, but not more than a taste for the virtuous affections, and both suppose that enlargement of mind which opens so many sources of mental pleasure.'

She advocated a 'Course of Sexual Education' during which children should be informed about the organs of reproduction as freely as about any other bodily function. The purpose of sexual intercourse should be explained and warning given about its abuse. This section of the book was responsible for the publication of a work by Thomas Taylor called *Vindication of the Rights of Brutes* and led to other scurrilous attacks on Mary as an immoral author.

She further recommended primary schools which would abolish all distinctions of class. She thought instruction should be made interesting and vivid, and advised methods towards this end now used in modern kindergartens but which in her time were almost unknown. For older pupils she believed in the Socratic method: education through discussion; religion, history, politics made 'real' and meaningful by the expression of personal opinion.

According to her, sport should be practised by boys and girls alike, and no child should be forced to sedentary employment for more than an hour at a time, however wide the curriculum, which included the three Rs, botany, mechanics, astronomy, natural history and natural philosophy.

She took into account the varying gifts of young people. After the age of nine a process of selection should take place; mechanically-minded children should be separated from those of superior abilities, each sort attending the establishment which best suits them, with boys and girls still together. But Mary feared it might be a long time before 'the world will be so far enlightened that parents, only anxious to render their children virtuous, shall allow them to choose companions for life themselves'.[22]

The wide scope of her views, particularly those affecting her sex, aroused much hostility. Women, it was considered, were best left unawakened to the possibilities that life opens up to the cultivated mind. They must not realize what they are missing.

'The education which women now receive,' Mary pointed out, 'scarcely deserves the name. My very soul has often sickened at observing the sly tricks practised by women to gain some foolish thing on which their silly hearts were set. Not allowed to dispose of money or call anything their own, they learn to turn the market penny.'[23]

One aspect of Talleyrand's *Report on Public Instruction*, which is still being debated at the present time, is that of making children and youths independent of their teachers in respect of punishments. Mary approved this idea and adopted it. She thought it would fix sound principles of justice in the mind and have a happy effect on the temper which is early soured or irritated by tyranny.

This for some readers of the book was the last straw, particularly when applied to women. So much latitude would favour the libertine in woman, they alleged. She would deteriorate; she would become unsexed by acquiring strength of body and mind, and 'that beauty, soft bewitching beauty, would no longer adorn the daughters of man'. 'I am of a very different opinion,' Mary declared. It was not freedom that would unsex women. 'Make them free,'[24] she urged. 'Reason and experience convince me that the only method of leading women to fulfil their peculiar duties is to free them from all restraint by allowing them to participate in the inherent rights of mankind. Women should be taught the elements of anatomy and medicine ... [become] acquainted with the anatomy of the mind, by allowing the sexes to associate together in every pursuit, and by leading them to observe the progress of the human understanding in the improvement of the sciences and arts—never forgetting the science of morality, or the study of the political history of mankind.'

She summed up her observations on public and private education with these words: 'I think the female world oppressed; yet the gangrene, which the vices engendered by oppression have produced, is not confined to the morbid part but pervades society at large. I wish to see my sex become more like moral agents, my heart bounds with the anticipation of the general diffusion of that sublime contentment which only morality can diffuse.'[25]

As always, Mary saw the rights of woman in the context of the rights of man, with benevolence towards humanity at large. Her ideas on education reached far beyond what was then usually accepted. Religion was implicit in her social philosophy and in her schemes of education. She put her faith in the goodness of God,

'For what man of feeling and sense could doubt it. . . . When that wise Being who created us and placed us here, saw the fair idea He willed by allowing it to be so that the passions should unfold our reason, because he could see that present evil would

95

produce future good. . . . A curse it might be reckoned if the whole of our existence were bounded by our continuance in this world; for why should the gracious fountain of life give us passions and the power of reflecting only to embitter our days and inspire us with mistaken notions of dignity. . . . Finally persuaded that no evil exists in the world that God did not design to take place, I build my belief on the perfection of God.'

Mary was forthright in her confession of belief, firm in her conviction that all reforms, whether or not they affected the position of women, must take into account the spiritual realities. 'Woman must never forget, in common with man, that life yields not the felicity which can satisfy an immortal soul.' But she had little place for organized sanctity. With Milton she cried: 'Faith and not the law is our rule. . . . The rule of judgment will be the conscience of each individual.' 'I can bear anything but my own contempt,' she confessed later in life when her independence of spirit was saving her from moral disaster. Her individualism was supreme. Tradition, the councils of any visible Church, the edicts of any magistrate, had little influence on her in matters of conduct. The voice of Nature, of Reason and of God were for her one and the same thing. 'To submit to Reason is to submit to the nature of things, and to that God who forms them so, to promote our real interest.' Children, she said, should not endure 'a slavish bondage to parents [which] cramps every facility of mind'. She quoted Locke: 'If the mind be curbed, if their spirits be abused and broken much by too strict a hand over them, they lose all their vigour and industry.' She pointed out that this in some degree accounts for the weakness of women, for girls are more kept down by their parents. Warning was given against too much exultation:

'The religion which consists in warming the affections and exalting the imagination is only the poetical part and may afford the individual pleasure without rendering it a more moral being. . . . Men will not become moral when they build airy castles in a future world to compensate for the disappointments they meet in this.'

Her idea of what was essential for a belief in God was that it should spring from reason and be based on a perfect understanding of his attributes. Instead of according him blind adoration for his supreme power, he should be adored as the source of all wisdom and goodness, the only sort of adoration that had any meaning for those desirous of virtue and knowledge. The future life was an undoubted reality, and present life but a preparation for the next, and a state of infancy during which care must be taken not to sacrifice hopes that alone justify earthly existence. Our plan of life should enable us to carry some knowledge and virtue into another world. Yet, she admitted, few have sufficient foresight or resolution to endure a small evil at the moment to avoid a greater hereafter.

'I know,' she wrote, 'that many devoted people boast of submitting to the will of God blindly as to an arbitrary sceptre or rod, on the same principle as the Indians worship the devil. In other words, like people in the common concerns of life, they do homage to power, and cringe under the foot that can crush them. Rational religion, on the contrary, is a submission to the will of a Being so perfectly wise that all he wills must be directed by the proper motive—must be reasonable.'

Mary's faith in a Being perfectly wise, governed by reason, must be taken as the core of her religion at this time. She had not yet experienced in life a degree of injustice and sorrow which, it would seem, no Being governed wholly by reason could tolerate. This simplification of a great and still unresolved mystery satisfied her for the moment. Moreover there were several aspects of the positon of women in society she had not examined. One was the legal position, with its inequalities in standards of conduct and degree of responsibility. But she had dealt with the fundamentals governing the female condition, which depended on conventional values and had degenerated into a code for slaves.

Her book is not well planned. She reiterates her arguments without strengthening them, suddenly returning on her steps to insist on some point which previously she had not sufficiently stressed. Although she is scornful in attacking 'the mould of prim littleness', she rarely indulges in anger. However, in her final summing-up she abandons some of her moderation, and a note of irony and anger is heard. She had not, she explains, written her book to extenuate the faults of women but to prove them to be the natural consequence of their education and station in society.

'Let women,' she wrote in her penultimate paragraph, 'share the rights and she will emulate the virtues of man; for she must grow more perfect when emancipated or justify the authority that chains such a weak being to her duty. If the latter, it will be expedient to open a fresh trade with Russia for whips; a present which a father should always make to his son-in-law on his wedding day, that a husband may keep his whole family in order by the same means, and without any violation of justice reign, wielding this sceptre, sole master of his house, because he is the only thing in it who has reason: the divine, indefeasible earthly sovereignty breathed into man by the Master of the universe. Allowing this position, women have not any inherent rights to claim; and, by the same rule, their duties vanish, for rights and duties are inseparable.'

8

To Paris for the Revolution

Soon after the appearance of Mary's masterpiece in the book-
shops of London it was translated into French and German. She
had every reason to be satisfied with herself; she was now on a
more equal footing with other authors in the radical group, with
Godwin and his *Political Justice*, Paine and his *Rights of Man*,
Blake and his *Songs of Innocence*. Along with these gifted writers
she had exposed some of the evils of the times and suggested ways
of removing them. There was no longer any need to hang back and
keep her opinions to herself. She liked discussion and the company
of men of intellect and progressive ideas, and she could now indulge
her taste.

Lavater, the physiognomist and friend of Fuseli, was in London
and she often joined their company, along with Johnson, for parties
and visits to the theatre and other festivities. When she heard that
Johnson and the Fuselis were planning a six weeks' stay in Paris
to study the Revolution at first hand, it seemed the most natural
thing in the world to suggest to them that she should make one of
the party. A visit to Paris at this time of far-reaching development
—1792—was essential for any social reformer; moreover many of
the French radicals, members of the Girondin Party, had often
visited England in the past and were on familiar terms with the
habitués of Johnson's upper room.

Mary had hoped she might profit by her presence in the French

99

capital to promote her sisters' interests by finding them situations there. Full of enthusiasm, she wrote to Everina, but the latter, who seems to have been aware of her sister's infatuation for a well-known artist, was full of doubts and confided in Eliza, who replied:

'So the author of the Rights of Woman is going to France! I dare say her chief motive is to promote her poor Bess's comfort! or thine, my girl, or at least I think she will thus reason. Well, in spite of Reason, when M^{rs} W reaches the Continent she will be but a woman. I cannot help painting her in the height of all her wishes, at the very summit of her happiness, for will not ambition fill every chink of her Great Soul (for such I really think hers) that is not occupied by Love. . . . And you actually have the vanity to imagine that in the National Assembly personages like M. and F. will bestow a thought on two females whom Nature meant to "suckle fools and chronicle small beer".'

This ill-natured letter reveals how little warmth of heart Mary could expect from her own family, who looked upon her as the natural provider of their well-being. Indeed, Mary was not particularly concerned about finding places for her sisters; her own affairs and those of France overwhelmed such considerations.

Meanwhile her passion for Fuseli consumed most of her vitality. Apart from her writing for the *Analytical Review* she did little creative work. For the *Review* she continued to criticize works on a great variety of subjects: education, history, travel, poetry, drama, novels, biography and sermons. But her deep concern was for two subjects only: Fuseli and the French Revolution. More and more her thoughts became inflamed by the news from France. Writing about the *Letters of the Countess du Barré* she remarks:

'These letters develope, in an interesting manner, the polished villainy of court intrigue, and that fatal system of *profusion* and *oppression*, which, in the latter part of the reign of Louis XV, hurried France to the brink of destruction, and at length brought the affairs of that Kingdom to the crisis which gave birth to the present revolution. The French patriots have been reviled, even to a degree of execration, by the *admirers* of *despotism*; but this collection of letters might alone serve as an apology for National assembly, were any apology necessary for the *glorious* labours of that *patriotic body*.'[1]

She took upon herself to address William Pitt and enlighten him on the revolutionary spirit in England. 'A spirit is abroad,' she wrote, 'to break the chains that have hitherto eaten into the human soul, which bids fair to mould the body-politic of Europe into a more proportional form, if we may be allowed the phrase, than has yet been seen on earth.'[2] Needless to say, Pitt did not reply; in any event none of this was news to him.

Her affair with Fuseli did not prosper; Mrs Fuseli had become hostile and told Mary she was no longer welcome in their home. It was not surprising, given Mary's almost ungovernable feelings for the artist; yet she still deceived herself and thought Mrs Fuseli was being unreasonable. Nevertheless, it was difficult for her not to see she was disrupting a marriage which at the best of times was not on too firm a foundation. The journey to France in good company had to be abandoned. It was obvious that if she went she must go alone, and she wrote a humble letter to her reluctant friend and hoped-for lover, pleading for forgiveness for having disturbed 'the quiet tenour of your life'.

It is hard to imagine in what spirit she undertook that sad and solitary journey to Paris, a tragic city still shuddering from the effects of the September massacres. The Revolution was no longer an uprising of middle-class idealists and uneducated, exploited workers; it was now a dangerous explosion of the mob in which mingled the professional assassins. Uncontrollable violence was dominant, and the King was no longer safe. The old Legislative Assembly had been dissolved and replaced by the National Convention, which proclaimed the French Republic. There were two rival parties for power, the Girondins and the Montagnards. The former were moderate intellectuals of Mary's own stamp; while they were in control the King was in no physical danger. But at about the time Mary reached Paris the Montagnards, that is to say the radical extremists led by Robespierre, Danton and Marat, were rapidly gaining upon the moderate Girondins and putting pressure upon them to bring the King to trial. It was a turning-point, a crisis which should have persuaded Mary to retrace her steps, for this was no time to visit Paris, least of all for a woman alone.

But she did not retrace her steps, although she was unprepared for the terrible situation which now reigned in the French capital. She was still capable of writing rhetorical descriptions of what seemed to be passing evils out of which merit would surely proceed. She was still unrealistic, filling her imagination with desirable images She saw good and evil clearly defined, and made rule-of-thumb judgments. Not intimidated by the entanglement of passions, ambitions, betrayals, hopes and fears, she felt herself carried along by the tide of history.

Everina and Eliza had taught at a school in Putney run by a Mrs Bregantz and it was a daughter of this lady, a Madame Fillietaz, who offered Mary a home in Paris. The Fillietaz house was now occupied only by servants, but Mary was told she could stay there as long as she pleased. It was gloomy living alone in that large empty place, but at least it provided shelter in a city in a state of dangerous disorder. She profited by this uneventful (for her) period by studying the French language so assiduously that she never went to bed without a headache. But that at least was better than a heartache; through her assiduity in work and contemplation of the stupendous events amidst which she was living the image of Fuseli was pushed to the back of her mind.

This moment was critical for the course of the Revolution. The struggle between the Girondins, men of moderation, and the Montagnards, men of varying degrees of violence and extremism, was at its height. Madame Roland and Danton were opponents in the struggle for power. They were the outstanding figures in the Convention, although of course Madame Roland worked behind her husband's name. But the truth was known; most of the pamphlets, appeals and warnings which Roland signed were the work of his wife.

Mary attended the meetings of the Convention and through the member for Calais, Thomas Paine, was introduced to Madame Roland and other leaders of the Girondins. As we have seen Thomas

Paine had left England a few months before Mary in order to escape imprisonment. The most eminent of the Girondins were Brissot, Vergniaud, Pétion, Buzet, Condorcet and the Rolands. These were the men who were Paine's daily companions, and Mary must have met many of them. Several of the Girondins had visited England and were already known to those who forgathered in Johnson's room. Meeting the same figures now in French homes and assemblies Mary would have felt at ease with them. They were well-educated, well-meaning middle-class people who had read Plutarch and Rousseau and, like herself, were full of enthusiasm. Indeed they had too much enthusiasm and reading, according to Madame Roland, and too little action to counter the ruthless moves being made by her rival, Danton.

For Mary the most interesting figure of the Government must certainly have been Madame Roland, for the reason that here was a woman, deprived by the law as much as any English woman could be, of her rights to education, economic freedom and equality of legal status, yet who had risen to the topmost ranks of power. Had Madame Roland come to terms with Danton, who, though a Montagnard, was far less extreme than Robespierre, emergent leader of the Jacobin faction of the group, it is possible that these two might even have ridden the storm and guided France into still waters. But Danton was—wrongly—held responsible by Madame Roland for the unspeakable September massacres, and this she could never forgive.

The events of Madame Roland's life offered a great contrast to Mary's, yet the two women had much in common in the fundamental qualities of intelligence, strength of soul and breadth of sympathy.

Manon Roland, née Phlipon, was born in 1754, five years earlier than Mary, and she was to die four years before Mary. Her father was a master-engraver and enameller, her mother a well-educated woman, daughter of a wine merchant. The family lived in the heart of Paris, near the Pont Neuf. Manon was given great liberty and as good an education as her parents could contrive for her. Tutors taught her history and geography, and an uncle, Latin. But the chief virtue of her upbringing was her liberty to read whatever she chose. At nine years of age she discovered Plutarch, and her favourite book was *Candide*. Descartes, Fénelon and Locke were known to her. In fact, she was a precocious and highly intelligent child encouraged by both parents in her explorations into great literature.

She married Roland de la Platière, an Inspector-General of Commerce, a dull, honest, conscientious man many years older than herself whom she did not love but always respected. He augmented his income by writing articles for the *Dictionnaire des Manufactures, Arts et Métiers*, a subdivision of the great *Encyclopédie*. Manon participated in this work, which prepared her for composing many of the political pamphlets and other publications which appeared later under her husband's name. More and more she became the power behind the façade of Roland's bland unimpassioned presence, which had earned him the sobriquet of 'Virtuous Roland'.

He was, however, one of the leading Girondins and was elected Minister of the Interior in March 1792. He had had no more ex-peri ence of office than had any other member of the Government, but with his wife behind him he cheerfully made his début in this new sphere of activity. They had been living in a modest flat in the rue de la Harpe and now they moved to the Hôtel de l'Intérieur. It was one of the most magnificent mansions in Paris. The entrance beneath the archway led into a paved courtyard, with arcades on each side of the great door, and a superb staircase mounting to the *grand salon* with its portrait of Louis XIV. The room in which Manon slept was decorated with frescoes of gods and goddesses, and the bed was crowned with white plumes. She chose for her study a small room which soon became crowded with petitioners and any who sought her influence. She was in fact that creature little esteemed in France, *la femme politique*.

By the time Mary arrived in Paris Roland was in his second term of office. Terrible things had happened between the two terms. Roland had resigned in June and returned with his wife to live in the modest apartment in the rue de la Harpe. In September occurred the massacres, possibly in part the work of professional assassins but probably largely the result of mass panic caused by the fear of foreign invasion and counter-revolution, in which about 1,400 people perished. Both husband and wife were profoundly shocked, particularly Madame Roland, who never wholly recovered from her horror. Anarchy now reigned in the capital; neither person nor property was respected, and people walking in the streets were attacked and robbed of their jewellery and purses. The Girondins, now known as the 'new aristocrats', went about armed; there was no government worthy of the name.

The King had been deposed in August and was now a prisoner. A Provisional Executive Council held office and elected new ministers, and Roland soon found himself back in the magnificent mansion of the Intérieur which he had left two months before, but with only the semblance of his former authority.

Now Madame Roland was engaged on that life and death struggle with Danton which was to bring down both. Neither of them really liked the mob; 'verminous insects rising from the slime' as one eminent Girondin described them. No; lacking any love for the people Madame Roland preferred to be surrounded by educated, well-turned-out citizens who knew how to behave. She was a snob, but nobody could say that of Danton, who was at this time the most powerful and talented figure in French politics. No one at this time equalled him in power of leadership, and nothing would persuade the Rolands to hold out to him the hand of reconciliation.

The Rolands gave dinner parties twice a week, on Mondays and Fridays. They began at 5 o'clock and ended at 9. Fifteen people sat at table to enjoy these sumptuous 'feasts of Circe'. Did Mary ever make one of the fifteen? There is no record that this was so, but she must surely have been present on similar occasions. The effect of coming into contact with men who were at the heart of government and held the lives of thousands of their fellow creatures in their hands was not lost on her. But where did the question of justice for women come in when the overriding question of survival was being debated?

True, Madame Roland had written: 'I am much annoyed at being a woman. On every hand my spirit and heart find the shackles of opinion, the iron of prejudice, and all my strength is wasted in vainly shaking my chains.' But at the moment she had neither time nor energy to consider this particular aspect of the general enslavement of mankind. Moreover she had worked for so long through her husband, composing many of his political declarations, inspiring his actions, taking upon herself under his name much of the responsibility for directing Girondin policy, that she lost sight of the woman vainly shaking her chains. Mary was a witness to all this, which, had she cleared her mind of the intense longing for personal happiness, might have changed her approach to social philosophy and life in general. Madame Roland's detachment from personal claims, her whole-hearted dedication to *la chose politique* could have been an example for the Englishwoman to follow. And, had Mary known it, Madame Roland was battling with an affair of the heart every bit as fierce as Mary's infatuation for Fuseli. The wife of the Minister of the Interior loved Buzot, Deputy for Evreux, with a depth of feeling the more profound for its being rooted in the same ideal of public service cherished by both.

The position of the Girondins worsened daily. As Buzot reported, there was not a department nor a town nor a miserable club in all France that did not at once denounce Girondins as Royalists. The infamous Comité de Salut Public began to operate in March, and on the 31st of that month it intruded upon the Rolands' privacy and seized all their papers.

At about the time of Mary's arrival in France, the King appeared at the bar and heard the inventory of his crimes read out. After this many who could afford to do so began to leave the country. On 15th January the Assembly had been required to vote on the guilt of the King. The more moderate Girondins had tried in vain to prevent a fatal vote by suggesting a referendum; but when voting began it was clear that the extremists were now dominant. M. Roland together with five of his colleagues was obliged to sign a proclamation announcing the time of the King's execution. This was to be the last time Roland signed a document in his official capacity. On 21st January 1793 the King was guillotined. The coach bearing the royal prisoner passed beneath Mary's window and she recorded what she saw in a letter to Johnson.

'About nine o'clock this morning the king passed by my window, moving silently along (excepting now and then a few strokes on the drum, which rendered the stillness more awful) through empty streets, surrounded by the national guards, who, clustering around the carriage, seemed to deserve their name. The inhabitants flocked to their windows, but the casements were all shut, not a voice was heard, nor did I see any thing like an insulting gesture. —For the first time since I entered France, I bowed to the majesty of the people, and respected the propriety of behaviour so perfectly in unison with my own feelings. I can scarcely tell you why, but an association of ideas made the tears flow insensibly from my eyes, when I saw Louis sitting, with more dignity than I expected from his character, in a hackney coach, going to meet death, where so many of his race have triumphed. My fancy instantly brought Louis XIV before me, entering the capital with all his pomp, after one of the victories most flattering to his pride, only to see the sunshine of prosperity overshadowed by the sublime gloom of misery. I have been alone ever since; and, though my mind is calm, I cannot dismiss the lively images that have filled my imagination all the day.—Nay, do not smile, but pity me; for, once or twice, lifting my eyes from the paper, I have seen eyes glare through a glass-door opposite my chair, and bloody hands shook at me. Not the distant sound of a footstep can I hear. . . . I wish I had even kept the cat with me!— I want to see something alive; death in so many frightful shapes has taken hold of my fancy.—I am going to bed—and, for the first time in my life, I cannot put out the candle.' [3]

What effects had all these appalling events upon Mary's heart and mind? She was living alone in the big deserted house, and fear was her constant companion. There were other English people in Paris, trusting to their nationality to escape the assassins' attention. Tom Paine was among them, living in the Faubourg St Denis in an hotel once patronized by Madame de Pompadour. Through Paine she was introduced to Helen Maria Williams, a poet known for her extreme liberalism. She was then barely twenty-one years of age and had been brought up by a mother with a fanatical devotion to the Revolution, which she imparted to her daughter. But the appalling September massacres had cooled the ardour of mother and daughter. Later on, when all persons of English or foreign origin became suspect, both were thrown into prison, where they had time to reconsider their early enthusiasm for events they little understood.

Paris was 'crammed with foreigners from nowhere', as Madame Roland complained; people drawn to the centre of the storm without at first realizing its malevolent power. Soon Tom Paine was to join the Williamses in prison, where he barely escaped the tumbrils that led to the guillotine. For now the 'strange beast with several heads' was raging through the streets attacking wherever it scented blood.

Another figure with whom Mary made contact at this historical moment was Count von Schlabrendorf, a radical philanthropist, son of a prime minister of Silesia. At first he was not impressed by her, thought her affected, but gradually he acquired a truer appreciation of her quality, when her goodness of heart broke through the varnish of manners. 'She was the noblest, purest and most intelligent woman I have ever met,' he wrote. He was to remain her good friend to the end of her life.

Tom Paine, the complete idealist, was unmoved by the evidence of deterioration in the ideals and conduct of the Revolution. He knew of the appalling events that had occurred during the September massacres but did not allow them to disturb his faith, standing firm for democracy, liberty and humanity. He defied Marat and the Montagne by voting against the King's death, an act of the greatest courage for which later he nearly paid with his life. He was flung into prison and destined for the guillotine. But with his customary courage, he refused to lose heart or lose time, and employed himself in writing his last book, *The Age of Reason*, in which he advocated freedom of the expression of opinion; it also contained a destructive criticism of Christianity. Eventually this work, together with his *Rights of Man*, became the Bible for those who in England struggled for the freedom of the Press. He escaped the guillotine by an accident; the open door of his cell concealed the red cross which indicated that the occupant was destined for execution. After the collapse of the Montagne and the end of the Reign of Terror, he was restored to his seat in the National Convention, and at the end of the Revolution went to the United States, where he died.

It was of course through Tom Paine that Mary had met some of the finest men thrown up by the Revolution, as well as distinguished foreigners whose ideals for a reformed society had brought them to Paris. Her own ideals had been temporarily shaken by events, she was at grips with the problem of good and evil, and the difficulty in assigning each ideal or personage to its relevant place. She tried to establish the virtues and vices in this great national upheaval as she had in the struggle for the rights of women, but the situation in France was far less accessible to precise judgment. At one time it had seemed simple to say such things were good and such things evil, but now no classification seemed possible. For a brief period she seemed to lose all faith in the radical ideals which had been her inspiration and to be totally disillusioned with the Revolution.

She wrote to Johnson:

'Before I came to France I cherished, you know, an opinion that strong virtues might exist with the polished manners produced by the progress of civilization; and I even anticipated the epoch when, in the course of improvement, men would labour to become virtuous, without being goaded on by misery. But now the perspective of the golden age, fading before the attentive eye of observation, almost eludes my sight; and losing thus in part my theory of a more perfect state, start not my friend if I bring forward an opinion, which at the first glance seems to be levelled against the existence of God! I am not become an atheist, I assure you by residing at Paris: yet I begin to fear that vice or, if you will, evil, is the grand mobile of action, and that when the passions are justly poised we become harmless and in the same proportion useless.' [4]

The horrors and sublimities of the Revolution were piercing her heart. She was tortured by anxiety for her friends among the Girondins. She heard the tolling of the midnight bell and the tramp of feet in the streets. Fresh disasters were reported daily. In the Vendée and Finisterre chaos reigned. In Lyons 800 patriots were massacred. The Girondins knew their end was near and some of them were trying to escape from Paris; those who remained were obliged to proscribe themselves. Finally the names of twenty-two

Girondins were read out in the Assembly by Marat; among them were those whom Mary knew personally, such as Brissot, Vergniaud, Pétion. It was obvious that the Rolands were now in great peril and that representative government in France was at an end.

9

The Meeting with Imlay

In January 1793 Madame Roland wrote to Lavater:

'The violent situation in which we are does not leave me a moment's liberty. Always in the tempest, always under the hatchet of the people. . . . Courage is but a habit.'[1]

With her it was one that had become second nature, for she remained the calmest of all the members of the Party, each one of whom was awaiting his turn to be struck by the 'hatchet'. On the 19th of that month M. Roland composed an address which was posted up in the streets of Paris. 'I expect,' he wrote, 'to be dismissed and sacrificed, but I demand to be judged.'[2] Danton took up the challenge. According to him it was Roland who was responsible for the faults of the Government and the desperate state of the country. His 'acrimonious temper', his pamphlets in which he 'spread his own mistakes broadcast over the land'. He was the source of calamity, but once this source had been dammed 'you may devote yourself with some hope of success to the salvation of the country'.[3]

Others joined in the indictment of one who had held the pursestrings of the country during critical months, and who had been utterly scrupulous in rendering an account of his expenditure.

'Devoted to liberty even under despotism, too simple in my habits to need money, too old to desire anything save glory, enthusiastic for my idol—the public good—I have striven for it with an energy and firmness which no obstacle could affright,' he replied in defence. It is easy to detect the prompting of his wife in the last paragraph: 'It is not enough that a man in office should merely be clean-handed—he must not even be the object of suspicion. I call the whole severity of the Convention down on my administration. I do not fear the result. I shall await it within the walls of Paris. I present myself to my contemporaries as to posterity with my works; they speak for me.'[4]

After the dispatch of this letter for reading in the Assembly the Rolands immediately left the magnificent Hôtel de l'Intérieur and returned to rue de la Harpe. Danton now became the dominant figure in France. Blown up by a sense of his measureless power he made a declaration to the effect that the limits of the country were marked by nature: 'The frontiers of the Republic are the ocean, the shores of the Rhine, the Alps and the Pyrenees.'[5]

Mary followed these developments with considerable anxiety. Since February England and France had been at war; it was impossible for her to return home, and equally impossible to get more money for her maintenance in France. Many of her friends had left Paris as the Terror grew daily more menacing. There was no justice to be had, no respect for the truth, no hope of mercy from the Revolutionary tribunals, which dispatched large numbers of innocent persons to their death. Most members of the former Government remained in the capital and attended the Assembly, although a few had fled into the country and were given hospitality by friends at great risk. Mary, walking through the streets of Paris in a mood of despondency, came upon pools of blood. She was near the place where the guillotine had been set up and this evidence of its work was more than she could pass in silence. She broke out into cries of protest and denunciation of those who were responsible for such appalling inhumanity. So strong were her terms, so impassioned her tone that she was warned by an onlooker to hold her peace or she would soon find herself in prison, awaiting a similar fate. It was only too obvious that those pools of blood must lie until they dried up or were washed away by rain. They could inspire no plea for mercy; they could only be mutely eloquent of moments of unspeakable agony. Mary was haunted by them. She thought of friends recently met at various socio-political gatherings. The guillotine had been at work all the time, and she had accepted the dreadful fact as part of an historical necessity.

Now as she listened to the good advice given her she realized she was no longer in Johnson's house, where opinions, however highly coloured, were not tainted with blood. To meet on the streets a tumbril with its load of doomed human creatures was a reminder that hell on earth was here in Paris and not some lurid illustration in a book. There was nothing in this city to mend a shattered human heart. Paris was drenched in a sweat of agony; any survival in an individual breast of hope and disinterestedness was a miracle, belief in which required strong faith. However, such faith was to be found in the occupant of a modest apartment in the rue de la Harpe where Madame Roland, upheld by a sense of history and her own high destiny, calmly watched events move to their inevitable conclusion. Nothing could persuade her to seek security. No Girondin sat on the Comité de Salut Public; there was no friend to curb Danton's ferocious hostility to the recent Government.

Mary found it difficult to live in the centre of such terrible events. As a British national she was in danger of being imprisoned, but since she mixed in American circles and was a friend of the Silesian Count von Schlabrendorf, of the Swiss Jean Schweitzer and of other members of the international group she was left in peace. But her financial difficulties were increasing. Food was scarce and prices were rising: how was she to survive?

It was at this moment she met the man who was to change the course of her life and turn her attention away from public affairs. She had by now quite recovered from her infatuation for Fuseli, whose stature had dwindled in comparison with the figures of power and tragedy she was meeting daily.

She first met Gilbert Imlay, an American apostle of Rousseau, during a visit to the Thomas Christies; he was not a conventionally handsome man but that did not, in his own estimation, count against him. He was full of vitality and initiative; was well read, liberal and had modelled himself on his master's *Émile*. In his *Topographical Description of the Western Territory of North America* he wrote:

'We [the Americans] have more of nature, and you more of the world. Nature formed our features and intellects very much alike; but while you have metamorphosed the one and contaminated the other we preserve the natural symbols of both. You have more hypocrisy—we are sincere. You are more cunning and adroit, which your laws and habits have rendered part of your natures. We are not so stupid as not to see through the veil, but when an European does us the honour to visit us, we have both too much hospitality and suavity of manners to inform them they have neither sentiment nor religion.'

Such complacency and the style of its expression should have warned Mary to keep her distance. At first she did, but the man had a powerful physical attraction for her and was esteemed by the people she liked; by Joel Barlow, for instance, with whom he was collaborating in a scheme for importing timber from Norway and Sweden; by Helen Maria Williams whom Mary admired and trusted. Also he had written books, such as the *Description of the Western Territory of North America* quoted above. But here again she should have found unfavourable auspices rather than encouragement, for he announced on the first page that his greatest pleasure in composing this work was due to its having afforded him an

'opportunity of contrasting the simple manners and rational life of the Americans in these back settlements with the distorted and unnatural habits of the Europeans, which have flowed no doubt from the universal bad laws which exist on your continent, and from the pernicious system of blending religion with politics which has been productive of universal depravity.'

Impressed by the flights of his own imagination, he saw himself as a liberator. 'Heavens! what charms there are in Liberty,' he wrote.

'Man born to enslave the subordinate animals has long since enslaved himself. But reason at length, in radiant smiles and

MARY WOLLSTONECRAFT
From the painting by Sir John Opie in the Tate Gallery, London

JEAN JACQUES ROUSSEAU, 1712–78 from the painting of 1766 by Allan Ramsay in the National Gallery of Scotland. The Mansell Collection

One of the leading writers of the French Enlightenment. Mary, like other English radicals, was profoundly influenced by his thought, but fiercely contested his 'anti-feminism' in her *Vindication of the Rights of Woman*

JOSEPH PRIESTLEY, 1733–1804 from the painting by Ellen Sharples in the National Portrait Gallery

Chemist of genius and Unitarian minister, Priestley's belief in the supremacy of Reason epitomized the intellectual climate of the day. Mary's first contact with his ideas was through his follower, the philosopher Richard Price, but she later met Priestley himself in London

JOHN WILKES, 1727–97
from an engraving after Hogarth. The Mansell Collection

Political agitator and parliamentary reformer, Wilkes was
a prominent member of the
radical group which Mary
frequented

THOMAS PAINE, 1737–1809
om the portrait by Auguste
illière in the National Portrait
Gallery

ne of the most influential
nglish political writers of the
ntury, whose *Rights of Man*
ickly became the radicals'
ble. As a member of the
tional Assembly, Paine was
le to introduce Mary to many
the leading Girondins while
she was in Paris

THOMAS HOLCROFT, 1745–1809 from the painting by Sir John Opie in the National Portrait Gallery

Playwright, social reformer, and a close friend of William Godwin. When Holcroft and eleven others were indicted in the Treason Trials of 1794, Godwin's open letter, *Cursory Strictures*, swayed public opinion in their favour and ensured their acquittal

WILLIAM BLAKE, 1757–1827 from the painting by Thomas Phillips in the National Portrait Gallery

Self-taught artist, poet and revolutionary, Blake was an ardent protagonist of social and political reform. He and Mary were not impressed with one another, but he illustrated two of her books, *Original Stories from Real Life* and her translation of Salzmann's *Moralisches Elementarbuch*

MADAME ROLAND, 1754–93
at the guillotine. The Mansell
Collection

Mme Roland was the leading
spirit of the liberal Girondin
party which dominated the
early years of the Revolution
in France. Mary's visit to Paris
coincided with her decline from
power and eventual overthrow
by the extremist Montagnards

FRANCIS PLACE, 1771–1854
om the painting by Samuel
rummond in the National
Portrait Gallery

self-educated reformer of
e artisan class, Place was one
the twelve defendants in the
reason Trials of 1794. After
quittal, largely as a result of
odwin's intervention, he con-
ued to be politically active
d was later a prominent
Chartist

HENRY FUSELI, R.A., 1741–1825
from the painting by Sir John Opie in the National Portrait Gallery

Mary developed a strong attachment to this brilliant and highly original
Swiss painter; but, eighteen years her senior and already married, he
ignored her feelings and her many passionate letters

WILLIAM GODWIN, 1756–1836
from the painting by James Northcote in the National Portrait Gallery

As the author of several important reformist works, including the famous *Political Justice*, Godwin made a significant contribution to the intellectual life of the period. Mary married him in 1797 and found him 'the kindest, best man in the world'

MARY WOLLSTONECRAFT, 1759–97
shortly before her death, from the painting by Sir John Opie in the National Portrait
Gallery, London

with graceful pride, illumines both hemispheres; and FREEDOM in golden plumes and in her triumphal car must now resume her lost empire.'

Soon after his first meeting with Mary he published a novel entitled *The Emigrants* in which he paints the heroine, Caroline,

'Half unzoned, setting in the marquee to receive the cool breeze which seemed to wanton in her bosom as if enraptured with its sweets, while her conscious thoughts diffused their roseate charms over her heavenly face.'

Even given the fashion of the period for lush description when it came to matters of the heart, such a piece of prose should have warned Mary. But at present she was not seeking refinement of taste or sincerity of feeling; she was seeking masculine intimacy, now become for her an overwhelming need.

She was highly sexed, emotional, rash and generous. No restraints of orthodox religion or convention were now left to put the brake on intense natural desires. All her reading pointed in one direction: liberation. Liberty for her soul, mind and body, and in the strength engendered by letting loose these forces, whole-hearted dedication to the cause of freedom in general. Memories of the past; her pitiful mother and sisters, the unnecessary death of her friend Fanny, to whom she remained faithful in memory, the empty lives of most women she knew, now became more than ever eloquent. The example of Madame Roland's steadfast devotion to a great social ideal did not, unfortunately, bear any special message for Mary. Unlike the French woman she did not realize that an over-insistent claim for personal satisfactions may limit growth of soul as much as does misery. There had been too little joy to enlighten Mary's understanding. She had never been given the chance to develop her character in the benign climate of a protracted happiness. From the beginning all had been struggle, and now she was starving for sensual release. Not to take advantage of this piece of unsolicited good fortune was beyond her power.

From Imlay's point of view here was a distinguished woman who offered uncritical devotion. Her personal attraction had increased with the years and the patina of success. It was a triumph for him to have in his train this outstanding writer with an international reputation. At the time he was working in collaboration with Brissot and Joel Barlow on a project to wrest Louisiana from Spain. Mary's support, her friendship with other members of the French Government, were all grist to his mill. The two seemed destined to be partners; Mary at least had no doubts on that score.

For the moment Mary, blossoming in her new-found happiness and still unaware of its flimsy foundation, carried them both along by virtue of her own strong faith. In a letter written to her sister Everina some time later she describes Imlay as

'a most worthy man who joins to uncommon tenderness of heart and quickness of feeling a soundness of understanding and reasonableness of temper rarely to be met with. Having been brought up in the interior parts of America he is a most natural unaffected creature'.

It must be assumed that the 'most worthy man' was all too familiar with the weak defences of the feminine heart, for, as was later revealed, he had already had many successes in that domain. But Mary suspected nothing. Relating this period of her life, Godwin wrote in his *Memoirs*:

'Her whole character seemed to change with a change of fortune. Her sorrows, the depression of her spirits, were forgotten, and she assumed all the simplicity and the vivacity of a youthful mind. . . . She was playful, full of confidence, kindness, and sympathy. Her eyes assumed new lustre, and her cheeks new colour and smoothness. Her voice became chearful; her temper overflowing with universal kindness; and that smile of bewitching tenderness from day to day illuminated her countenance, which all who knew her will so well recollect; and which won, both heart and soul, the affection of almost everyone that beheld it. . . . She gave a loose to all the sensibilities of her nature.'

The Terror was making life extremely hazardous and Mary thought it advisable to move away from Paris where every day new prospects of horror opened out, and new possibilities of disaster for anyone who still cherished the hopes of a normal existence. In such conditions how could anyone give himself up to the labour of literary composition? History was to be read in the frenzied faces of men and women, in pools of blood, the ringing of bells and the visible fear of even those who seemed most secure. Few indeed could have echoed the words that Madame Roland wrote while in prison: 'Death, torment, pain are nothing to me; I can defy them all. . . . I shall live to my last hour without wasting a single minute in the trouble of unworthy agitation.'[6]

Having surrendered to Imlay's advances, Mary needed a retreat, somewhere to cherish undisturbed her awakened sensibilities and put her intellectual powers to work once more. There was a cottage in Neuilly, a few miles from Paris, which, with Imlay's help, she could rent. A forest lay just beyond the cottage walls and an old gardener, who offered his services from time to time, assured her of his protection but advised her not to penetrate too far into it.

She now enjoyed a brief period of calm and happiness. Always courageous, fear was banished from her mind; fear of the enraged people around her, of the stray assassin in the forest, of isolation in a country at war with her own, of poverty and future uncertainties; and above all, of her own impulsive and impressionable nature. She never doubted her judgment, so great was her need, so overwhelming the effect of good fortune suddenly breaking through the gloom. At last it was her turn to taste a little pleasure. 'Death and misery in every shape of terror haunt this devoted country,' she wrote to her sister, willing to paint the picture black without restraint because now no blackness could dim her own inner joy.

For months she played this game of hide and seek with reality. Imlay was no advocate for marriage, either from the sentimental or from the practical angle. In *The Emigrants* he had written that he proposed 'to place a mirror to the view of Englishmen that they may behold the decay of these features [ravages in the Western Territory of N. America] that were once so lovely, and to prevent the sacrilege which the present practice of matrimonial engagements necessarily produce.'

He owned no property and Mary had only debts. It was not the best of conditions for a union which was regarded by one of the partners at least to be as sacred and enduring as marriage. Mary did not want to burden her lover with financial and family entanglements. Such matters were of no importance set beside the glow in her heart and the sweet repose of satisfied nature.

Imlay came frequently to her cottage in Neuilly, and together they explored the forest. It was spring and the veil of green on the trees and the chanting of birds seemed to them omens of bliss. The old gardener was pleased that she had a protector. He brought her fruit and flowers and became increasingly devoted to the attractive woman who was so grateful for his attentions. The isolation of the cottage was a great advantage; no neighbours destroyed her privacy and she could await Imlay's visits in peace of mind, passing the time between his visits in work upon her *Historical and Moral View of the French Revolution*, which she had planned while in Paris. When Imlay could not come the whole way to the cottage, they would meet at the toll-gate near Neuilly and wander in the countryside. Here Mary's child was conceived, the 'barrier girl' as they called her.

Her pregnancy put an end to this idyllic phase. Imlay had now informed his Embassy that Mary Wollstonecraft was his wife and henceforth an American citizen, thus saving her from the dangers of British nationality. He advised her to return to Paris under the protection of his name.

This she did, and found Paris even more agitated than when she left. The struggle between the Montagne (Danton) and the Girondins had reached a new climax. On the first day of June Madame Roland was arrested in her home and conveyed in a cab to the prison of l'Abbaye to wild cries from her neighbours of '*À la guillotine!*' She had not been given the time to seek her husband and say farewell; in fact he had already made his escape without informing her, knowing that the Government was doomed. That same day the names of twenty-two Girondins were read out by Marat in the Assemblée and all condemned to the guillotine. When Mary heard this news she fainted. How could she lose herself in dreams of happiness when her friends were caught in this terrible trap? M. Roland was not among the twenty-two names read out, but Buzot,

Madame Roland's lover, was. Fortunately he too had made his escape. When in prison Madame Roland wrote to him:

'As for me, I know how to wait equally for the return of justice and how to submit to the last excesses of tyranny in such a way that my example shall not be altogether useless. If I feared anything it is that you might do something rash on my behalf. My friend, it is in saving your country that you save me. I do not want the latter without the former. I shall die satisfied in knowing that you really are saving your country.'[7]

Mary's shock on hearing of the fate of her friends did not prevent her from dwelling upon plans for her own future happiness with Imlay. So deeply immersed was she in this personal dream that she could not predict that the very nature of its context would destroy its chance of materialization. She tried to forget the tragedy all around her by immersing herself in her work on her new book on the Revolution.

Unfortunately, this *Historical and Moral View* deals only with events up to 1789, over three years before Mary's arrival in France. The reader is therefore denied any first-hand description of many of the stirring, terrifying and appalling events through which Mary herself had lived. However, it is clear that, by the time of writing, much of Mary's faith and composure, so shaken at the time of her letter to Johnson, had returned. Her belief in the basic rectitude of the Revolution and its principles has been fully restored: it is the human element, she points out, that has so far failed abysmally to live up to the ideals set it.

The French, she thought, lacked the purity of heart and maturity of judgment necessary to bring the Revolution through its initial phase of chaos to one that would justify the exorbitant price being paid. In her opinion the leaders were 'inebriated with the doctrines of the liberal writers who had roused them to action'. She had small sympathy with the Gallic temperament in spite of its admirable dynamism.

'We have seen the French engaged in a business the most sacred to mankind, giving by their enthusiasm splendid examples of their fortitude at one moment, and at another, by their want of firmness and deficiency of judgment, affording the most glaring and fatal proofs of the just estimate which all nations had formed of their character.'

She was disillusioned by the cruelty of mob rule and it seemed to her the people ignored their debased condition, all the while insisting upon a degree of freedom in government which could only lead to further disasters. This, she maintained, was due to deficiencies in the French character. They had no idea what citizenship implied; no sense of justice founded upon long experience and rigorous self-discipline. The abrupt change from tyranny to so-called freedom had gone to their heads and they had failed to meet the challenge of power. They were guilty of moral depravity; however, she predicted that with an improved system of education and domestic affairs 'the French will insensibly rise to a dignity of character far above that of the present race; and then the fruit of their liberty, ripening gradually, will have a relish not to be expected during its crude and forced state.'

She lacked the detachment and discernment of a trained historian, and personal feelings ran away with her respect for fact. More favourable to philosophers than to politicians, she pointed out that the philosopher 'dedicates his exertions to promote the welfare and perfection of mankind, carrying his views beyond any time he chooses to mark'; whereas the politician does not 'sacrifice any present comfort to a prospect of future perfection'. For Mary, future perfection was always her goal. She could endure any hardship as long as her eyes were fixed upon a beckoning ideal. It was the effort to reach the ideal rather than the perfect state itself which kept her courage high.

Mary's pregnancy did not alarm her unduly, for her confidence in Imlay was as yet unshaken. Other men might succumb to the poisonous atmosphere of France, but not her 'dear love'; as a man of reason he was not to be shaken by the mishaps of daily existence or the exigencies of live history.

'True love,' she had written, 'spreads this kind of mysterious sanctity round the beloved object, making the lover most modest when in her presence. So reserved is affection that, receiving or returning personal endearments it wishes not only to shun the human eye as a kind of profanation, but to diffuse an encircling cloudy obscurity to shut out even the saucy sparkling sunbeams.'

When writing this passage in earlier years in her *Vindication*, Mary may have had a premonition of the hazards of a love between unequal protagonists. Now she confessed that she saw Imlay in 'encircling cloudy obscurity' and that the 'saucy sparkling sunbeams' were becoming more rare. This change of view was owing to the fact that their love was entering on a phase which entailed responsibility for a new life.

Back in Paris, living openly with Imlay, all went well at first. She knew he was planning their future together in America. Once he had accumulated £1,000 they would leave France and buy a farm somewhere in the States. How far away would the Revolution and all its horrors then seem! How she longed for that end to their tribulations!

Unfortunately Imlay's schemes for earning money were not turning out well, although Mary did not yet suspect it. He and Joel Barlow were trying to set themselves up as importers of ammunition, timber and grain, but there were great difficulties of transport which necessitated many absences from Paris. Soon he had to leave for Le Havre, telling her it would not be for long, but days lengthened into weeks, horrible weeks of the Terror in Paris. By good chance she had not shown to anyone the manuscript of her book on the Revolution, otherwise her life would have been in great peril. In August she wrote to Imlay:

'I obey an emotion of my heart which made me think of wishing thee, my love, good-night, before I go to rest, with more tenderness than I can tomorrow, when writing a hasty line or two under Colonel . . .'s eye. You can scarcely imagine with what pleasure I anticipate the day when we are to begin almost to live together; and you would smile to hear how many plans of employment I have in my head, now that I am confident my heart has found peace in your bosom.—Cherish me with that dignified tenderness, which I have only found in you; and your own dear girl will try to keep under a quickness of feeling, that has sometimes given you pain.—Yes, I will be *good*, that I may deserve to be happy; and whilst you love me I cannot fall again into the miserable state, which rendered life a burthen almost too heavy to be borne. But, good-night!—God bless you! Sterne says that is equal to a kiss—yet I would rather give you the kiss into the bargain, glowing with gratitude to Heaven, and affection to you. I like the word affection, because it signifies something habitual; and we are soon to meet, to try whether we have mind enough to keep our hearts warm. . . .' [8]

Now that she was pregnant she longed for the presence of a 'husband' to support her in the coming ordeal. But Imlay, after a short stay in Paris, had departed again for Le Havre; it seemed that they were to be separated for several months, and Mary was to be left alone in Paris at the height of the Terror. She wrote to him in September:

'I have been following you all along the road this comfortless weather; for, when I am absent from those I love, my imagination is as lively as if my senses had never been gratified by their presence—I was going to say caresses—and why should I not? I have found out that I have more mind than you, in one respect; because I can, without any violent effort of reason, find food for love in the same object, much longer than you can. The way to my senses is through my heart; but, forgive me! I think there is sometimes a shorter cut to yours.

'With ninety-nine men out of a hundred, a very sufficient dash of folly is necessary to render a woman *piquante*, a soft word for desirable; and, beyond these casual ebullitions of sympathy, few look for enjoyment by fostering a passion in their hearts. One reason, in short, why I wish my whole sex to become wiser, is, that the foolish ones may not, by their pretty folly, rob those whose sensibility keeps down their vanity, of the few roses that afford them some solace in the thorny road of life. . . .

Of late we are always separating. Crack! crack! and away you go! This joke wears the sallow cast of thought; for, though I began to write cheerfully, some melancholy tears have found their way into my eyes, that linger there, whilst a glow of tenderness at my heart whispers that you are one of the best creatures in the world. When we are settled in the country together, more duties will open before me, and my heart, which now, trembling into peace, is agitated by every emotion that awakens the remembrance of old griefs, will learn to rest on yours, with that dignity your character, not to talk of my own, demands.'[9]

There is a hint of despondency in these lines; old griefs were mixing with present care. Was Imlay, in fact, 'one of the best creatures in the world'? She has misgivings. Had she, in her eagerness to snatch happiness, made a disastrous decision? The child in her womb seemed restless.

'Write to me, my best love,' she urged, 'and bid me be patient —kindly—and the expressions of kindness will again beguile the time as sweetly as they have done to-night. Tell me also over and over again, that your happiness (and you deserve to be happy!) is closely connected with mine, and I will try to dissipate, as they rise, the fumes of former discontent, that have too often clouded the sunshine which you have endeavoured to diffuse through my mind. God bless you! Take care of yourself, and remember with tenderness your affectionate Mary. ... I am going to rest very happy, and you have made me so. This is the kindest good-night I can utter.'[10]

10

From Feminist to Humanist

The year 1793, when at Neuilly Mary and Imlay joined their destiny, was the nadir of the Revolution. It is strange that the passionate, warm-hearted Mary makes no reference in her letters to the appalling events taking place then, probably for reasons of safety. Like other British nationals, Tom Paine, Helen Maria Williams, Archibald Hamilton Rowan, she was in constant danger of imprisonment and worse. Her safety depended upon her obscurity. In fact these three friends all found themselves in one horrible place of confinement or another, where generally the only release was by way of the tumbril.

In July of that year a remarkable French woman mounted the scaffold and died with sublime calm. Charlotte Corday was the great-niece of Corneille. She was nourished, spiritually speaking, on extensive reading of her great-uncle's works and those of Plutarch and Rousseau. She had taken Rousseau's admonition, put into the mouth of Émile, to submit to necessity and behave as if one's conduct were to be an example to the universe.

For her the Girondins represented, *par excellence*, the cause of liberal government, the only cause that interested her, and when she heard of the horrific struggle between what she saw as the forces of good (the Girondins) and evil (the Montagne) she decided with innocent and disinterested simplicity to eliminate the chief instigator of evil: Marat. To her it seemed a requisition of the highest authority:

he must disappear and leave the government of the country to men who would not dishonour France and humanity! She decided to assassinate him, and in July 1793 travelled alone to Paris, gained admittance to Marat's home and stabbed him to death.

For this act she died by the guillotine. She was prepared for this terrible end; it was all exactly what she had foreseen. Her pride and patriotism sustained her. When she appeared before the Revolutionary Tribunal the evidence against her was duly mustered but she waved it all aside as unnecessary. 'I killed one man to save a hundred thousand,' she stated, as quoted by Carlyle in his *French Revolution*, 'a villain to save innocents; a savage wild beast to give repose to my country.'

Madame Roland a few months later was likewise waiting to appear before the Revolutionary Tribunal and her thoughts turned to the young woman who had never flinched. When Sophie Grandchamp, Madame Roland's friend and the companion of her last days, was asked by Madame Roland whose death had made the deepest impression on the people of Paris she replied that it was Charlotte Corday's. Madame Roland, well-read in Plutarch, Tacitus and Plato, considered that this time at least the people of Paris had shown good judgment.

M. Roland escaped to Rouen, M. Buzot to various places in the provinces, and Madame Roland was left alone in Paris to face her enemies. Most of her supporters were in hiding or dead—Sophie Grandchamp was free for she had no political significance. At first she was confined in the Abbaye, a 'respectable' prison, from which she was removed to La Pélagie, the prison of the prostitutes. Here she occupied herself writing her *Mémoires particulières* and *Dernières Pensées*.

'I have experienced generous and terrible sentiments which never flame more brightly than in times of political unrest, and in the confusion of all social relations. I have not been unfaithful to my principles. . . . I have had more virtues than pleasures' is one of her most moving observations. She spent some time trying to comfort Madame Pétion, whose mother had recently been guillotined; when alone and not writing she read Tacitus. 'I have taken a sort of passion for Tacitus; I read him through for the fourth time with a new delight, soon I shall know him by heart, and I cannot go to bed without having savoured a few of his pages.'[1]

Manon Roland felt her life had been a failure. The ideals for which she worked and inspired others to work likewise, her husband, and Buzot, along with many other Girondins, were being swept away. The vision of liberty was fading. 'O Liberty,' she cried at her death, 'what crimes are committed in thy name!' Yet she never allowed her own spirit to be darkened for long. Her love for Buzot, fervent idealist yet the one Girondin who tried to translate ideals into acts, was the mainspring of her hope.

'When men say that the morale of love is worth just nothing, they make a big proposition very lightly, which if true might be applied to all human passions which produce splendid and brilliant results; take away this morale and life is reduced to physical needs and appetites. . . . If the morale of love is admitted, I believe it to be the most fertile as well as the purest source of great virtue and splendid action.'[2]

Within a few hours of the execution of the twenty-two Girondins she was taken to the Conciergerie, the prison which preceded death.

She was tried on 8th November 1793 and died at 3.30 the same day. She made a pact with Sophie Grandchamp to exchange farewell glances on the route to the guillotine. Sophie, fainting with terror and pity, was waiting at the agreed place and watched the tumbril approach. She at once detected her friend, who at the moment was trying to comfort a man seated beside her who was at the end of his courage. Sophie reported these ultimate moments: 'Her eyes sought me out and I read in them the satisfaction she experienced at seeing me at this last, this ineffable tryst.'[3]

Thus died two French women for the ideals Mary Wollstonecraft held, many of which she outlined in her *Vindication*. Mary could have echoed Madame Roland's remarks on the morale of love. It must indeed have been her utter absorption in her love for Imlay which made her remain silent in face of these heroic examples of women dying for *la chose publique*. It is possible she felt she could not meet the challenge they gave, but it is only fair to add that it was not quite an equal one.

Neither of the French women had known years of poverty, petty misery and intellectual starvation. Neither had experienced what it was to be at the mercy of men brutalized by drink and incapable of reasoning. They were spared a debasing youth of slavery, although it was in opposition to political slavery that they died. It must be remembered that Madame Roland disliked the lower orders; she equated nobility with style and misery with incompetence. Yet the lessons she had learned from Rousseau were not forgotten. Man is born free and everywhere he is in chains. That the chains upon women were still more heavy than those upon men had not entered much into her consideration. Like the Blue Stockings, she had not suffered from the pressure of economic circumstance. It had never been for her a question of the next meal, a roof over one's head, the debtors' prison. The cramping misery of English women wholly dependent upon fathers, husbands or brothers for a reasonable existence was less evident in a country where family life was held in higher esteem than civic responsibilities, and women were the centre of the family. Also, French women were able to exercise their charms over men to their own advantage, whereas the general run of English women, largely because of a long tradition of puritanical restraint, were not so versed in these arts, which in fact Mary condemned in her *Vindication*.

There was a fundamental difference in the masculine attitude towards femininity in Latin countries. Whatever their legal standing, French women had, on the whole, happier relationships with the opposite sex. They were equally subordinated by custom and law, but by fully realizing men's dependence upon them and susceptibility to their charms they contrived to get a great deal of what they wanted. Rousseau gave warning: 'Educate women like men and the more they resemble our sex the less power they will have over us.' This is just the point Mary stressed in her book. In forceful language she asks were women born 'only to procreate and rot?' and in the course of doing so, bend men to their wills by sexual blackmail? The idea was abhorrent to her.

'We might as well never have been born unless it were necessary that we should be created to enable men to acquire the noble privilege of reason, the power of discerning good from evil, while we lie down in the dust from whence we were taken, never to rise again.'

Yet Mary must surely have been moved and influenced by the nobility of the sacrifice made by Madame Roland and Charlotte Corday. They were great humanists in the modern sense of the word. For them the feminist cause, in so far as they realized its existence at all, was part of the general liberation. For them the sex question was overwhelmed by the struggle between the classes, of the rich and the poor, of the over-privileged and the under-privileged, of enslaving custom and tradition and equal rights for all. But it is interesting to note that, sympathetic though the characters of Manon Roland and Charlotte Corday are, they are today considered to have had only negligible political influence overall, whereas Mary's views have subsequently had global re-percussions.

Mary too was a fervent advocate of the libertarian ideals of the Revolution, but she saw no reason why the struggle for female liberation should not take place simultaneously, since women were the cradle of the race. Parental affection could have great dangers. To be a good mother a woman must have an independent mind. Meek wives made foolish mothers. A child brought up to obey a parent only 'on account of his being a parent is shackled in his intelligence and prepared for a slavish submission to any power but reason'. Important as it was for men to be set free, was it not of even greater importance for women? This was an ancient cause going back to early centuries. Had not Plato insisted that women should be placed on an equal standing with men? The knowledge of the injustice done to one half of the population rankled with enlightened people; frequently it broke through the crust of masculine (and in lesser degree feminine) indifference and complacency. In England various talented women, such as those who led the Peti-tioners of the seventeenth century, had raised their voices and demanded the only weapon that they felt might lead to a lasting improvement in their lot, the right to an education at least as comprehensive as that given to boys.

It was Mary's glory that she canalized this recurrent sense of injustice, assembled the evidence in life and literature, and gave proof in her own life-story of the remedies she advocated. The education that had enabled her to pass on to the world her message (the *Vindication* had been translated into many languages) had been acquired by her own efforts, but it had been an unnecessarily hard struggle. She was in fact, although she would not have recognized herself as such, the first effective feminist-humanist in the Western world, forerunner of a great movement still alive today.

Mary was now alone in Paris and it was becoming daily more difficult for her to provide herself with food and other needs. She missed Imlay increasingly and public events disturbed her. Altogether she was at a low ebb. Imlay had written, scolding her for not making more effort.

'You will tell me,' she wrote, 'that exertions are necessary. I am weary of them! The face of things, public and private, vexes me. The "peace" and clemency which seemed to be dawning a few days ago, disappear again. "I am fallen," as Milton said, "on evil days"; for I really believe that Europe will be in a state of convulsion during half a century at least. Life is but a labour of patience: it is always rolling a great stone up a hill; for, before a person can find a resting-place imagining it is lodged, down it comes again, and all the work is to be done over anew! . . . My head aches, and my heart is heavy. The world appears an "unweeded garden" where "things rank and vile" flourish best.

'If you do not return soon—or, which is no such mighty matter, talk of it—I will throw my slippers out at window, and be off—nobody knows where. . . .

'Considering the care and anxiety a woman must have about a child before it comes into the world, it seems to me, by a *natural right*, to belong to her. When men get immersed in the world, they seem to lose all sensations, excepting those necessary to continue or produce life! Are these the privileges of reason?

Amongst the feathered race, whilst the hen keeps the young warm, her mate stays by to cheer her; but it is sufficient for man to condescend to get a child, in order to claim it. A man is a tyrant.'[4]

The cause of her despondency was Imlay's protracted absence. It seemed strange to her that he should leave her alone in her present condition in a city so full of horror and danger. When she had discussed marriage with Archibald Rowan, one of her few remaining English friends in Paris, she had shocked him by persisting that no motive upon earth ought to make a man and wife live together a moment after mutual love and regard were gone. It had been easy to make such positive statements when she was confident of Imlay's devotion, but at the present moment there seemed to be need for further reflection on the subject.

In October Marie Antoinette had been driven through the streets of Paris in a tumbril, her hands bound behind her. She was wretchedly dressed, a mob-cap on her head, her hair cut short roughly, her cheeks thin and colourless and in her eyes a look of fathomless grief. So David, the artist, sketched her as he watched her pass on her way to the last humiliation. If Mary saw her she made no mention of the fact in her letters. She seemed to have withdrawn from public life and deliberately refrained from dwelling upon the horrors she witnessed. Beyond rare meetings with former English friends she saw no one. Wherever Mary turned her eyes she found misery. Her only consolation lay in Imlay's letters, all too rare and all too desperately awaited.

'I have just received your kind and rational letter, and would fain hide my face, glowing with shame for my folly. I would hide it in your bosom, if you would again open it to me, and nestle closely till you bade my fluttering heart be still, by saying that you forgave me. With eyes overflowing with tears, and in the humblest attitude, I entreat you. Do not turn from me, for indeed I love you fondly, and have been very wretched since the night I was so cruelly hurt by thinking that you had no confidence in me.'[5]

She wrote to him continually to relieve her over-burdened heart.

'Yesterday, my love, I could not open your letter for some time; and, though it was not half as severe as I merited, it threw me into such a fit of trembling, as seriously alarmed me. I did not, as you may suppose, care for a little pain on my own account; but all the fears which I have had for a few days past, returned with fresh force. This morning I am better; will you not be glad to hear it? You perceive that sorrow has almost made a child of me, and that I want to be soothed to peace.'[6]

Such appeals eventually convinced Imlay that she was in no condition to be left alone in the desolation of Paris. He was not a cruel man, but shallow in feeling and without much imagination. He had never bargained for the sort of relationship Mary thought had been established between them and into which she had poured all her aspiration. But these hopes held small reality for him. It is true he was doing his best to make money and, in theory, this was to provide for their future together. His was the sort of temperament that dispels gloom. He was vital, active and cheerful: it was not surprising she clung to him in a world full of despair. Yet she was beginning to see him in a clearer light and her letters reveal the note of doubt. 'Knowing I am not a parasite-plant, I am willing to receive the proofs of affection that every pulse replies to, when I think of being once more in the same house with you.'[7]

She received a letter from him to say he had engaged lodgings for her in Le Havre and she had only to come to him when she felt well enough for the journey. She replied immediately with an '*avant-courier* without jack-boots' in which she asks,

'What is the reason that my spirits are not as manageable as yours? Yet, now I think of it, I will not allow that your temper is even, though I have promised myself, in order to obtain my own forgiveness, that I will not ruffle it for a long, long time —I am afraid to say never. . . . I am well, and have no apprehension that I shall find the journey too fatiguing, when I follow the lead of my heart. With my face turned to Havre my spirits will not sink, and my mind has always hitherto enabled my body to do whatever I wished.'[8]

It was the beginning of February 1794 when she made the journey to the coast and resumed daily life with Imlay. 'My lodgings are pleasantly situated,' she wrote to Ruth Barlow, wife of Joel Barlow, Imlay's business partner, 'and I have hired a maid servant, so that I am very comfortably settled, and shall remain so, if the high price of all the necessaries of life, do not ruin us.'[9] She was still busy on her *Historical and Moral View of the Origins of the French Revolution*, the first volume of which was almost ready to be dispatched to London, but it would be difficult to make further progress, for all her books were in Paris. However, life for the moment was pleasant and with Imlay at her side doubts about the wisdom of her alliance vanished. Now that she was happy she felt it was safe to write to her sister Everina, who was more understanding and approachable than Eliza.

> 'I am certainly glad that I came to France because I never could have had else a just opinion of the most extraordinary event that has ever been recorded, and I have met with some uncommon instances of friendship which my heart will ever gratefully store up, and call to mind when the remembrance is keen of the anguish it has endured for its fellow creatures at large—for the unfortunate beings cut off around me—and still more unfortunate survivors.'[10]

Among the unfortunate survivors was Buzot, who had been in hiding at Saint Émilion. As long as Madame Roland escaped the guillotine life had meaning for him, but when he heard of her end his courage and patriotism died with her. He wrote to a friend, Letellier, a man with whom she had worked in the *Bureau de l'Esprit Publique*: 'She is no more—she is no more, my friend. Judge if there is anything now left for me to regret upon this earth.'[11] Both Letellier and Buzot committed suicide, the first while in prison and Buzot while hiding in the countryside. M. Roland, who had taken refuge with friends in Rouen, when he heard of his wife's death also decided to take his own life. At his feet was found a piece of writing: 'Whosoever thou art that findest me lying, respect my remains; they are those of a man who consecrated all his life to being useful; and who died as he lived, virtuous and honest.'[12]

It might have been the epitaph of the Girondins as a whole. They were virtuous and honest and they upheld the cause of liberal government. Too much influenced by ancient history, particularly by the lives of classical heroes, they were strong in learning but weak in action, not lacking in conviction but lacking in drive. Only Madame Roland and Buzot had any of the qualities of real leadership.

Imlay had to leave for Paris a few weeks after Mary had joined him in Le Havre, but this separation did not alarm her now that she was reassured about the stability of their union.

'I knew that you were to stay such a short time and I had a plan of employment'; she wrote to him without any resentment, 'yet I could not sleep. I turned to your side of the bed, and tried to make the most of the comfort of the pillow, which you used to tell me I was churlish about; but all would not do. I took, nevertheless, my walk before breakfast, though the weather was not inviting—and here I am, wishing you a finer day, and seeing you peep over my shoulder, as I write, with one of your kindest looks—when your eyes glisten, and a suffusion creeps over your relaxing features.'[13]

Now that she had finished the first part of her book she had nothing to do but await the birth of her child. Imlay was not absent for long and since his work was to ensure their future together in America she had no reason to complain.

On 14th May 1794 her daughter was born and named Fanny after the friend of Mary's youth. The child was healthy and the mother blissfully satisfied. Childbirth was 'not smooth work,' she confessed to a friend, but 'this struggle of nature is rendered much more cruel by the ignorance and affectation of women'.[14] In this observation she proved herself yet again in advance of her times, for most women of her class treated the occasion as a major illness. She confined herself to bed for one day only and was out walking within the week. Imlay was delighted by her quick recovery and touched by the little creature with whom Mary presented him. 'The constant tenderness of my most affectionate companion makes me regard a fresh tie as a blessing,' she confided to Mrs Barlow.

'My little girl begins to suck *so manfully* that her father reckons saucily on her writing the second part of the *R - - - ts of Woman*.'

But a shadow fell on her happiness due to Imlay's lack of business success. As he pointed out, 'business and love will not chime together'. He had two faces, she told him; his money-making face and the 'barrier' face with which he used to welcome her when they met to spend happy hours together in the countryside. 'Be not too anxious to get money,' she warned him. 'For nothing worth having is to be purchased.'

The demon of doubt was beginning once more to haunt her. She began to pay visits to some of Imlay's business acquaintances. But her dislike of commercial affairs and the people engaged in them was too strong to allow of any enjoyment.

'The house smelt of commerce from top to toe—so that his abortive attempt to display taste, only proved it to be one of the things not to be bought with gold. I was in a room a moment alone, and my attention was attracted by the *pendule*. A nymph was offering up her vows, before a smoking altar, to a fat-bottomed Cupid (saving your presence), who was kicking his heels in the air. Ah! kick on, thought I; for the demon of traffic will ever fright away the loves and graces that streak with rosy beams of infant fancy the *sombre* day of life; whilst the imagination, not allowing us to see things as they are, enables us to catch a hasty draught of the running stream of delight, the thirst for which seems to be given only to tantalize us.'[15]

The split between her tastes and Imlay's was beginning to interfere seriously with their contentment in each other. Mary loathed what she called 'square-headed money-getters'.

'Common life,' she wrote to him, 'is scarcely worth having, even with a *gigot* every day, and a pudding added thereunto. I will allow you to cultivate my judgment, if you will permit me to keep alive the sentiments in your heart, which may be termed romantic, because, the offspring of the senses and the imagination, they resemble the mother more than the father, when they produce the suffusion I admire. In spite of icy age, I hope still to see it, if you have not determined only to eat and drink, and be stupidly useful to the stupid.'[16]

This was an unwise letter for her to write; she was showing a side of her character which must have appealed little to a man of Imlay's disposition. It was inevitable that with all the family responsibilities she had assumed, keeping her father solvent, directing her brothers and sisters into the right channels of usefulness, rescuing them when their difficulties became too great, she should adopt occasionally a hectoring tone. Few men, certainly not Imlay, would appreciate their activities being described as 'stupidly useful to the stupid'. Although she assured him in a subsequent letter, 'I want you to promote my felicity, by seeking your own', and with the next breath, 'Whatever pleasure it may give me to discover your generosity of soul, I would not be dependent for your affection on the very quality I most admire,'[17] she was none the less dangerously dependent. At odds with herself she could not disentangle the humiliating truth from her philosophic stand. To her very real doubts were now added torments of the imagination. Did Imlay, the father of her child, cherish her with anything like the intensity of her feeling for him? It was impossible to believe as much. In fact Imlay was drifting away, but the full realization of this was too fearful to bear. She continued to fool herself. There was always the little damsel to bridge the widening gap between her parents. 'She certainly looks very like you,' she wrote to him, 'but I do not love her the less for that, whether I am angry or pleased with you.'[18]

11

'The More I Think the Sadder I Grow'

Mary was enjoying a period of calm and happiness with Imlay when little Fanny broke the spell by falling ill with smallpox. Her mother, who had lost confidence in French doctors, followed the suggestions of her own reason, as she explained in a letter to Everina, and 'probably saved her [Fanny's] life, for she was very ill, by putting her twice a day into a warm bath'. Very soon Imlay had to leave for London on business, which he reckoned would mean an absence of two months, and Mary again became disturbed by a feeling of insecurity. Why was Imlay so frequently separated from her?

'When I am sad,' she wrote to him, 'I lament that all my affections grow on me, till they become too strong for my peace, though they all afford me snatches of exquisite enjoyment. This for our little girl was at first very reasonable—, more the effect of reason, a sense of duty, than feeling—now she has got into my heart and imagination, and when I walk out without her, her little figure is ever dancing before me. You too have somehow clung round my heart. I found I could not eat my dinner in the great room, and, when I took up the large knife to carve for myself, tears rushed into my eyes. Do not, however, suppose that I am melancholy, for, when you are from me, I not only wonder how I can find fault with you, but how I can doubt your affection. ... You are the friend of my bosom, and the prop of my heart.'[1]

Meanwhile Volume One of *An Historical and Moral View of the Origins and Progress of the French Revolution* appeared in London and had a mixed reception. It was obvious that the author was disappointed by the way the Revolution had developed. It was not, she pointed out, the principles that were wrong but the character of those responsible for the events consequent upon the principles. She had no admiration for the rabble and little confidence in their leaders, however talented and inspired. She thought the French people were depraved and unequal to the great task of liberation. She did not understand the Gallic temperament and wrote of it in a carping vein that detracted from the book's value as history. When speaking of 'lascivious pictures in which grace varnishes voluptuousness' she gives way to a censorious spirit now gaining upon her, much to the detriment of her relationship with Imlay. The bleak mood caused by his frequent absences was due to painful insight into the true nature of the relationship. Just as there was so much to deplore in the Revolution, such as horrible acts claiming to be those of justice, so was there in her lover's conduct a like deceptive quality. She was becoming disillusioned with all. Public events and private hopes were equally infected with an inner rot. She wrote to him at this time begging him to allow her to 'look into a heart, which my half-broken one wishes to creep into, to be revived and cherished'.[2]

She was alone in Le Havre; all the friends who remained to her were in Paris, and she decided to return there and defeat her loneliness by seeking their company. The journey by stagecoach was no small matter for someone in charge of a sick child, and in fact the coach overturned no less than four times. But she was determined not to be beaten by the accidents of fortune. They had survived the four breakdowns of their conveyance; she preferred now not to dwell in her letter upon the fright this had caused her and the little girl, but rather to pour out how much Fanny adored to ride in a coach, to see a scarlet waistcoat and to hear loud music. Her mother added to these joys by adorning the child with 'a sash, the first she has ever had round her', given in honour of Rousseau, for 'I have always been half in love with him'.

She rambled on in her letter but lacked confidence in his mood on receiving it.

> 'Believe me, sage sir,' she wrote, 'you have not sufficient respect for the imagination ... it is the mother of sentiment, the great distinction of our nature, the only purifier of the passions ... imagination is the true fire stolen from heaven to animate this cold creature of clay.... If you call these observations romantic ... I shall be apt to retort, that you are embruted by trade and the vulgar enjoyments of life.'[3]

Lapses into moments of cold criticism such as 'embruted by trade', 'vulgar enjoyments', were not calculated to bring Imlay back to her arms. She realized it and tried to control her outbursts of resentment, knowing she could not afford to give herself this relief. 'For you seem to pervade my whole frame, quickening the beat of my heart,'[4] she had written in the last of three unanswered letters. She tried to vary the reproachful tone by alluding to current events. Public affairs, she tells him, are rapidly improving. There is a certain liberty of the press which she foretells will result in the overthrow of the Jacobins. There are gleams of hope in *la chose publique*—if only she could detect a few in her own affairs! 'After you return, I hope indeed that you will not be so immersed in business, as during the last three or four months past—for even money, taking into account all the future comforts it is to procure, may be gained at too dear a rate.'

But even *la chose publique* was developing in a way not to inspire confidence. 'The liberty of the press will produce a great effect here —*the cry of blood will not be in vain*! Some more monsters will perish —and the Jacobins are conquered. Yet I almost fear the last flap of the tail of the beast.'[5] She refused, however, to be too down-hearted and threatened him:

> 'I have almost *charmed* a judge of the tribunal, R—— who, though I should not have thought it possible, has humanity, if not *beaucoup d'esprit*. But let me tell you if you do not make haste

back I shall be half in love with the author of the *Marseillaise*, who is a handsome man, a little too broad-faced or so, and plays sweetly on the violin.'[6]

She waited at home expecting him, trying to keep her spirits from sinking. 'Will you not then be a good boy and come back quickly to play with your girls? . . . My heart longs for your return, my love, and only looks for, and seeks happiness with you.'[7] But he did not come and she carried on alone in autumnal Paris, where so many mourned their dead and the living were not sure they were truly spared. Her Christmas of 1794 must have been a sad day. She had heard from him; he was still in London separated from her by the sea and wild storms. Many vessels had been driven on the rocks, but he was safe, although dissatisfied with his business affairs. She swept this consideration aside: 'I will not regret that your exertions have hitherto been so unavailing.' What did money matter as long as the beloved one was still on earth, still striving to secure their future together, still longing to rejoin her. On the day after Christmas she was assailed by doubts. Had fate done persecuting her? she asked. Unable to give an answer she cried out in despair,

'Come to me my dearest friend, husband, father of my child! All these fond ties glow at my heart at this moment, and dim my eyes. With you an independence is desirable; and it is always within our reach, if affluence escapes us—without you the world again appears empty to me.'[8]

It is hard to believe that a man of the least sensibility could resist such an appeal, though he had good, practical reasons to remain where he was and leave her to struggle with her agony of mind. He had a business friend in Paris who was working against Mary's desires and who urged her to have a little patience. Things would surely pick up; to let go now would spoil everything. And there were other possibilities of making money to be considered.

Imlay agreed with this and wrote to Mary accordingly. She replied begging him to listen to reason (her reason, not his) and come home.

'When we meet, we will discuss this subject. You will listen to reason, and it has probably occurred to you, that it will be better, in future, to pursue some sober plan, which may demand more time, and still enable you to arrive at the same end. It appears to me absurd to waste life in preparing to live.'[9]

This was her strongest argument. Life flows on and does not wait for the propitious moment. One cannot *prepare* to live; life is immediate and insistent. She had been bitterly schooled by circumstances and knew how few and fleeting were the chances of happiness. She was not angry, she assured him, but hurt and apprehensive. 'I will not importune you,' she writes, when every word did nothing but that. Yet what did it matter if there was no logical sequence in her words?

'I will not importune you, I will only tell you that I long to see you. . . . Having suffered so much in life, do not be surprised if I sometimes, when left to myself, grow gloomy, and suppose that it was all a dream, and that my happiness is not to last. I say happiness, because remembrance retrenches all the dark shades of the picture.'[10]

These letters of Mary make pitiful reading. Where is the strong-minded woman who separated her half-demented sister from her insensitive husband, who took upon herself to support a despairing wife rather than let her perish in humiliation? Where is the bold writer of the *Vindication*, the proud author who claimed that women were not born to suckle fools and chronicle small beer; that they should take part in the major tasks of life?—in medicine, as physicians as well as nurses; in politics, the making of history; in business, in order not to be forced to marry for support or sink to the level of prostitution; in the arts; and in education, not as ill-paid governesses almost as ignorant as their pupils, but as trained specialists?

On occasion she went back in mind to her former independence of spirit.

'Say but one word,' she wrote, 'and you shall never hear from me more. If not, for God's sake let us struggle with poverty—with any evil, but these continual inquietudes of business, which I have been told were to last but a few months, though every day the end appears more distant.'[11]

She could not face what the facts were crying aloud to her. Few letters from him, at most a scribble of lines which related nothing of what she longed to hear. Indifference to her health: 'a neglected cold, and continual inquietude ... have reduced me to a state of weakness I never before experienced.' Indifference to the child: 'God preserve this poor child, and render her happier than her mother!' She should have dropped her pen and ceased writing, for each word opened a new wound and led into the slough of self-pity.

'I deserved a better fate ... I am sick at heart; and, but for this little darling, I would cease to care about a life, which is now stripped of every charm.'[12]

Eventually Imlay was impelled, not so much by the desire to see her and his child as by the fear of where her powerful emotions might lead her, to write and suggest that she should join him in London. But it was only too obvious that he was not moved by the affection she longed to awaken. 'You talk of permanent views and future comfort,' she wrote. 'Not for me, for I am dead to hope. The inquietudes of the last winter have finished the business, and my heart is not only broken, but my constitution destroyed.'[13]

She could not go to him on such terms. Imlay, goaded by her outcry, offered what should have come from a free heart, but it was too much for her to accept and she made plans to live more economically in France, alone if necessary. She would give up her lodging and share the apartment of a friend, a German lady who had a child of the same age.

'I can live much cheaper there, which has now become an object. . . . I shall endeavour to procure what I want by my own exertions. I shall entirely give up the acquaintance of the Americans. . . . X [Imlay's business partner in Paris] and I have not been on good terms for a long time. Yesterday he very unmanlily exulted over me, on account of your determination to stay. I had provoked it, it is true, by some asperities against commerce which have dropped from me when we have argued about the propriety of your remaining where you are; it is no matter, I have drunk too deep of the bitter cup to care about trifles.'[14]

In July of that year Robespierre had died on the guillotine to which he had condemned so many innocent victims. His death ended the Reign of Terror, but Paris was like a man who has been brutally stunned and on recovering is divided in mind between thankfulness at having survived and anger that he cannot return the blow. The disappearance of the tyrant meant the opening of the prisons. Men issuing from dark cells thronged the streets, together with others who had been hiding in cellars and attics, and fugitives from abroad. Thousands of wronged and embittered people roamed the city demanding restitution and justice. But the machinery of justice no longer existed. The Revolutionary Committees had faded out of existence, and the institutions that they had replaced were not in a state to function. Terror no longer reigned, but there was great unrest and fear; fear of the general disorder, of poverty, hunger and homelessness.

In such a Paris Mary was more than ever alone. At first, on her return to the capital, she had been reasonably happy, seeing the friends who still remained there; her pleasure in meeting them and in making a few new contacts cheated her loneliness. A glimpse of her is given in a letter of a Swiss friend, Madeleine Schweizer, who wrote:

'I passed one evening with her in the country. The blending of the various tints of colour in the sky were of a marvellous poetical beauty. Mary was sitting with the Baron W. beneath a tree gilded by the rays of the setting sun. I was opposite them, and was so enraptured by the scene that I said to her: "Come, Mary, come nature lover, and enjoy this wonderful spectacle, this constant transition from colour to colour." But to my great surprise Mary was so indifferent that she never turned her eyes from him by whom she was at the moment captivated.'[15]

This certainly paints a different picture of the deserted woman, but it was a superficial impression. To enjoy conversing with a male meant more to her at this moment than the beauty of the sky. 'She never turned her eyes from him' portrays a woman for whom masculine contact had now become a craving that curbed wider sympathies and narrowed her interests to a very fine point.

There is another impression of her given by her one remaining friend in Paris: Archibald Hamilton Rowan, a member of the international circle she had frequented before going to Le Havre. He was an ardent revolutionary, lacking depth and a sense of proportion but generous and warm of heart. Writing to his wife he described his first meeting with her:

'On the day of the celebration of one of the numerous feasts with which this country has abounded. . . . Mrs B. who was with me joined a lady who spoke English, and who was followed by her maid with an infant in her arms which I found belonged to the lady. Her manners were interesting and her conversation spirited, yet not out of her sex. B. whispered me that she was the author of *The Rights of Woman*. I started. "What," said I within myself, "this is Miss Wollstonecraft parading about with a child at her heels, with as little ceremony as if it were a watch she had just bought at the jeweller's. So much for the rights of woman", thought I. My society which before that time was wholly male, was now agreeably increased, and I got a dish of tea, and an hour's rational conversation whenever I called on her.'[16]

Hamilton Rowan was an admirer of the *Vindication* and had even put some of its principles into action. He had married a French woman, reputed to be a daughter of Philippe Égalité, and had ten children, now left with their mother in Ireland. An impractical idealist, he had hopes of liberating Ireland by landing French troops there. For this activity he was sentenced to imprisonment but escaped to France, where instead of being welcomed as a revolutionary he was taken for an English spy. But for being recognized by an Irish Inspector for Prisoners of War he would have ended on the guillotine; instead he was immediately released and offered a suite of apartments in the Palais Royale, together with a pension. Such abrupt reverses of fortune made him cautious, for he refused the splendours of the Palais Royale and the pension, preferring to retire to a modest flat in the rue de Mousseau. Mary visited him here and they exchanged views on the Revolution, with which both were disillusioned. He began to doubt its principles but she remained faithful to them, though mistrusting the men who had put those principles into action.

As time went on they met less and Mary was reduced strictly to her own company. She wrote to Imlay:

'This has been such a period of barbarity and misery, I ought not to complain of having my share. I wish one moment that I had never heard of the cruelties that have been practised here, and the next, envy the mothers who have been killed with their children. . . . You will think me mad: I would I were so, that I could forget my misery—so that my head or heart would be still.'[17]

Imlay wrote again urging her to return to England, yet she still hesitated. Wretched as she was in France, in England she would meet with difficulties of a different nature, not so harsh but less easily to be borne. In France her social position as an unmarried woman with an illegitimate child caused her no embarrassment. There were too many in like circumstances, and in any event this situation met with more understanding than in her own country. In England she would be called a 'kept woman' and the thought was odious to her.

'When I determined to live with you,' she wrote to Imlay, 'I was only governed by affection. I would share poverty with you. . . . I have certain principles of action; I know what I look for to found my happiness on. It is not money. With you I wished for sufficient to procure the comforts of life, as it is, less will do. I can still exert myself to obtain the necessaries of

life for my child, and she does not want more at present. I have
two or three plans in my head to earn our subsistence; for do
not suppose that, neglected by you, I will lie under obligations
of a pecuniary kind to you! No; I would sooner submit to
menial service.'

She feared what she hardly dared to express in writing, that he
had found someone to replace her in his affections.

'If a wandering of the heart, or even a caprice of the imagination detains you, there is an end of all my hopes of happiness.
I could not forgive you if I would. . . . Say but one word and
you shall never hear of me more.'

Tossed between her longing to be with him and an intuition that
held her back from facing what would be a deadly blow to her,
she declared that the thought of living once more in England filled
her with 'a repugnance that almost amounts to horror'.

'The more I think the sadder I grow,' she confessed during a
period of self-examination.

'Society fatigues me inexpressibly. So much so, that finding
fault with everyone, I have only reason enough to discover that
the fault is in myself. My child alone interests me, and, but for
her, I should not take any pains to recover my health.'

Then, in forlorn surrender, she summed up:

'I have not found a guardian angel, in heaven or on earth, to
ward off sorrow or care from my bosom.'[19]

12

Back in London

Burke had published in 1790 his *Reflections on the Revolution in France*, not long before Mary left England for France. This book, in which he upheld the divine right of kings and sternly reproved the aspirations of the people, so revolted her that she was inspired to write immediately afterwards her *Vindication of the Rights of Men*. It had a certain success but was eclipsed the following year by her far more important *Vindication of the Rights of Woman*. However, in the first of these two works she defined the Rights of Man as: 'Such a degree of liberty, civil and religious, as is compatible with the liberty of every other individual with whom he is united in a social compact.' The corollary that all men are born free was one of Rousseau's sweeping precepts which figured largely in Mary's social philosophy. But the axiom, which derived from an over simplification, was unsound, since man's conduct is inevitably subject to the exigencies of society, to questions of tradition, behaviour and current morality. In trying to fit the profound desire for freedom of action into such a coercive form, Rousseau falsified the issue. Man is *not* born free. Mary came to this conclusion at a later date, but at this moment faith in the liberty of the individual was paramount with her. It was on such a premise that she founded her union with Imlay.

How far had she any rights over him? Legally she had none, but on the higher plane of humanity she had many. Although she

146

treated conventional values and current morality lightly, she was none the less deeply concerned with virtue. It was virtue, or reason with which she equates it, that was the key to everything. Without reason combined with virtue man is spiritually lost. Reason combined with virtue, together with Nature and God are the triumvirate reigning over the inner world of men. 'Oh! virtue,' she wrote, 'thou are not an empty name! All that life can give—thou givest. . . . For it is the right use of reason alone which makes us independent of everything—excepting the unclouded reason whose service is perfect freedom.'

But Mary's strong natural passions were not as docile as her mind would have liked them to be.

'Why,' she asked, 'should the gracious fountain of life give us passions and the power of reflection only to embitter our days? Why should he lead us from love of ourselves to the sublime emotions which discovery of his wisdom and goodness excites, if these feelings were not set in motion to improve our nature of which they make a part, and render us capable of enjoying a more godlike portion of happiness?'[1]

It was obvious that she was going to find it difficult to force her passionate nature to keep within the bounds of her stern philosophy, and this perhaps is one reason why her letters to Imlay portray such anguish. In some way the two forces must be reconciled. Since the passions unfold the faculties, they are sacred fire and must be cherished. Yet cannot the imagination reduce the passions to mere appetite? But reflection will counteract this, for it shows, she wrote, that 'the governing passions implanted in us by the Author of all good . . . strengthen the faculties of each individual and enable it to attain all the experience that an infant can obtain who does things it cannot tell why'.

This is an argument to which she reverts more than once. She was clear-sighted enough to take account of the dangers inherent in passion. Yet passion may be purified and given force by reflection, that

'noble distinction of man . . . an instrument to raise him above

147

the earthly dross, by teaching him to love the centre of all perfection whose wisdom appears clearer and clearer in the works of nature, in proportion as reason is illuminated and exalted by contemplation'.

But where did Imlay come in all this? Try as she might she could not fit him into her personal philosophy. His love for her, if indeed it existed, was so different in quality from hers for him that she was forced to question it, yet if in fact she had been mistaken in him, then all her life in Paris fell to dust. It was more than she could bear to contemplate.

The despairing note in her letters drove Imlay to put some warmth into his and again urge her to join him in London. He assured her that 'business alone has kept me from you. Come to any port and I will fly down to my two dear girls with a heart all their own.' She found it hard to believe in such bliss. It was too much. She had expected dry crumbs and had received a freshly baked loaf; but her enfeebled being could not absorb such abundance.

'I sit, lost in thought, looking at the sea; and tears rush into my eyes when I find that I am cherishing any fond expectations. I have indeed been so unhappy this winter, I find it as difficult to acquire fresh hopes, as to regain tranquillity. Enough of this; lie still, foolish heart.'[2]

The truth was she had lost faith, in him and in happiness for herself. Even now as she was preparing to cross the sea to go to him, she was unable to feel joy. In her heart she knew that he had retained little true affection for her or the child. In order to oblige some friend of his she had to delay her departure for a short while. This small upset drew from her a bitter observation: 'I have not quite as much philosophy, I would not for the world say indifference, as you.'

These words were written at Le Havre on 7th April, and four days later she wrote more hopefully:

'Here we are, my love, and mean to set out early in the morning; and, if I can find you, I hope to dine with you to-morrow. I shall drive to ——'s hotel, where —— tells me you have been

—and, if you have left it, I hope you will take care to be there to receive us. I have brought with me Mr ——'s little friend, and a girl whom I like to take care of our little darling. . . . But why do I write about trifles, or anything? Are we not to meet soon? What does your heart say?'[3]

She knew that he would have few words of comfort for her, yet she continued to ask the question, not only in written words but also in speech when finally they met at an hotel in London. Here it seems he had the courage to hint at the reason for his lack of warmth. A young actress now attracted him and his best thoughts and affections were no longer for Mary and their child. It was now that Mary's former proud words demanded her endorsement, but she failed herself. 'I find,' she wrote to him, 'that tranquillity is not to be obtained by exertion; it is a feeling so different from the resignation of despair! . . . There are arguments that convince the reason, whilst they carry death to the heart.'[4]

She could not steer a straight course through so many fierce currents. She failed to steer at all. 'A strong conviction seems to whirl round in the very centre of my brain, which, like the fiat of fate, emphatically assures me that grief has a firm hold of my heart.'[5]

In a previous letter she had exhorted him: 'My friend—my dear friend—examine yourself well. I am out of the question; for alas! I am nothing, and discover what you wish to do—what will render you most comfortable—or, to be more explicit, whether you desire to live with me, or part for ever!'[6]

Imlay compromised. In truth he did not want to live again with her but could not reconcile his conscience to a brutal separation. He had never intended a union of such depths. He fell so far short of the standard she set in her ardent imagination, and none of her appeals could possibly restore him to what in fact he had never been, except in the fervour of her love and desire. He was not her equal in anything and he did not want to continue with the useless effort to attain her level. It was not his fault, he argued, that she had created an imaginary lover to fit her needs. She was a mature woman and should know what was the nature of most men. He could not be held responsible for the fantasies she had invented.

He was what he was, and as an intelligent woman she did not need to have all the i's dotted and the t's crossed.

He installed her in a furnished house at 26 Charlotte Street, Rathbone Place, prompted by conscience rather than by love. After more than a month in England she still lacked any assurance about their future together.

> 'We have had too many cruel explanations, that not only cloud every future prospect, but embitter the remembrances which alone give life to affection. . . . It seems to me that I have not only lost the hope, but the power of being happy. . . . I shall expect you to dinner on Monday, and will endeavour to assume a cheerful face to greet you.'[7]

She tried to turn the course of her thoughts by getting in touch once again with her sisters, but she shrank from letting them know the true state of affairs between herself and Imlay. She knew that Eliza cherished the hope of being able to make her home with her eldest sister and her husband, and it was too hurtful to Mary's pride to reveal the true state of affairs. She wrote to Eliza in a way far from justifiable by the facts.

> 'When Mr Imlay and I united our fate together he was without fortune, since that there is a prospect of his obtaining a considerable one; but though the hope appears to be well-founded, I cannot yet act as if it were a certainty. He is the most generous creature in the world, and if he succeed, as I have the greatest reason to think he will, he will in proportion to his acquirement of property enable me to be useful to you and Everina. I wish you and her could adopt any plan in which five or six hundred pounds could be of use. I know you will think me unkind, and it was this reflection that prevented my writing to you sooner, not to invite you to come and live with me. But Eliza, it is my opinion, not a readily formed one, the presence of a third person interrupts or destroys domestic happiness. Excepting this sacrifice there is nothing I would not do to promote your comfort. I am hurt at being obliged to be thus explicit and do indeed feel severely for the disappointments you have met with in life.'[8]

This is an astonishing letter in view of the facts of the situation. Since writing it her relations with Imlay had further deteriorated and her hope of reviving his affection was rapidly vanishing, and with it her own desperate courage. Eliza wrote a disagreeable reply, the nature of which may be inferred by a letter she sent to Everina.

'How have I merited such pointed cruelty? I may say insolence. When did I wish to live with her? At what time wish for a moment to interrupt their Domestic happiness? Was ever a present offered in so humiliating a style? Ought the poorest domestic to be thus insulted? I am positive I will never torment our amiable friend in Charlotte Street.'[9]

Eliza's character excluded hope of comfort. She was jealous of her sister's brilliant position in the literary world and was unaware of the trials Mary had overcome and those that still faced her. Nor did she appreciate how much the eldest sister owed it to her own efforts that she had arrived, speaking from the point of view of literary success, to the present high point. Her family considered that she had been treated favourably by fortune and that she owed them a share in her exceptional luck. Their letters to her were full of envy and false pride. They contained no warmth of heart and Mary was only humiliated by this attempt to get on closer terms. This was yet another discouraging fact to be added to what already filled her cup. Where could she look for strength of soul?

13

The Treason Trials and
Godwin's Intervention

Mary's interest in public affairs was still very much alive. It had been something more than an 'interest', for she had identified her own life with the struggle for social justice. She had no difficulty in understanding the artisan who had endured years of deadening toil for which he received a pittance, and who was punished if he dared to raise a voice in protest, more severely if he dared to combine with his fellows in an attempt to secure a better wage. The rule of law in England was superior to the will of the rulers. It had been greatly strengthened in a spontaneous reaction to the excesses of the French Revolution and judges were the independent umpires between the King and his subjects.

The Treason Trials of 1794, in which some of Mary's friends—who had forgathered in Johnson's house—were involved, give a vivid impression of 'revolutionary' England at this time. Fearful of a repetition in England of the events in France which had culminated there in the Terror and the breakdown of law and order, Parliament had recently added many new repressive statutes to the code of English law. Suspicion was rife in every stratum of society: the expression of a moderately liberal view might now put its author at risk, and any attempt by the skilled worker to improve or even maintain his position by the most rudimentary bargaining was liable to be construed as treason. Death or transportation to the wilds of Australia was usually the consequence for anyone who dared to bargain for better conditions of work. Such daring spirits were in fact very few and far between: the docility with which the penal legislation of this period was accepted implies that the masses regarded it as necessary in a time of national crisis. After war with revolutionary France had broken out, popular feeling was in fact so anti-Jacobin that there seems little doubt that, had manhood suffrage, and not the vagaries of the rotten borough system, then prevailed, radicals such as Charles James Fox would rapidly have lost their seats.

Nevertheless from time to time there was an undercurrent of passive discontent. A series of bad harvests had accelerated the drift to the towns; the increase in population and the conflict with France produced a rise in the prices of essential commodities. The small minority of radical thinkers of mainly middle-class or even, occasionally, of upper-class origins—preachers, politicians and writers—was now joined by a number of individuals of a slightly different social background. Such men came from the artisan class, but they were very far from being unskilled labourers: most of them already possessed, or were in process of acquiring through apprenticeship, their own small businesses. They thus possessed a degree of economic independence which the agricultural labourers and the growing number of urban workers lacked. In the true tradition of historic English radicalism questions of reform, both political and economic, began to occupy the minds of some such people, even though the risks were terrible for anyone who tried to interfere with the prevailing conditions of labour. Despite popular disapproval and distrust, they worked assiduously to further their aims by peaceful methods of persuasion. The inevitable consequence soon followed.

In 1794 the charge brought against twelve men of 'certain High Treasons and Misprisions of Treason' read that they 'maliciously and traitorously with force of arms did amongst themselves and together with others make war upon the King'. In the atmosphere of the times, such charges did not at first sight seem far-fetched to most onlookers.

All the twelve men were members of one or the other of those clubs and societies which were coming into being, particularly in London, to assist the disfranchised in their struggle for political

and economic justice. The chief of these was the London Corresponding Society, of which Thomas Hardy, a shoemaker, was the
secretary. Other organizations were the Friends of the People, and
the Society for Constitutional Information; but the London Corresponding Society, with a subscription of 1d. a week, was the most
important and the most accessible to those of low incomes. Members
were drawn chiefly from the most poorly paid group of reformers,
but also included a number of lawyers and teachers. It was a pioneer
political organization with nation-wide branches. It looked for its
inspiration to France, and in November 1792 John Frost, a lawyer
and one of its co-founders, had presented addresses from the Society
to the French Convention, in which the French were assured that
the British people would never support a war against liberty, i.e.
against revolutionary France. It was hardly surprising, therefore,
especially after 1793, that many came to believe that the Society
was the thin end of the wedge of an English Revolution along
French lines. Hence the charge of treason and the deep suspicion
aroused by the clubs and societies in general, where discussion of
grievances, the publication of radical literature and the general
encouragement to reform were the order of the day.

A verdict of guilty could entail a sentence of death and dis-
embowelment, although the latter extreme measure was now seldom
carried out. But the lesser penalty of transportation to the wilds of
Australia, where prisoners were deprived of all that constituted
civilized existence, was fearful enough. In Scotland in August 1793
a trial in similar circumstances had resulted in Thomas Muir, a
lawyer and founder of the Scottish Friends of the People (a Scottish
version of the Corresponding Society) being condemned to fourteen
years' transportation. The following month Thomas Palgrave, a
leading Scottish Unitarian, was sentenced to be transported for seven
years. The precedent of such sentences boded ill for the defendants
in the English case, even though English judges tended to be less
severe than their Scottish counterparts.

Most of the twelve men in the London dock derived from the
independent artisan class: they were largely self-made and self-
educated, and were grateful to their clubs and societies for the
little knowledge they had. But among them was a sprinkling of

intellectual radicals of the more traditional sort, men who had from time to time visited publisher Johnson. Two of them were Horne Tooke and Thomas Holcroft, close friends of William Godwin and supporters of John Wilkes. Tooke, a philologist, used to keep open house in Wimbledon on Sunday evenings for progressive thinkers and writers. He had been a clerk in Holy Orders but 'overlooked' the fact in view of his present concentration on social conditions. Though a scholar he was far from blind to all else but his chosen subject. He had detected one of the members of the Corresponding Society as a government spy, which did little to endear him to authorities. In fact when he appeared at the trial he had already spent six months in jail, during which his health had deteriorated. His remark that 'The law is open to everyone—like the London Tavern' (a very select establishment) tersely summed up a situation which did no credit to those in power.

Thomas Holcroft was a playwright whose *Road to Ruin* had been a theatrical triumph in recent years. So deep were his sympathies with ordinary working men, who had no other means of improving their lot but to combine together, that he forced himself upon a prosecution reluctant to have to deal with an educated person of his wit and spirit. The more uneducated man (like the uneducated woman, Mary would have interposed) was a far easier victim.

Francis Place, a self-educated tailor, also one of the twelve, was certainly not 'easy'. He had outstanding ability and would in due course make social history in England. At this time only twenty-three years of age, his face was already lined and his cheeks sunk from the effects of overwork and undernourishment. His was an indomitable spirit. As yet no more than a journeyman, a maker of leather breeches, his hands scarred by the strong thread he used in his trade, he frequently worked the night through, in order to have time for his socio-political activities. He had already organized an unsuccessful strike amongst his fellow workers. The secretary of the London Corresponding Society, Thomas Hardy, when arrested entrusted the papers of the Society to Place with orders to prepare the defence.

Charles Grey, later Earl Grey, of the Reform Bill, who attended the trial, seated comfortably near the judge, remarked of Thomas

Hardy, 'If this man is hanged, there is no safety for any man. Innocence no longer affords protection to a person obnoxious to those in power.'

Another of the twelve was Jeremiah Jones, tutor to the third Earl of Stanhope, who liked to be called Citizen Stanhope. The arrest of this member of high society had caused a flutter in aristocratic circles. It was described by Citizen Stanhope's daughter, Lady Hester: 'He was getting up in the morning and was just blowing his nose, as people do the moment before they come down, when a single knock came to the door and in bolted two officers with a warrant and took him off without my father's knowledge.'

The elaborate charges laid against the prisoners by the Lord Chief Justice on 2nd October, and on which a grand jury duly returned a bill of indictment, amounted in effect to high treason and were so worded that they gave a clear impression that the government had indeed discovered a conspiracy of gigantic proportions. In the tense atmosphere prevailing at the time, public reaction to the defendants therefore tended to be extremely hostile even before the trial proper commenced.

Among those radicals not arrested was the writer William Godwin; but he knew most of the prisoners well and shared their ideals. He also knew the charge of treason to be false, but he was well aware that they were in grave danger of conviction, nevertheless. In an effort to illustrate the speciousness of the charges brought against them Godwin wrote in great haste his *Cursory Strictures on the Charge delivered by Lord Chief Justice Eyre to the Grand Jury*, and this was duly published by the *Morning Chronicle* on 20th October, five days before the trial was due to begin, as an open letter to Lord Eyre. It was one of Godwin's masterpieces of cogent, practical argument. He pointed out that there was no proof whatsoever of any form of disloyalty to the Crown. Were men to risk death or transportation for such unsubstantial crimes?

The letter had considerable effect, for it swayed informed public opinion to the side of the defendants: the Crown case was made to appear ridiculous. It was 'one of the most acute and seasonable political pamphlets that ever appeared', commented Hazlitt, the essayist.

Godwin, along with Samuel Taylor Coleridge, the poet, and a good-looking young woman of radical principles, Amelia Alderson, attended the trial in the public gallery. Witnesses for the defence included Fox and Sheridan. In the end, all the defendants were acquitted.

Godwin's letter had been timely indeed. The trial became a turning-point in English social history. Amelia Alderson, unable to contain her enthusiastic feelings, pushed her way to where Horne Tooke was standing and flung her arms round his neck. She also paid a tribute to Godwin, who responded after a short interval of time by proposing marriage. He was refused, but the friendship suffered no harm. When eventually Mary became Godwin's wife it was with Amelia's blessing.

Godwin had given proof of considerable courage by his letter, although his authorship of it was kept secret for several months afterwards. It would not have been difficult for the authorities to have linked him with it, however. He was known as a convinced radical, and anarchist of a sort. He wanted a well-conceived form of society without government. But as he had already made clear in his *Political Justice*, he did not want lawlessness or the sort of anarchy that Robespierre had fathered. *Political Justice*, first published in 1793 at three guineas, was, fortunately for its author, an expensive volume to buy. William Pitt remarked that this was providential, since few people would be prepared to pay so much for so little comfort; its price, together with its condemnation of revolution by violence, undoubtedly saved Godwin from prosecution. In fact, despite its cost, *Political Justice* was widely read for its searching inquiry into the principles of government and of morals.

Of all the gifted men welcomed by Johnson to his home William Godwin was one of the most remarkable, although Mary at the time of first meeting him was little aware of it. When seated he was impressive to look at, with his broad forehead, thoughtful eyes and well-cut lips. But his legs were short, so that when he stood up he lost much of the impressiveness of his appearance. But his book established him as a major prophet. He had been paid seven hundred guineas for it, and three hundred more were due to him after the sale of three thousand copies, a big price for the times, which added still further to the respect he received. In argument Godwin went wide of Rousseau, who stood for man's natural gifts. For Godwin, social justice founded upon correct principles dominated all his ideas of reform. The consideration of the general good should be the concern of individuals and not of governments 'which only give substance and permanence to our errors'. The less governments interfere the better. 'Whatever each man does for himself is done well; whatever his neighbour or his country undertake for him is done ill.'

This was heady wine for those whose ears were still ringing with the explosive axioms of the French Revolution and who had not followed too closely subsequent events. And Godwin's view of property, 'that a loaf belongs to him who most wants it', was even headier. Under the subject of Property came consideration of marriage, the high point of all possessiveness.

'So long as I seek to engross one woman to myself,' he wrote, 'and to prohibit my neighbour from proving his superior deserts and reaping the fruits of it, I am guilty of the most odious of all monopolies.' Mary in her *Vindication* had revealed too much of the dark side of conventional marriage for this view to cause her and her readers much surprise, but when Godwin, warming to his subject, declared conventional marriage a 'fraud', a form of respectable prostitution, he was on more dangerous ground. However, the price of three guineas acted as a useful buffer for the book's survival and the liberty of the author. Godwin, a liberal humanist of the first water, would not be easy to convict of subversiveness. He believed in 'perfectibility', in human progress by man's own individual effort, to such a degree that it would be a brake on morality to penalize him.

The book stirred up considerable enthusiasm among a certain section of its readers. Southey having closed its covers observed: 'I read and almost worshipped Godwin.' And Hazlitt: 'No work in our time gave such a blow to the philosophical mind of the country.' Godwin's summing up: 'To a rational being there can be but one rule of conduct—justice, and one mode of ascertaining that mood—the exercise of the understanding.'

Godwin was the son of dissenting parents, his father being a Unitarian minister, and he was educated at Hoxton Academy with the idea that he should follow in his father's footsteps. It will be remembered that he was at Hoxton at the time Mary was living there with her parents. Steeped in the works of the French philosophers, he soon found he could not continue along the lines laid down by his father. When he joined a club in London called the 'Revolutionists' he became a close friend of Horne Tooke and Holcroft and cut himself off completely from the organized religion of his youth.

One of Godwin's most strongly held opinions was the futility of every form of punishment, above all that of death. His hatred of restrictions on liberty and his trust in the power of reason were the twin supporting towers of his philosophy. He gave artistic expression to them in his outstanding novel, *Things as They Are, or, The Adventures of Caleb Williams*, published a year after *Political Justice*. *Caleb Williams* just failed to be one of the great novels of the century. It was highly original in concept and constructed with much deeper psychological insight than was usual for the times. It established his literary reputation and he became a much sought after guest for social and philosophical gatherings. He was on friendly terms with Fox and Sheridan, and the latter told him he should become a member of parliament. Horne Tooke did not forget the debt he owed the author of *Political Justice*. At a dinner party he took Godwin's hand and kissed it. 'I can do no less for the hand that saved my life.'

Godwin was a rebel with a difference. If he was out of sympathy with a man in difficulties and disliked his acts, if the latter were not of 'indispensable utility' he advised resignation. 'How senseless and idiot-like to be angry with what we know to be a mere passive instrument, moved according to certain regular principles and in no degree responsible for its operation.' Godwin held that every man should be 'the ingenuous censor of his neighbour', and that it was a duty 'to tell a friend in person and to publish to the world his virtue, his good deeds, his meanness and his follies'.

He failed to appreciate the fact that such principles would hardly make him popular. Charles Lamb blamed this type of sincerity as 'forward-talking, half-brother of Truth . . . uncalled for'. None the less Godwin had many distinguished friends, among them Dr Richard Price, the radical dissenter and Mary's old acquaintance, the man whose writing provoked Burke to his *Reflections on the Revolution in France*; Thomas Lawrence, the celebrated portrait painter; and John Opie, a young artist who eventually painted the best portrait of Mary in existence. He went out frequently to meals in feminine company and on occasion met Mary Wollstonecraft, or Mary Imlay as she was now known.

Mary now made a good impression on Godwin but he still considered her the wife of Imlay and there were the rival charms of other gifted and attractive women. While staying in Norwich where Amelia Alderson lived with her father, he asked Dr Alderson for Amelia's hand and was refused. Soon afterwards he turned his attention to other of the brilliant female writers who surrounded him. Without acknowledging the fact to himself he was already attracted to Mary Wollstonecraft, although at this moment she was hardly to be seen, were it not for a rare visit to Johnson's upper room.

Even anxiety about Fanny's future had faded out of Mary's mind. Without Imlay's love there was little to interest her on this earth and she sought release. Godwin, quite unaware to what depths she had fallen, considered that intellectual women, like intellectual men, could not be reduced to despair as long as their reason held. Had he been able to read her letters to Imlay it would have seemed to him that Mary's reason was as good as ever, for she was still exhorting her lover to find out for himself what would make him most happy. But the letters did not reveal the whole woman, and so Godwin went about his usual ways and Mary, caged in misery, was hardly aware of him. It was at this point that she obeyed an impulse and sought to kill herself, but Imlay saved her from ultimate disaster just in time. It is not known by what means he was warned to prevent the final act, whatever it was, for that too has not been recorded.

Imlay was quite at a loss to know what to do with this passionate woman whom he no longer loved. He had expected her to go on writing books and meeting old friends, leaving him in peace. Yet he could not wholly forget her charm and the stimulus of her company. She was, as he knew, outstanding and not to be abandoned lightly. But her depth of character served now only to alienate him. He could not match her; his qualities were tinsel to her gold. She made an analysis of his character in a letter she wrote to him at this time in which she makes it quite clear she has no illusions left.

'I shall always consider it as one of the most serious misfortunes of my life, that I did not meet you, before satiety had rendered your senses so fastidious, as almost to close up every tender avenue of sentiment and affection that leads to your sympathetic heart. You have a heart, my friend, yet, hurried away by the impetuosity of inferior feelings, you have sought in vulgar excesses for that gratification which only the heart can bestow.

'The common run of men, I know, with strong health and gross appetites, must have variety to banish *ennui*, because the imagination never lends its magic wand, to convert appetite into love, cemented by according reason. Ah! my friend, you know not the ineffable delight, the exquisite pleasure, which arises from an unison of affection and desire, when the whole soul and senses are abandoned to a lively imagination, that renders every emotion delicate and rapturous. Yes; these are emotions over which satiety has no power, and the recollection of which, even disappointment cannot disenchant; but they do not exist without self-denial. These emotions, more or less strong, appear to me to be the distinctive characteristic of genius, the foundation of taste, and of that exquisite relish for the beauties of nature, of which the common herd of eaters and drinkers and *child-begetters* certainly have no idea. You will smile at an observation that has just occurred to me:—I consider those minds as the most strong and original whose imagination acts as the stimulus to their senses. . . . These are not common sorrows.'[1]

No, it was not easy to deal with a woman capable of writing such a letter. It could not have pleased him to hear that she considered he had none of the characteristics of genius, and that along with the rest of the common herd of 'eaters and drinkers and child-begetters' he had no idea of the 'ineffable delight of those gifted with a lively imagination'. Obviously he was of inferior clay, but that did not make her any less unhappy, and she still counted on hearing from him. She was in a turmoil of contradictory emotions.

Imlay had business interests in the timber trade in Scandinavia which demanded his personal attention. It occurred to him that Mary could take his place and collect certain sums of money which were due. Her thoughts would be taken off her own troubles by the complete change of scene and occupation. He would reward her by a promise to meet her in Switzerland and spend a holiday with her. Mary would have preferred to settle their future together and take steps towards some positive solution, instead of running away from the trouble. But this was Imlay's choice. He could not bear to face the straight issue that Mary put to him: 'Do you desire to live with me, or part for ever?' After her attempt at self-destruction, he feared to do, as Mary put it, 'what will render you most comfortable'.

Having urged her strongly to take on the Scandinavian project, he went so far as to execute a document to the effect that 'Mary Imlay, my best friend and wife', was to be his agent in 'all my affairs which I had placed in the hands of Mr Elias Backman, negociant, Gottenberg, or in those of Messrs Myburg and Co., Copenhagen'.

On 9th June Mary and the child Fanny with her nursemaid left London for Hull to await there the boat's departure on favourable winds. At first the change of scene was far from working a cure. 'Am I always to be tossed about thus? Shall I never find an asylum to rest *contented* in? How can you love to fly about continually, dropping down, as it were, in a new world—cold and strange—every other day! Why do you not attach those tender emotions round the idea of home, which even now dim my eyes? This alone is affection—every thing else is only humanity, electrified by sympathy.'[2]

They had to wait in Hull nearly three weeks, a miserable period of frustration when 'all nature seems to frown, or rather mourn with me. Everything is cold'. At last on the morning of 16th June, the captain warned her to be on board, for they were soon to sail.

Mary felt the moment of parting had really arrived and she became very agitated. Would Imlay forget her once she was right out of sight? 'My hand seems unwilling to add adieu,' she wrote, for she had a superstitious fear it might seal the separation. 'Well, let it come—I care not. What have I to dread, who have so little to hope for?' It was, however, a false alarm and they were still detained in Hull by unfavourable winds. She fell into profound depression, unable to sleep, or if she slept, tormented by appalling dreams. 'One thing let me tell you,' she wrote, 'when we meet again— surely we are to meet?—it must be to part no more. I mean not to have seas between us; it is more than I can support.'[3]

Next day, however, the moment of departure arrived in all earnest. She just had time to write a valedictory note.

'Adieu! Adieu! my friend. Your friendship is very cold—you see I am hurt. God bless you! I may perhaps be, some time or other, independent in every sense of the word. Ah! there is but one sense of it of consequence. I will break or bend this weak heart, yet even now it is full.'[4]

14

Letters from Scandinavia

The captain had promised to put her ashore at Arundall or Gothenburg on his way to Elsinore, but contrary winds obliged them to pass both places during the night and in the morning they had lost sight of the entrance to the bay. The vessel was becalmed and the captain put out a signal for the pilot. But no pilot was forthcoming and Mary persuaded the captain to let her have the ship's boat with sailors to row her to the lighthouse at which she had been staring for the last two hours. The captain consented and soon Mary with Fanny, the nurse and luggage were being rowed to this point, hoping to find there a means of getting conveyed round the rocks. Marguerite, the nurse, was full of misgivings but not Mary, whose courage was as usual high. None the less the silence that greeted them at the lighthouse was disturbing. At last, however, they discovered two old men who informed them that on the other side of the rocks some eight or ten miles away was a pilot's dwelling; whereupon they all got into the boat and the sailors rowed her to the other side of the island where they saw the pilot's hut.

'There was a solemn silence in this scene, which made itself be felt,' Mary wrote.

'The sun-beams that played on the ocean, scarcely ruffled by the lightest breeze, contrasted with the huge, dark rocks, that looked like the rude materials of creation forming the barrier of unwrought space, forcibly struck me; but I should not have been sorry if the cottage had not appeared equally tranquil. Approaching a retreat where strangers, especially women, so seldom appeared, I wondered that curiosity did not bring the beings who inhabited it to the windows or door. I did not immediately recollect that men who remain so near the brute creation, as only to exert themselves to find the food necessary to sustain life, have little or no imagination to call forth the curiosity necessary to fructify the faint glimmerings of mind which entitle them to rank as lords of the creation.'[1]

The pilot who came to the call of the sailors refused to act without directions from his chief, a lieutenant retired from the service who spoke English. Once more Mary's party rowed off in search of this man who, to their relief, they soon detected coming towards them in a boat. This saw the end of their troubles about setting foot on land. Soon Mary and her party were transferred to the lieutenant's boat and were conveyed to where his home was situated, and here they were made welcome by his wife. The first step was over; Mary at last stood on Swedish soil.

The early impression was good: a clean house, beds 'dazzlingly white', and the floor strewed over with little sprigs of juniper. Very soon they were seated at a table spread with dishes of fish, milk, butter, cheese and brandy—'the bane of the country', as Mary learned.

She had decided to keep notes of her travels intended not only as an account for Imlay's benefit but also as a work to be published as *Letters, written during a short residence in Sweden, Norway and Denmark*. So her eyes were kept busy and her mind alert. All seemed to be going well. 'The gaiety of my babe was unmixed. . . . She found a few wild strawberries more grateful than flowers or fancies.' The English-speaking lieutenant was agreeable and pleased to have such an appreciative visitor.

'I gazed around with rapture', she wrote, 'and felt more of that spontaneous pleasure which gives credibility to our expectation of happiness, than I had for a long, long time before. I forgot the horrors I had witnessed in France, which had cast a gloom over all nature, and suffering the enthusiasm of my character, too often, gracious God! damped by the tears of disappointed affection, to be lighted up afresh, care took wing while simple fellow feeling expanded my heart.'[2]

The friendly lieutenant suggested a visit to a family the head of which spoke English. Here Mary was welcomed with almost too much exuberance. Her baby risked being killed with kindness, and she was entertained by childish practical jokes, such as being offered snuff out of a box to which an artificial mouse was attached. At this place arrangements for her journey to Gothenburg were quickly made. The expense for travelling twenty-two English miles would not amount to more than twelve shillings. Mary insisted upon paying a guinea and a half, which led her host to suggest he should accompany her to prevent any trouble. She retired to rest early that night, for they had to be up at six next morning.

'Nothing, in fact,' she wrote in her notes, 'can equal the beauty of the northern summer's evening and night; if night it may be called, that only wants the glare of day, the full light, which frequently seems so impertinent. . . . I contemplated all nature at rest; the rocks, even grown darker in their appearance, looked as if they partook of the general repose, and reclined more heavily on their foundation.'[3]

They set off in a cart along a rocky road and all went well until they stopped at a little inn to bait the horses. Here it was discovered that Mary was not provided with a passport, and the customs officer who now appeared proved that professional zest can efface pleasant character. But Mary could not obtain her passport until she was actually in Gothenburg, and the officer blustered for money. The lieutenant opposed him; none the less Mary was obliged to walk to the town. Finally all was settled and that night in Gothenburg she wrote an account of her adventures.

'I have now but a moment before the post goes out to inform you we have got here; though not without considerable difficulty, for we were set ashore in a boat about twenty miles below. What

I suffered in the vessel I will not now descant upon—nor mention the pleasure I received from the sight of the rocky coast. This morning, however, walking to join the carriage that was to transport us to this place, I fell, without any previous warning, senseless on the rocks, and how I escaped with life I can scarcely guess. Twenty miles in the rain after my accident has sufficiently deranged me—and here I could not get a fire to warm me, or anything warm to eat; the inns are mere stables—I must nevertheless go to bed.'

It had been a rough start. Having got over her first keen interest in new impressions and the friendliness of the people she grew more critical. The politeness she so much appreciated she found to be not the polish of cultivated minds but consisted largely of 'tiresome forms and ceremonies'. There being little education behind the elaborate manners, these only served to stress their flimsy foundation. But in the peasantry she found the true politeness that seemed absent in the higher grades of society. Here life was a caricature of the French; the cooking, for instance, was aimed at destroying the natural taste of the food. Spices and sugar were put into everything and all dishes were highly seasoned, which brought about a constant use of spirits.

'Before dinner and supper, even while the dishes were cooling on the table, men and women repair to a side-table and, to obtain an appetite, eat bread and butter, cheese, raw salmon or anchovies, drinking a glass of brandy.'

To Mary's dismay meals lasted two and three hours.

'A never-ending, still-beginning feast. . . . Let me, my kind strangers, escape sometimes into your fir-groves, wander on the margin of your beautiful lakes, or climb your rocks.'

Her heavy heart was lightened as she progressed through new scenes and met more people whose habits she observed closely. The treatment of servants, for instance, showed her 'how far the Swedes are from having a just conception of rational equality'. They were not termed slaves,

'yet a man may strike a man with impunity because he pays him wages; though these wages are so low that necessity must teach them to pilfer, while servility renders them false and boorish. Still the men stand up for the dignity of man, by oppressing the women. The most menial, and even laborious offices, are therefore left to these poor drudges. . . . In the winter, I am told, they take the linen down to the river, to wash it in the cold water; and though their hands, cut by the ice, are cracked and bleeding, the men, their fellow-servants, will not disgrace their manhood by carrying a tub to lighten their burden. . . . You will not be surprised to hear that they do not wear shoes or stockings, when I inform you that their wages are seldom more than twenty or thirty shillings per annum.'[4]

She was hardly surprised to discover that here in the far north poor people suffered the same tyrannical treatment as had produced revolution in France and unrest in England. Taxation was heavy and wages extremely small. War, she noted, saps the vitals even of neutral countries. Here the French Revolution had decreased respect for the nobility. The peasants had lost their blind reverence for their lords and 'complain in manly style of oppressions which before they did not think of designating as such because they were taught to consider themselves as a different order of beings'.

Mary went about, her eyes growing ever more perceptive of unusual and significant details. The effect of the severe climate on the way people were clothed and the quality of their food struck her forcibly. The children, for instance, appeared to be 'nipped in the bud'. Their clothes were too heavy and too seldom aired. Even in summer they were loaded with flannels, which kept in the moisture of continual perspiration. To make matters worse, babies, even at the breast, were given brandy and salt fish. The women took insufficient exercise and grew fat at an early age. They had fine complexions, but indolence 'makes the lily displace the rose'. They absorbed quantities of coffee and spices, and with want of care allowed their teeth to decay 'and contrast ill with their ruby lips'. The men pleased her more. They were a robust, healthy race, distinguished for their common sense and humour; in the lower classes she found much to admire, for here was no aping of good breeding, no artificial refinement.

'The sympathy and frankness of heart conspicuous in the peasantry produces even a simple gracefulness of deportment, which has frequently struck me as very picturesque. I have often also been touched by their extreme desire to oblige me, when I could not explain my wants, and by their earnest manner of expressing that desire. . . . Still, my good friend, I begin to think that I should not like to live continually in this country, with people whose minds have such a narrow range.'[5]

She had now to leave Sweden for Norway. Her destination was Strömstad, a frontier town, to reach which she had to pass over the most uncultivated part of the country. Fortunately she was able to share the expense of a carriage and a servant who could speak the language with two gentlemen, one of whom had a German attendant able to drive well. In order to avoid having to wait for horses it was necessary to send a courier ahead the night before. The expense of all this did not amount to more than a shilling the Swedish mile, which was nearly six English miles.

The inns were reasonably good and the food tolerable, although Mary could not digest the rye-bread. Neither could she accustom herself to the down beds, in which she felt suffocated. People seemed to be afraid of air at night. Windows were kept closed and she found it hard to sleep. But in spite of everything she kept cheerful.

They arrived the second evening at a little village called Quistram just as the sun was beginning to decline.

'The road was on the declivity of a rocky mountain, slightly covered with mossy herbage and vagrant firs. . . . As we drew near, the loveliest banks of wild flowers variegated the prospect, and promised to exhale odours to add to the sweetness of the air, the purity of which you could almost see, alas! not smell, for the putrefying herrings, which they use as manure, after the oil has been extracted, spread over the patches of earth, claimed by cultivation, destroyed every other.'[6]

She had left Fanny and the nurse in Gothenburg and now she began to long for the comfort of her affectionate little companion.

'I grow more and more attached to my little girl. . . . She is an interesting creature. On ship-board, how often, as I gazed at the sea, have I longed to bury my troubled bosom in the less troubled deep; . . . and nothing but the sight of her—her playful smiles, which seemed to cling and twine round my heart—could have stopped me.'[7]

She was writing two sets of letters. One was a continuation of her usual correspondence with Imlay, in which she described her experiences and feelings and sought to retain his affection by dwelling upon her improved condition. 'I am more alive than you have seen me for a long, long time. I have a degree of vivacity, even in my grief, which is preferable to the benumbing stupor that, for the last year, has frozen up all my faculties.'[8] The other set were the *Letters* destined for publication, which she was composing daily during the progress of her journey. She calculated that these *Letters* would find a ready public, for at that time a woman travelling to the far north, accompanied by a small child and nurse, was indeed a rare visitor, especially a woman of Mary's ability and varied interests.

As they approached the frontiers, and the sea, 'nature assumed an aspect ruder and ruder'.

'Surely,' she wrote, 'if the sun ever shines here, it cannot warm these stones. . . . Man must therefore have been placed in the north, to tempt him to run after the sun, in order that the different parts of the earth might be peopled.'

The farms were small and most of the houses indicated poverty. They drew near to Strömstad and found here accommodation in the house of a merchant. Mary's companions wished to visit Fredericshall, the first town in Norway, and she agreed to accompany them. They had to scale some of the most mountainous cliffs in Sweden on their way to the ferry which separates the two countries.

'Entering among the cliffs,' she wrote, 'we were sheltered from the wind; warm sunbeams began to play, streams to flow, and groves of pines diversified the rocks. Sometimes they became suddenly bare and sublime. Once, in particular, after mounting the most terrific precipice, we had to pass through a tremendous defile, where the closing chasm seemed to threaten us with instant destruction, when turning quickly, verdant meadows and a beautiful lake relieved and charmed my eyes.'

They were now in Norway, and Mary noticed at once the difference in the manners of the inhabitants. The Norwegians were more industrious and more opulent. The Swedes were not on good terms with them and accused them of knavery. Both countries vied in claiming the best attributes, but as Mary observed 'the natural, I believe, will be found to consist merely in the degree of vivacity or thoughtfulness, pleasure, or pain inspired by the climate, whilst the varieties which the forms of government, including religion, produce are much more numerous and unstable'. She was on her guard against what she called factitious natural characters which have been supposed permanent, though only rendered so by the permanency of ignorance.

They visited Fredericshall but had time only for a transient view, for soon it was necessary to return to the ferry. When they had regained their carriage and Mary's companions had fallen asleep, she remained awake to enjoy

'a night such as I had never before seen or felt to charm the senses, and calm the heart. The very air was balmy, as it freshened into morn, producing the most voluptuous sensations. A vague pleasurable sentiment absorbed me, as I opened my bosom to the embraces of nature; and my soul rose to its author, with the chirping of the solitary birds, which began to feel, rather than see, advancing day. . . . The grey morn, streaked with silvery rays, ushered in the orient beams,— now beautifully varying with purple!—yet I was sorry to lose the soft watery clouds which preceded them, exciting a kind of expectation that made me almost afraid to breathe, lest I should break the charm. I saw the sun and sighed.'

They arrived back in Strömstad at five in the morning, to find the wind had changed in the night, and Mary's boat to take her to

Norway was ready for her. After refreshment she set off again, proposing to land much higher up the coast. She wrapped the folds of her greatcoat around her and reclined on some sails at the bottom of the boat until a wave sprayed her and obliged her to rise. Her solitariness now began to weigh on her.

Their destination was Laurvig, where they arrived towards three o'clock in the afternoon. She was deadly tired through lack of sleep, lonely without Fanny, but being met with great kindness she took courage. Her immediate need was for a carriage to continue her journey to Tönsberg, and eventually the 'good people of the inn procured a rude sort of *cabriole* and driver half drunk'. She was accompanied by a Danish captain and his mate, 'the former to ride on horseback ... and the latter to partake of my seat'. To Mary's mind they presented a grotesque trio, but what matter since they went forward at full gallop, the horses being very good. Mary, catching sight of a gentlemanlike man in a group who had crowded to watch them pass and seeing a smile on his face, burst into laughter to allow him to do so too, 'and away we flew'.

It was late when they reached Tönsberg. Next morning after conversing with the gentleman with whom she had business to transact, she found she would be detained in this town three weeks, and she regretted having left Fanny behind. But it was as well to have a little peace and quiet, for she was getting over-tired. The inn was comfortable and her room commanded a view of the sea. No one in the place could speak English or French, but this suited her, for it gave her a pretext to dine alone at a later hour than was usual. Having thus gained time for writing she composed a letter to Imlay.

'I will try to write with a degree of composure. I wish for us to live together, because I want you to acquire a habitual tenderness for my poor girl. I cannot bear to think of leaving her alone in the world, or that she should only be protected by your sense of duty. Next to preserving her, my most earnest wish is not to disturb your peace. I have nothing to expect, and little to fear in life. . . . When we meet again you shall be convinced that I have more resolution than you give me credit for. I will not torment you. If I am destined always to be dis-appointed and unhappy, I will conceal the anguish I cannot dissipate, and the tightened cord of life or reason will at last snap, and set me free. Yes; I shall be happy. This heart is worthy of the bliss its feelings anticipate and I cannot even persuade myself, wretched as they have made me, that my principles and sentiments are not founded on nature and truth.' [9]

She continues in a more cheerful vein and describes her life in Tönsberg, where she has never been so much in the air.

'I walk, I ride on horseback, row, bathe, and even sleep in the fields. My health is consequently improved. . . . I have enjoyed some tranquillity, and more happiness here, than for a long, long time past. (I say happiness, for I can give no other appella-tion to the exquisite delight this wild country and fine summer have afforded me.) Still, on examining my heart, I find that it is so constituted, I cannot live without some particular affec-tion—I am afraid not without a passion—and I feel the want of it more in society, than in solitude.' [10]

She returned to her professional writing and gave an account of Tönsberg, the oldest town in Norway. The Norwegians appeared to her the most free community she had ever observed. The mayor of each town exercised an authority almost patriarchal. 'They have no time to learn to be tyrants,' a gentleman informed her. The farmers were a manly race, 'for not being obliged to submit to any debasing tenure, in order to live, or advance themselves in the world, they act with an independent spirit'. There were four sheriffs in Norway, and from their sentences an appeal could be made to Copenhagen. Near most of the towns were commons on which the cows of all the inhabitants were allowed to graze. To render living more easy, all the people went out to fish in their own boats. The lower class of people in towns were in general sailors. Politics did no tinterest them, but the French Revolution was having its effect and the people, while remaining much attached to their Prince Royal, sang many revolutionary songs. The laws were mild and did not punish capitally for any crime but murder, which seldom occurred. The first and second conviction produced a sentence of a limited number of years. After the third the prisoners were whipped, branded on the forehead and condemned to perpetual labour. The total number of slaves did not amount to more than a hundred.

'The happiness of the people', Mary commented, 'is a substantial eulogism; and, from all I can gather, the inhabitants of Denmark and Norway are the least oppressed people of Europe. The press is free. They translate any of the French publications of the day, deliver their opinion on the subject, and discuss those it leads to with great freedom, and without fearing to displease the government.'

She was painfully impressed by the little attention paid to education except in reading, writing and the rudiments of arithmetic. The catechism was carefully taught, and the children obliged to read in the churches to prove that they were not neglected. There was no university, and degrees to enable anyone to practise a profession had to be taken at Copenhagen. But preparations were being made to establish a university in Norway. It was thought preferable to have the centre of learning at Tönsberg rather than in the metropolis. Tönsberg would then recover its pristine consequence. Once it had contained nine churches; at present there were only two. In one of them, St Mary's, there was an inscription importing that King James VI of Scotland and I of England, who came to escort his bride home, stood there and heard divine service. In St Mary's was a little recess full of coffins containing very old embalmed bodies. The idea of embalming filled Mary with 'disgust and horror'. Dust to dust, she thought; 'if this be not dissolution it is something worse than natural decay'. The contemplation of those coffins moved her to bemoan all vain attempts to snatch from decay what was destined so soon to perish.

Tönsberg, which was formerly the residence of one of the petty sovereigns of Norway, had the remains of a fortress on an adjacent mountain. Mary liked to walk among the ruins of the fortress and look down on the sea, following the course of white sails which seemed to take shelter under the pines covering the islands. It was a peaceful scene which brought relief to her troubled spirit. The fishermen calmly cast their nets, while the gulls hovered over the unruffled deep. Everything seemed to harmonize into tranquillity. She gazed and gazed again, her 'very soul diffused in the scene'. Its beauty and her lonely appreciation of it filled her with new delight and grief.

'I must love and admire with warmth,' she wrote, 'or I sink into sadness. . . . My bosom still glows. Do not saucily ask, repeating Sterne's question, "Maria, is it still so warm?"'

She discovered a new pleasure in bathing. A young woman from the hotel at which she was staying accompanied her to serve as interpreter and to row her across the water. But as the girl was pregnant Mary took one of the oars and learned an enjoyable exercise. A pleasing forgetfulness overcame her, or 'fallacious hopes'. 'But', she reminded herself,

'how fallacious! yet, without hope, what is to sustain life? . . . It appears to me impossible that I should cease to exist, or that this active. restless spirit equally alive to joy and sorrow should only be organised dust. . . . Surely something resides in this heart that is not perishable.'[11]

She would take up the oars and disturb the innumerable young starfish which floated just below the surface. They looked like thickened water; 'touching them the cloudy substance would turn or close, first on one side, then on the other, very gracefully'. The sea became her friend, showing her its half-hidden beauties as she floated on it or rowed across it.

She met the mayor, who spoke English, and was willing to give her much information. He invited her to spend the day with his family at the house of one of the richest merchants. She did not expect to find the company richly dressed and the young women so attractive. 'Rosy cheeks, sparkling eyes, and light brown or golden locks.'[12] The women thought her unaccompanied state terrible but it filled them with admiration. They gathered round her, sang to her, kissed her. Alas, their minds were 'totally uncultivated'; however, much affectionate warmth passed between the parties. 'They said it was a pleasure to look at me, I appeared so good-natured.' Real contact could not be made; nor was it possible to do much better with the men, whose interest was firmly centred on their own affairs and who knew little and cared less about matters of general interest.

Illegitimate children were supposed to be supported by both parents, but the father frequently disappeared. Mary's compassion was deeply stirred by 'this painful state of widowhood'. She thought of her little Fanny and the sadness of a deserted house: the poverty, the struggle for the mother to keep the baby. The business of living was complicated by the fact that there were no markets even in the large towns. When the farmer had anything to sell he would hawk it from house to house, and people often had to buy food when they did not want it. There was so much Mary saw that needed improving: the care of the children, the care of the sick, suitable clothes for the changing seasons, a simpler and more healthy way of preparing food. She could do so much for them if she could stay for some length of time. But she did not want to stay; she was longing to have Fanny once more in her arms; none the less it made her feel sad to leave Tönsberg, where she had received so much kindness.

'I never, my friend, thought so deeply,' she wrote, 'of the advantages obtained by human industry as since I have been in Norway. The world requires, I see, the hand of man to perfect it; and as this task naturally unfolds the faculties he exercises, it is physically impossible that he should have remained in Rousseau's golden age of stupidity. And, considering the question of human happiness, where, oh! where does it reside? . . . What a long time it requires to know ourselves; and yet almost every one has more of this knowledge than he is willing to own, even to himself. I cannot immediately determine whether I ought to rejoice at having turned over in this solitude a new page in the history of my own heart.' [13]

15

An Ever-growing Heap of
Discarded Hopes

She had now been seven weeks on her mission, a period of mixed feelings, of interest and sad reflection. The inner calm she sought evaded her, however much she tried to impose serenity. 'Friendship and domestic happiness are continually praised; yet how little is there of either in the world, because it requires more cultivation of mind to keep awake affection, even in our own hearts, than the common run of people suppose.'[1] Musing thus she sat in the boat as it twisted in and out of the rocks, her thoughts so vivid and troubling that it seemed she was engaged in a never-ending dialogue with one who made little response. 'Why am I talking of friendship after which I have had such a wild-goose chase? I thought only of telling you that the crows, as well as wild-geese, are here birds of passage.'[2]

She had left Tönsberg and was on her way to Moss. They glided along meadows and through woods, not forests of vast pines but light and graceful oaks, ash and beech. There seemed to be an air of contentment everywhere. 'The arbitrary government ... the king of Denmark, being the most absolute monarch in Europe ... seeks to hide itself in a lenity that almost renders the laws nullities.' Once more she was at the ferry which led to Moss, where the scenery lost much of its grandeur. The roads were like paths made in pleasure-grounds, the meadows like lawns. 'Never was a southern sky more beautiful, nor more soft its gales. Indeed, I am led to conclude, that the sweetest summer in the world, is the northern one.'[3] In Moss she met—*rara avis*—a literary man who was anxious to gather information relative to the past and present situation of France. The Norwegians were most sympathetic to the republican cause and could excuse anything that disgraced this struggle for freedom. 'I could hardly persuade them that Robespierre was a monster.'[4]

They were now approaching Oslo, then called Christiania. The situation of the capital city was very fine but somewhat spoiled by depredations committed on the rocks to make alum. Mary was given a polite reception when she landed, and supped that evening with some fashionable people of the place. Here she saw 'the cloven foot of despotism'. The grand bailiffs, mostly noblemen from Copenhagen, were 'political monsters', dependent upon their relations and connections at the Danish court, aping a degree of courtly parade. This aspect of things was far from pleasing her and she quickly got into the open air and walked towards the fortress, where the slaves (prisoners with more than three convictions) were working with chains on their legs; a sight which embittered her, for 'there was a degree of energy in some of their countenances which unavoidably excited my attention and almost created respect'. In her opinion the stars and gold keys of polite society disgraced the wearers as much as the fetters she was viewing.

She would have liked to journey farther to the north, but the advancing season warned her it was almost time to depart. She had acquired much respect for the Norwegian character, particularly for the farmers, who were superior to the people on the coast. Inland there was such a high degree of honesty that a man detected in dishonesty could no longer live among them. He was universally shunned and shame became the severest punishment.

Near Fredericshall she viewed the celebrated cascade, which so impressed her by its grandeur that she felt unequal to describe the beauty and elegance of the scene. Her exploring eye produced equal activity of mind. She asked herself why she was chained 'to life and its misery'. 'Still the tumultuous emotions this sublime object excited, were pleasurable; and, viewing it, my soul rose with renewed dignity, above its cares, grasping at immortality. . . .

I stretched out my hand to eternity, bounding over the dark speck of life to come.'

Norway had its Loch Ness monster, which greatly intrigued Mary. No captain she talked to had ever heard any traditional description of it although many claimed to have seen it. 'Till the fact be better ascertained,' Mary observed, 'I should think the account of them ought to be torn out of our Geographical Grammars.'

Near Strömstad, the frontier town, the pilot lost the way, and to Mary's alarm confessed that he was accustomed to the coast only along the Norwegian shore. He had no compass and a friend upon whom he relied to help him appeared no better equipped; so the boat dallied amidst a labyrinth of rocks. They entered creek after creek merely to find themselves running aground. Darkness was falling and the rocks cast their shadows; it seemed they might pass the whole night wandering to and fro. Then Mary discerned a light on a summit, which became their beacon, and they landed finally at Strömstad a little after one in the morning. The next day they set off for Quistram by land only to find a fair in progress.

'No bed to be had, or even a quiet corner. . . . All was lost in noise, riot and confusion.'

She managed to get some food and then set off again.

'Quitting Quistram, I met a number of joyous groups, and though the evening was fresh, many were stretched out on the grass like weary cattle; and drunken men had fallen by the road-side. On a rock, under the shade of lofty trees, a large party of men and women had lighted a fire, cutting down fuel around to keep it alive all night. They were drinking, smoking and laughing, with all their might and main.'[5]

They pressed on. The horses went well until suddenly the postilion stopped short and refused to continue. He had received orders not to go any farther, and Mary was obliged to stay at a nauseous inn where they had halted. She was almost driven back by the stench issuing from an apartment in which eight or ten people were sleeping.

'Two or three of the men and women were lying on the benches, others on old chests; and one figure started half out of a trunk to look at me. . . .'[6] After scaling a ruinous staircase she was shown a bedchamber, and found rest in spite of her previous disgust.

Next morning she set off again. It was Saturday and everywhere preparations for Sunday were on foot. She arrived at Gothenburg and there found Fanny and her nurse, which soothed her heartache for a while. Next day they set off for Trollhätten to observe the progress of the stupendous attempt to form a canal through the rocks. The work would take five years to complete and appeared to afford the country people great satisfaction. Not so Mary, who found it 'a grand feat of human industry but not calculated to warm the fancy'. She was far more impressed by the cataract and was stunned by its noise. 'I listened, scarcely conscious where I was, when I observed a boy, half obscured by the sparkling foam, fishing under the impending rock on the other side.'[7] She contrasted this quiet human activity with the awful roaring of the impetuous torrent, the noise of human instruments, the bustle of workmen, and the blowing up of the rocks, when granite masses trembled in the darkened air.

She found the general condition of people in Sweden inferior to that of Norway.

'The Norwegian peasantry, mostly independent, have a rough kind of frankness in their manner; but the Swedish, rendered more abject by misery, have a degree of politeness in their address, which, though it may sometimes border on insincerity, is oftener the effect of a broken spirit.'[8]

The money was a further indication of the comparative condition of the two countries. In Norway there were no notes of less value than the Swedish *rixdollar*, which was a small silver coin not worth more than a penny. But in Sweden they had notes for a much lower sum.

The Swedes she saw were in general deeply attached to their families, but divorce was easy on proving infidelity. Mary was severe on the worsening of relations between the couples once the first years were over. 'The husband becomes a sot, the wife amuses herself by scolding her servants.' The fault lay in the lack of any cultivation of the mind. There was nothing to replace youthful beauty and animal spirits.

They had now arrived at Elsinore and were waiting, as usual, for horses. Although in the surrounding country agriculture was in a more advanced state than farther north, and the people more civil and more moderate in their demands, yet there was too little to please the eye or the senses to make a stay there agreeable. They pressed on to Copenhagen, around which was 'a perfect plain with nothing to recommend it, but cultivation, not decorations'. The city had been ravaged by a great fire. There was little to see but fallen bricks. The palace must once have been a spacious building, but that had been consumed by fire two years before and served now only as a refuge from the recent conflagration. One of the reasons for the widespread nature of the catastrophe was the unwillingness of the people to arrest the course of the conflagration by pulling down houses. The people would not consent to this and the prince dare not insist. Even the fire-engines were out of order. She became more and more disillusioned with the people.

> 'The men of business are domestic tyrants . . . and so ignorant of the state of other countries, that they dogmatically assert that Denmark is the happiest country in the world. . . . The women are simply notable housewives, without accomplishments, or any of the charms that adorn more advanced social life.' [9]

Business obliged her to go a few miles out of town, and she met a troop of people who had just witnessed a man being executed, his body afterwards burned. This turned her sick with disgust. Women were accompanied by excited children; the whole scene had obviously been one of amusement for the gaping crowd. She was persuaded that capital punishment should be abolished for the evil effects it has on spectators. She even thought actors should not be allowed to die on the stage. Such spectacles only harden the heart of those who witness them; moreover she was convinced that the fear of an ignominious death never deters anyone from the commission of a crime. 'I am more and more convinced,' she wrote, 'that the same energy of character which renders a man a daring villain would have rendered him useful in society, had that society been well organised.'[10]

As she observed some of the commercial frauds practised she decided that the worship of property was the root of all evil. She thought the people were unenterprising, for there was little appearance of active industry, which was a great contrast to what she had observed in Norway. Here the paramount interest lay in hoarding property, for 'property is power in the shape of the respect it procures'. Wealth was not wanted in order to acquire the elegant luxuries of life. 'For a want of taste is very conspicuous at Copenhagen.'[11] The elegance which she (Queen Matilda) wished to introduce would be considered lasciviousness, but, as she observed,

> 'I do not find that the absence of gallantry renders the wives more chaste, or the husbands more constant. Love here seems to corrupt the morals, without polishing the manners. . . . The promiscuous amours of the men of the middling class with their female servants, debases both beyond measure.'

Women, she observed, were usually seduced by their superiors and men jilted by their inferiors.

She considered that the prevalent sensuality arose from indolence of mind. The degree of intimacy permitted to young people was remarkable. If a lover obtained the privileges of a husband it was only half by stealth because the family was wilfully blind. But these honorary engagements were rarely dissolved. To violate them was thought as disgraceful as violating the marriage vow.

Mary confessed that had she travelled towards the north before she visited France she would have been far less severe in condemning 'the depravity of the French'. Travel, she thought, ought to be the completion of a liberal education. The northern states ought to be visited before the more polished parts of Europe, 'to serve as the elements even of the knowledge of manners. . . . But, when visiting distant climes, a momentary social sympathy should not be allowed to influence the conclusions of the understanding'.

She visited the public library and museum as well as the palace of Rosenburg, then abandoned. Every object in the palace carried her back to past times, but the vacuum left by departed greatness was depressing. 'It seemed a vast tomb, full of the shadowy phantoms of those who had played or toiled their hour out.'[12]

The public library was well arranged and much larger than she had anticipated. The Icelandic manuscripts impressed her by showing what immense labour men will submit to in order to transmit their ideas to posterity. She gave a glance at the pictures, where the good were mixed indiscriminately with the bad, but she remarked that 'that same fault is conspicuous in the new splendid galleries forming at Paris. ... Specimens of natural history, and curiosities of art, were likewise huddled together without that scientific order which alone renders them useful'.[13] There were a number of respectable men of science but few of a literary character and fewer artists. The enterprising spirit of commerce and the parsimony of the royal prince led to dullness and eroded all activity of mind. Everything was reduced to an economical level; even the burning of the palace was esteemed a fortunate circumstance, since it reduced the establishment of the household, which was far too great for the revenue of the Crown.

She met Count Bernstorff and made a shrewd estimate of him.

'A worthy man ... more anxious not to do wrong ... than desirous of doing good ... inclining to that cautious circumspection which treads on the heels of timidity. ... Determined not to risk his popularity, for he is tenderly careful of his reputation, he will never gloriously fail ... or disturb, with the energy of genius, the stagnant state of the public mind.'[14]

Lavater had visited the Bernstorffs two years previously 'to fix the principles of the Christian religion firmly in the prince royal's mind', and found lines in his face to prove him a statesman of the first order. Mary sceptically attributes this to the fact that Bernstorff and Lavater agreed on their views about the French Revolution.

She wandered through shady walks and along pleasant streets, one of the best almost filled with hospitals. 'But whether hospitals, or workhouses, are any-where superintended with sufficient humanity' she frequently had reason to doubt. The autumn was exceptionally fine and she felt she should be making her way to Hamburg before the weather broke. Also she had forebodings about what awaited her at her journey's end. At times she found it impossible to write her travelogue, so hard did her personal problems press on her sensibilities.

'I am not, I will not be, merely an object of compassion—a clog, however light, to teaze you. Forget that I exist; I will never remind you. Something emphatical whispers me to put an end to these struggles. Be free, I will not torment, when I cannot please. I can take care of my child; you need not continually tell me our fortune is inseparable, *that you will try to cherish tenderness for me.* Do no violence to yourself! When we are separated, our interest, since you give so much weight to pecuniary considerations, will be entirely divided. I want not protection without affection; and support I need not, whilst my faculties are undisturbed. I had a dislike to living in England; but painful feelings must give way to superior considerations. I may not be able to acquire the sum necessary to maintain my child and self elsewhere. It is too late to go to Switzerland. But be not alarmed! I shall not force myself on you any more.'[15]

After writing this she received a letter from Imlay which showed such callousness that her bitterness overflowed.

'Gacious God, it is impossible for me to stifle something like resentment, when I receive fresh proofs of your indifference. ... I have not that happy substitute for wisdom, insensibility— and the lively sympathies which bind me to my fellow creatures, are all of a painful kind. They are the agonies of a broken heart; pleasure and I have shaken hands.'
'I am weary of travelling,' she went on, her heart becoming heavier as she took up her pen and tried to resume her travelogue, 'yet seem to have no home—no resting place to look to. I am strangely cast off. How often, passing through the rocks, I have thought, "But for this child, I would lay my head on one of them, and never open my eyes again." With a heart feelingly alive to all the affections of my nature, I have never met with

one softer than the stone that I would fain take for my last
pillow. I once thought I had, but it was all a delusion. I meet
with families continually, who are bound together by affection
or principle, and, when I am conscious that I have fulfilled the
duties of my station, almost to a forgetfulness of myself, I am
ready to demand, in a murmuring tone, of heaven, "Why am
I thus abandoned?"'[16]

She left Copenhagen by boat without much regret and passed
open cultivated country towards Korsør. She had joined forces with
a German gentleman, his friend and servant, which made pleasant
company. The child and Marguerite often slept, and when awake
the latter kept her amused by the stories she had treasured up for
her family, showing the pieces of money she had collected, and
stammering out a few foreign phrases. 'Happy thoughtlessness,
enviable harmless vanity, which thus produces a gaiety *du cœur*
worth all my philosophy,' Mary observed.

They were becalmed in the Little Belt, and Mary, having omitted
to bring food, could do nothing to calm the child's crying. Finally
they arrived and were lodged in a comfortable inn situated in a
countryside which resembled the most open part of England. Here in
Germany she found none of the wild charms of Sweden and Norway,
no terrific rocks but smiling herbage. The towns were superior to
anything she had seen on her northern tour; in the daytime there
was the busy hum of men, in the evening exhilarating cries of joy.
The weather was fine and the women and children were amusing
themselves at their doors or walking under the trees.

'The chearfulness of the people in the streets was particularly
grateful to me, after having been depressed by the death-like silence
of those of Denmark, where every house made me think of a tomb,'
Mary wrote. On arriving at Schleswig she decided that the King of
Denmark's German dominions were far superior to any other part
of his kingdom, none the less the sight of soldiers recalled unpleasing
ideas of German despotism. She looked at these men in uniform,
training to be sold to slaughter or be slaughtered, and reflected that
the design of the Deity was the preservation of the species and not
of the individual. 'Blossoms come forth only to be blighted; fish

lay their spawn where it will be devoured; and what a large portion of the human race are born merely to be swept prematurely away.'

They stood awaiting the arrival of the horses and observing the way people were dressed. The women appeared 'very grotesque and unwieldy'. The false notion of beauty consisted in 'giving a rotundity to a certain part of the body not the most slim, when nature has done her part', often leading them to 'toil under the weight of some ten or a dozen petticoats—which, with an enormous basket, literally speaking', serving as a bonnet, the whole outfit almost completely concealed the human form, 'as well as face divine, often worth showing'. However, Mary was pleased to note that the women seemed to take the lead in correcting manners everywhere; cumbersome clothes and enormous burdens did not prevent that essential part of the feminine role.

They pushed on, and were pleased to observe the general improvement in houses, farms and the aspect of the people. The farmhouses had huge stables and big living-rooms, and were all very clean and commodious. They were welcomed by a pretty young woman, 'dressed in a cotton jacket, ornamented with knots of blue ribbon', whose greeting completed the excellent impression already given. Everywhere there was a degree of comfort which shut out misery. As Mary continued on her way this experience was repeated, and the only complaint she could make was of the softness of the beds which prevented her from sleeping.

Hamburg disappointed her. They had great difficulty in finding accommodation, and determined to leave the city for Altona the following day. Her one night in the great port was enough to disgust her. The place reeked of commerce and great fortunes were amassed out of secret manœuvres of trade; mushroom fortunes, which were a side product of the war. The prosperous business men seemed to her 'of the species of the fungus; and the insolent vulgarity which a sudden influx of wealth usually produces in common minds is here very conspicuous,' she observed acidly. It contrasted with the distress of many of the unfortunate immigrants, fallen from their high estate, and 'gliding about "like the ghosts of greatness, with the *croix de St Louis* ostentatiously displayed, determined to hope, though Heaven and Earth their wishes crossed"'. But these

poor ghosts were for Mary much to be preferred to the sordid accumu-
lators of cent per cent. Her thoughts turned to Imlay, who belonged
to the latter category, and she suddenly threw off the covering of
the travelogue and cried out in protest:

'Ah, shall I whisper to you—that you—yourself, are strangely
altered, since you have entered deeply into commerce—more
than you are aware of—never allowing yourself to reflect and
keeping your mind, or rather passions, in a continual state of
agitation. Nature has given you talents, which lie dormant,
or are wasted in ignoble pursuits. You will rouse yourself, and
shake off the vile dust that obscures you, or my understanding,
as well as my heart, deceives me, egregiously.'[17]

When Imlay had first proposed this journey to her it was on the
supposition that she could advance his business affairs; having
done this they were to meet in Hamburg and enjoy a holiday together, perhaps in Switzerland. How far Mary had been upheld by
this prospect during the hardships and trials of the journey it was
not possible to say. It is true that in a recent letter to him she had
said it was too late for the Swiss holiday; but whatever the situation, it was hard to find no one to welcome her in Hamburg, and no
mention whatever made of any alternative holiday arrangement.
Such projects, it seemed, had been swept into the ever-growing
heap of discarded hopes. It became more and more difficult to
deceive herself. Imlay did not care what became of her and neither
he nor she had any plans for the future. She could not at first face
this too bitter truth, and stayed on in hateful Hamburg, writing her
book and trying to keep despair at a distance by observing other
foreigners, notably French refugees, with their own set of insoluble
problems. In fact Mary could hardly stir out of her lodging without
meeting 'interesting countenances, every lineament of which tells
you that they have seen better days'.

She met an acquaintance of Imlay's, St John de Crèvecœur,
author of *Letters from an American Farmer*, and they got into a
way of dining together; they had ideas in common and were loud
in declaiming against commerce and in particular against the Ham-
burgers thus employed. 'Why, Madam,' he said to Mary, 'you will

not meet with a man who has any calf to his leg. Body and soul, muscles and heart, are equally shrivelled up by a thirst of gain.'[18]

Mary did not seem to realize how plentifully she was feeding the fire that would destroy her relationship with Imlay. He was a man of commerce and she was travelling to promote his commercial interests. She had always known he was not of the learned tribe, but of men who bought in the cheapest market and sold in the dearest; a tribe she detested. She, who admonished human beings to live by reason and avoid despair, was outraging her own counsels. It was unbelievable she had not seen the situation from the angle from which Imlay had been viewing it for some time. She and he were not compatible and they were drifting farther apart. There was nothing in Imlay to respond to her fervent idealism and hopeful political philosophy. Men, at least most of them, were incapable of living on the principles she laid down. In a mood of bitter clearsightedness, she wrote:

'Men are strange machines; and their whole system of morality is in general held together by one grand principle, which loses its force the moment they allow themselves to break with impunity over the bounds which secured their self-respect. A man ceases to love humanity, and then individuals, as he advances in the chase after wealth; as one clashes with his interest, the other with his pleasures; to business, as it is termed, every-thing must give way, nay, is sacrificed; and all the endearing charities of citizen, husband, father, brother, become empty names. . . . Cassandra was not the only prophetess whose warning voice has been disregarded. How much easier it is to meet with love in the world than affection.'[19]

In these words Mary had penetrated to the heart of her trouble. Imlay had once felt physical love for her but not affection. There was not between them that affinity upon which lasting relationships are built. He had been the first to discover this. She had blinded herself to the lack in him of those feelings that knit man and woman together, such as the desire for development, the growing towards each other, the groping through the dark of untoward circumstances, the faith that dispels shadow. She had these qualities but not he, nor had he ever possessed them, a fact she should have discovered much earlier. Her angry protests against his occupation —'To commerce everything must give way; profit and profit are the only speculations—double—double, toil and trouble'—were in reality outcries against the man and her own self. She too had fallen out of love, but with her it was a far more serious matter, because love in all its aspects was the centre of her belief in all things. With reason and with love for safeguards she imagined she could not suffer. Yet here she was suffering with a greater intensity than she had ever known before. Yet she could still reason, could still love; why this anguish at her heart? She gave the answer herself in her last letter from Dover.

'I cannot calm my trembling heart. . . . That being who moulded it thus, knows that I am unable to tear up by the roots the propensity to affection which has been the torment of my life— but life will have an end.'[20]

16

The Break with Imlay

They arrived at Dover in October 1795 and again there was no one to meet them. Mary had written to Imlay from Hamburg, but the boat sailed very soon after she had dispatched her letter and probably he had not been able to come to Dover in time. She had had many forebodings; none the less it was a crushing disappointment. How often during her journey she had imagined their meeting at the end of it, their leaving together for a well-earned holiday in Switzerland, or England, or anywhere as long as they were together. Instead she had been greeted by emptiness and cold, and she found it almost impossible to bear up. But there was the little girl to consider. 'I even thought that you would be glad, some years hence, when the tumult of business was over, to repose in the society of an affectionate friend, and mark the progress of our interesting child,' she wrote to Imlay, and continued: 'This landing without having any friend to receive me, and even to be conscious that the friend whom I most wish to see will feel a disagreeable sensation at being informed of my arrival, does not come under the description of common misery. Every emotion yields to an overwhelming flood of sorrow.'[1] In a letter from him, his writing of 'the ties which bind you to me and my child' had momentarily raised her hopes and warmed her heart. But where was the evidence of those ties in his comforting presence after her months of travelling and effort on his behalf? Where the appreciative glance, the grateful touch of the hand as she described her adventures? His interest had completely gone. She rightly put the cause of this collapse to his having formed a new attachment. 'If it be so,' she wrote, 'let me earnestly request you to see me once more, and immediately. This is the only proof I require of the friendship you profess for me.'[1]

The real proof would have been his fulfilling his promise to accompany her on a holiday, but this idea belonged to a past that seemed impossibly remote and full of happy expectation. How could she ever have imagined such bliss? Instead she now held in her hand a letter from him 'written with extreme harshness ... with not a trace of tenderness of humanity, much less of friendship. I only see a desire to heave a load off your shoulders'.

At last she was facing reality, and finding it almost too much to bear. But she was determined to see Imlay once more.

'I now most earnestly intreat you to write to me, without fail, by return of the post. Direct your letter to be left at the post-office, and tell me whether you will come to me here, or where you will meet me. . . . Do not keep me in suspense. I expect nothing from you, or any human being.'[2]

Mary was losing her grip on herself and felt in an increasing state of mental collapse. Even the thought of her child had lost its restraining quality. Imlay did not come to Dover and she decided to go to London, where he consented to see her. They met, talked and came to an arrangement that for a while she should have what she had striven so desperately to obtain, that is, to share a home with Imlay and the child. But she could not congratulate herself on the success of this scheme, for his neglect of her and indifference to their common happiness became increasingly evident. Rashly she questioned their servant and learned that he had a mistress installed in another lodging. Rushing off to the address she had been given she verified the cook's statement; there could be no doubt: Imlay had deceived her and wanted above all to be rid of her.

It would have been easy enough to arrive at this conclusion without the help of the cook and her own rash inquiries. All had been obvious for months, yet she had not dared to face the situation.

This time evasion was no longer possible. She must be prepared for an end to every hope of happiness, to life itself.

'I write to you now on my knees, imploring you to send my child and the maid with —— to Paris. . . . Let the maid have all my clothes without distinction. Pray pay the cook her wages, and do not mention the confession which I forced from her; a little sooner or later is of no consequence. Nothing but my extreme stupidity could have rendered me blind so long. . . . I shall make no comments on your conduct or any appeal to the world. Let my wrongs sleep with me! Soon, very soon, I shall be at peace. . . . I would encounter a thousand deaths rather than a night like the last. Your treatment has thrown my mind into a state of chaos; yet I am serene. I go to find comfort, and my only fear is that my poor body will be insulted by an endeavour to recall my hated existence. But I shall plunge into the Thames where there is the least chance of my being snatched from the death I seek. God bless you. May you never know by experience what you have made me endure.'[3]

Mary was now set on a course of self-destruction. The idea had lurked at the back of her mind for some time; but she had argued that others had passed through this agony of defeat, alone and un-flinching, and she could too. There was, it must be confessed, a certain satisfaction in the knowledge that she would at last shake Imlay's indifference, at last find a way to his heart in the midst of business and sensual pleasure. She warns him: 'Should your sensi-bility ever awake . . . I shall appear before you, the victim of your deviation from rectitude.'[4] But this sort of cold comfort is not in keeping with her usual zest for living. Such wooden phrases as 'deviation from rectitude' did no justice to the torturing reality and were not those she would have chosen had not misery frozen the heart and checked the flow of understanding. Where was the freedom of spirit she so much vaunted? Whose and what rectitude was Imlay outraging? Every man was his own judge. She had written: 'While reason raises man among the brutal herd and death is big with promise, they alone are subject to blind authority who have no reliance on their own strength. They are free—Who will be free?' And now Imlay was giving her the opportunity to test those words by her own fortitude and suffering. At this terrible moment she must call upon her own strength and no other. All else passed from her mind, even her protective devotion to Fanny, even her longing to see the face of love once more; all were weaknesses induced by memory. Nothing remained but the resolve of a lonely heart to find Shelley's 'Elysian, windless fortunate abodes' that lie beyond the wilderness of living.

That night the rain was merciless, which suited both her mood and her purpose. She walked to Battersea Bridge, but meeting too many people for her liking, she hired a boat to take her up the Thames to Putney. Leaving the boat she made her way on to the Bridge and there paced to and fro to allow her clothes to become thoroughly sodden and lose their buoyancy. She passed no one, for which she was grateful. There was to be no break in those last conscious moments, no return to suffering, once she had made the final step. Her only care was to ensure that no act on her part would lead to her having to take up again the intolerable burden of living. When she judged that her clothes were sufficiently weighted with rain, she climbed the railing of the Bridge and flung herself into the water.

To her dismay her sodden clothes were not sufficient to sink her. She pressed them to her body, none the less they buoyed her up. Caught thus between life and death she endured an experience that wiped out all previous bitterness as a cloud-burst sweeps the land clear of ditches and puddles. The acute, individual, piercing pains of existence ceased and she was almost enveloped in blissful oblivion. Her mother's words, 'A little patience and all will be over', drifted through her mind. She opened her mouth and gulped down water; then consciousness faded out and she was at peace.

But her hopes were not realized. A man had seen her body floating and promptly took measures to rescue her. She was conveyed to the home of the Christies in Finsbury Park, where she was nursed back to health. She did not seem to have learned much from this terrible experience, for she played with the idea of repeating it. She wrote to Imlay:

'I have only to lament, that, when the bitterness of death was past, I was inhumanly brought back to life and misery. But a fixed determination is not to be baffled by disappointment; nor will I allow that to be a frantic attempt which was one of the calmest acts of reason.'[5]

Imlay did not wish to read any more of her letters, which had become an unbearable reproach. He forced his feelings to become numb; his one desire was to be rid of the whole affair. While Mary lay in Mrs Christie's hospitable home, recovering from shock, she seemed to be unable to refrain from writing to him. The proud woman who had so repeatedly expressed independence and self-sufficiency did not seem to realize how much she was betraying her better self. 'I have loved with my whole soul, only to discover that I had no chance of a return.' 'My heart thirsts for justice from you ... I am convinced you will not always justify your own [conduct].'[6] 'I am stunned. Your late conduct still appears to me a frightful dream. ... Principles are sacred things, and we never play with truth with impunity.'[7] 'In tearing myself from you, it is my own heart I pierce; and the time will come, when you will lament that you have thrown away a heart that, even in the moment of passion, you cannot despise. I would owe everything to your generosity, but, for God's sake, keep me no longer in suspense! Let me see you once more!'[8]

It was all of no use; it was astonishing that a woman of Mary's powers of understanding should have persisted in such a hopeless pursuit. Her judgment was warped, her pride in the dust. At times, however, it reasserted itself. 'You need not fear that I shall publicly complain. ... I shall be silent as the grave in which I long to forget myself.'

Imlay at this point moved to a new house, which gave Mary the mad hope that she might be asked to join him there, even if his mistress were present too. She would put up with any humiliation rather than live without him. She stripped herself of pride, and forced her high-flown feelings to subside.

'I have long ceased to expect kindness or affection from any human creature and would fain tear from my heart its treacherous

sympathies ... I ask impatiently, what and where is truth?
I have been treated brutally; but I daily labour to remember
that I still have the duty of a mother to fulfil.'

She was to see Imlay once more—before the final break came.
He was visiting the Christies in Finsbury Square when Mary called.
Mrs Christie tried to persuade her to go away, but Mary's combative
mood was on her; instead she grasped Fanny's hand and strode into
the dining-room where Imlay was. They were face to face; other
people were present and it was agony to make a semblance of
friendship. They both withdrew to another room and Imlay agreed
to see her later, going as far as to consent to dine with her the
following day. The event passed off without painful incident and
unfortunately this served to revive the fire under the cinders of
her love. She left London soon afterwards to visit a friend, Mrs
Cotton, at Sonning in Berkshire, and while there received a letter
from him of such callousness that she knew this was the end. He
said, without beating about the bush, that his 'delicacy of mind'
prevented him from remaining faithful to any one woman. This
'delicacy' seemed the releasing word, for it effaced the last traces
of the esteem which she still cherished for him. 'Your understanding
or mine must be strangely warped, for what you term "delicacy"
appears to me to be exactly the contrary. . . . I part with you in
peace.'[9]

It is painful to follow Mary in these humiliating months of despair.
She excused the uncontrollable force of her passion by declaring that
Imlay was not the man he seemed to be. 'It is strange that, in spite
of all you do, something like conviction forces me to believe that
you are not what you appear to be. . . .'[10] These were her last
written words to him and they justify to a certain degree her lowering of herself. In this matter of love she suffered her great defeat,
in truth her only defeat; for in this instance alone did she accept
the fact that she was beaten, but by someone who was 'better than
he seemed'. Somewhere in her heart the 'real' Imlay was enshrined.
Never to the end of her life would she listen to any adverse criticism
of him.

Since she had greater power of self-knowledge than these desperate letters reveal she must have known in her heart how incompatible she and Imlay were. The letters clearly show the immense gulf which separated their views on life. Their principles and values; their habits of thought; their judgment of people; their sense of responsibility; their hopes and in fact the entire range of their conception of life and its demands. The one thing they had in common was ardour in living. With Mary it rested equally on spiritual and physical grounds, with stress perhaps on the former, whilst with Imlay the material and physical aspect of human existence alone made sense. How could they have hoped to undertake the long journey of marriage with success? It was amazing that they had continued so far as to bring Fanny into existence. The tragic course of Fanny's short life suggests that it would have been better if Imlay's and Mary's passion had declined earlier under the strain of a profound division in quality of being.*

Mary had refused to accept any financial help from him.

'When you only allude to pecuniary assistance . . . I want not such vulgar comfort, nor will I accept it. I never wanted but your heart. . . . Had I only poverty to fear, I should not shrink from life. Forgive me then, if I say, that I shall consider any direct or indirect attempt to supply my necessities, as an insult which I have not merited, and as rather done out of tenderness for your own reputation, than for me.' [11]

These words written in disdain were perhaps her saving, for she was obliged to disentangle herself from the devitalizing coils of self-pity and recrimination. Had she continued to nourish an ignoble dependency, of which the material side was the least pernicious, she would have been lost.

Her first attempt to obtain a temporary supply of money failed, but that seemed so much part of the general misery which had settled on her that she almost welcomed the setback. 'An accumulation of disappointments and misfortunes seems to suit the habit of

* Fanny committed suicide by taking an overdose of laudanum at Bristol, on 9th October 1816. She was then twenty-two years old. A note she left said: 'I have long determined that the best thing I could do was to put an end to the existence of a being whose birth was unfortunate and whose life has only been a series of pain to those persons who have hurt their health in endeavouring to promote her welfare. . . .'

my mind.' However, she soon recovered some of her old courage. Having taken a first step towards recovery she soon found she was able to go forward. She wrote to her old friend Johnson the publisher and learned that her book, *Letters Written during a short residence in Sweden, Norway and Denmark*, was about to be published. Not many people had at that time travelled so far afield as she had, or had her powers of description and her lively interest in the details of living. The countries she described were unknown to most readers. She was right in her anticipation that this book would rescue her and Fanny from immediate need. Also it was good to make contact with Johnson again and meet with old friends. The liberal ideas that circulated in that 'upper room', the contact with vital personalities such as Godwin, Holcroft and Horne Tooke and other personalities of the Treason Trials, of sister souls such as Mary Hays and Amelia Alderson, served to release her from her obsession with the wrongs of love.

The wide interests which affected thousands of lives; unjust laws, the self-righteousness of pillars of society, the respectable middle and upper classes with their safe investments, both in this world and the next, the stirring consciousness of a small band of rebellious women, the movement against slavery, whether of the Negro in the fields of America, the labourer in the farms and factories or the dispossessed wife of an unscrupulous husband; all such questions, with their associations, began to overshadow her miserable affair with Imlay. He was reduced, if not in her heart then in her mind, by the limits of his understanding. She knew now that they could never have been companions in spirit. Gone was her conviction that in freedom man would obtain perfection. 'The world is still the world,' she declared, 'and man the same compound of weakness and folly, who must occasionally excite love and disgust, admiration and contempt.'[12]

While writing her book of travels she had, without knowing it, been gradually loosening the links of the chains that hung on her. Once her mind began detaching itself from the personal problem, the search for happiness to which she felt she had a right, her spirit revived. Her deep appreciation of natural beauty, which for her always illustrated the possible grandeurs of the human soul, was given full range by the northern scene, with its unparalleled majesty, its austerity melting into rare beauty. Grains of hope were maturing during that fervid, lonely wandering; although they were not enough to prevent the desperate act of self-destruction, once she had made that gesture and satisfied her sense of outraged justice, her recovery was quick.

The book was more favourably received than any of her previous works. The *Analytical Review*, the *Monthly Magazine* and the *British Critic* were all in favour of it. Extracts from the work were printed in the *Universal Magazine*, the *Scots Magazine* and the *New York Magazine*. An American edition was published in Wilmington, Delaware, in the same year as its appearance in London. A Dutch translation appeared in 1799, Portuguese selections from it in 1806, and German translations of the whole work were published, one at Hamburg and one at Leipzig, in 1893. Its success was balm to the raw misery in the author's heart. Robert Southey in a letter to Joseph Cottle asked: 'Have you ever met with Mary Wollstonecraft's *Letters from Sweden and Norway*? She has made me in love with a cold climate, and frost and snow with a northern moonlight.' Later on he was to meet Mary, and write:

> 'Of all the lions or *literati* that I have seen . . . Mary Imlay's [countenance] is the best, infinitely the best . . . her eyes . . . the most meaning I ever saw.'[13] But more important for Mary's destiny was Godwin's comment: 'If ever there was a book calculated to make a man in love with its author this appears to me to be the book.'

Godwin had, of course, first met Mary in 1791 and had not been much impressed either by her or by her *Vindication of the Rights of Woman*. Now he was no longer an obscure revolutionary. Since that first meeting with Mary he had written *Political Justice* and *Caleb Williams*, had vitally helped the defence in the Treason Trials, where he had been partly responsible for the freedom of his friends, Holcroft, Tooke and the other radicals. He had become a leading figure in the progressive world, very sure of himself, and above all of his female disciples. The delightful Maria Reveley, the artist, who had studied under Angelica Kauffmann, was married, unfortunately.

He liked Elizabeth Inchbald, but she was a widow who wrote and acted with much success, and was too pleased with her liberty to be tempted to lose it. And then there was impulsive Amelia Alderson from Norwich, who had flung her arms around Horne Tooke's neck when he was acquitted at the Trials. Amelia was very pretty and a flirt. She was always praising Godwin's friend Holcroft, which was not exactly encouraging, and she was not afraid of making fun of him.

'Godwin drank tea and supped here last night,' she wrote in a letter to a friend, 'a leavetaking visit, as he goes tomorrow to spend a fortnight at Dr Parr's. It would have entertained you highly to have seen him bid me farewell. He wished to salute me, but his courage failed him. ... "Will you give me nothing to keep for your sake and console me during my absence?" murmured the philosopher, "not even your slipper? I had it in my possession once, and need not have returned it." This was true; my shoe had come off and he had put it in his pocket for some time. You have no idea how gallant he is become; but indeed he is much more amiable than ever he was.'

Mary Hays, an enthusiastic collector of literary celebrities—who had much admired Mary's *Vindication of the Rights of Woman*— now thought it an excellent idea to bring Godwin and Mrs Imlay (as she was still called) together again. The latter was much subdued by suffering and far more inclined to rouse kindly feelings than in the old days when she had been over-sure of herself and her opinions. Certainly Godwin found her more attractive now than in those early days of her emancipation. Now the traces of suffering on her face added greatly to its dignity. 'Sympathy in her anguish,' Godwin wrote at a later period, 'added in my mind to the respect I had always entertained for her talents.'

He knew of her emotional entanglement and had little sympathy with a woman who could break her heart over an empty sensualist like Imlay. None the less a subdued, heartbroken Mary had far more appeal than the triumphant author of the *Vindication*.

Peace was at last beginning to settle on Mary's spirit. On a visit to Berkshire, Mrs Cotton and some of her friends surrounded her with attention and did all they could to banish the wretched Imlay from her mind. She spent hours walking in the fields, enjoying the wild flowers in the hedgerows and borders; the snowdrops, aconites, crocuses and primroses poking their questing faces through the rough grass had a special message for her. These bright, hopeful splashes of yellow, white and purple shamed her out of the grey uniformity of futile grief. Life must go on; nature's small duties could not be extinguished whatever the blasts of wind and hail they met, whatever the indifference of the beholder. The tiny flowers triumphed and she absorbed their message of courage, welcoming the healing process whatever form it took. At the end of the month of March 1796 she thought she had triumphed over her inner enemy and that it was time to return to London and hard work. She was not, however, so much restored to health as she imagined. Miss Hays wrote in a letter to Godwin: 'Mrs Imlay is returned. . . . I am sorry to add her health appears in a still more declining state. It does not signify what is the cause, but her heart I think is broken.'

Mary Hays certainly wrote the truth about Mary. She was defeated and had abdicated from happiness. Words of philosophy so easily composed for the consolation of others were now applicable to herself. She was left with her 'naked thinking' for her best companion.

She did not return to her old lodging in Finsbury Place but to Cumming Street, Pentonville, which was not far from Somers Town, Godwin's place of residence. Here she sought work from Johnson and began to live a lonely existence. She had no wish to settle in London, associated now with too much misery, but thought longingly of Italy and Switzerland. First, however, she must earn some money, although the success of her book of Scandinavian travel spared her from immediate financial anxiety. Johnson, knowing her present predicament and all the recent shocks she had experienced, introduced her to one of his friends who was acquainted with a man who would be delighted to offer her the security of marriage. The idea was odious to her. It seemed a form of prostitution and she turned disdainfully aside. No, she was not up for sale; she would prefer to die of starvation, she and Fanny together, but it would never come to that; her pen lay near at hand.

Godwin was living alone in his house in Somers Town; lately he had come to the conclusion that marriage had advantages he had overlooked when he had written *Political Justice*: 'Marriage is law, and the worst of all laws. The abolition of marriage will be attended with no evils. We may all enjoy the conversation of an accomplished woman, and we shall all be wise enough to consider the sensual intercourse a very tiresome object.'[14]

As we have seen he had been so much attracted by Amelia Alderson that he had asked her father for her hand, but neither Dr Alderson nor his daughter was favourable. Then he had considered the chance of Elizabeth Inchbald although it was still Amelia who held him most strongly, in spite of the fact that she liked to mock him.

The glow of the Treason Trials and the decisive part he had played in them still lingered on the air and strengthened his confidence in himself. Mary Hays, enthusiastic admirer of the author of the *Vindication*, was prominent in the circle of his friends. She it was who wrote of Mary Wollstonecraft: 'This lady appears to me to possess the sort of genius that Lavater calls the one in ten million. Her conversation, like her writing, is brilliant, forceful, instructive and entertaining. She is the true disciple of her own system and commands at once fear and reverence, admiration and esteem.'

Mary Hays much respected Godwin and had a truer appreciation of his qualities than Amelia. She decided that Mary Wollstonecraft and Godwin should make closer contact for their mutual benefit, and arranged a dinner-party. In spite of the reservations made by Godwin in his reply to her invitation—'I will do myself the pleasure of waiting on you on Friday, and shall be happy to meet Mrs Wollstonecraft, of whom I know not that I ever said a word of harm and who has frequently amused herself with depreciating me'[15]—she persisted in acting the benevolent fairy. This was the beginning of Mary Wollstonecraft's friendship with Godwin, which was to become the happiest human relationship of her life. After this encounter he began to read and admire most of her works.

Godwin did not shine in general conversation. He was slow and heavy, and Mary easily outshone him. But he did not take umbrage, for in fact he was already sensitive to her great charm; moreover suffering had lowered her voice and softened the aggressiveness that was apt to detract from her powers of persuasion. He was not cold by nature and his intellect was superior to hers. There was every reason for mutual admiration, although at first sexual attraction did not play much part. Mary possessed strong personal magnetism, but she was little conscious of this asset. Godwin, however, did not escape its power. Then she further amazed him by calling at his house in Somers Town.

From the point of view of convention it was not at all the right thing to do. But when had Mary been influenced by such considerations? Had she nurtured certain designs on his freedom, which she did not, it was a good strategic move; for she singled herself out from other women and showed a just appreciation of her own worth; all of which pleased him. From that time he was firmly caught, although neither of them was aware of it. He addressed her in verse, which amused and touched her. She was certainly not in love with him, but he had established himself in her affection. 'I want to remind you, when you write to me in verse, not to choose the easiest task, my perfections, but to dwell on your own feelings—that is to say, give me a bird's-eye view of your heart. Do not make me "a desk to write upon", I humbly pray—unless you honestly acknowledge yourself to be bewitched. Of that I shall judge by the style in which the eulogiums flow, for I think I have observed that you compliment without rhyme or reason, when you are almost at a loss what to say.'

This was certainly not the language of a woman in love, and in fact at this point she was a long way from feeling for him the strong passion that she had possessed for Imlay. There was little in Godwin's outer appearance to encourage such a growth. She knew that with his big head and large nose (which Southey said he was always tempted to cut off when they met), he presented an unheroic figure, yet in his grave expression and careful speech there was promise of those qualities she had so much longed to find in Imlay, sincerity, depth of feeling and true kindliness. Perhaps it was the latter quality more than all else that held her. Her heart, less raw with grief than previously, still could not tolerate any rough shock. The fits of deep depression, which she now managed to stave off, still lay near, and she feared lest they should return. When she was tempted to compare Godwin's unattractive physical appearance with more elegant forms she remembered how little happiness had come to her from this source. Everything he offered her was moderate in expression yet promising of reserves. Moreover she found in him something which awakened her protectiveness, which both Fuseli and Imlay had failed to do. To her surprise she found that here was a man who could understand her loneliness and would not condemn her for cherishing it rather than lowering her essential needs. She demanded companionship, high intelligence, generosity and courage. They did not seem to her extravagant demands, yet it had not proved easy to satisfy them. She did not willingly avow to herself how big a part sensuality played in her nature, but it was this sort of attraction that accounted for the hold Fuseli and Imlay had had upon her. She disguised her own sensuality from herself, speaking in terms of the heart's warmth rather than a strong physical pull. Yet she was her father's daughter, although she had nothing of his brutal self-indulgence. Still the claims of the flesh could not be ignored, and she began to feel that Godwin's strange nature might offer greater emotional satisfaction than she ever could have found in the two men who had previously captured her heart.

17

Godwin: 'Friendship Melting into Love'

Mary was now seriously at work again. She had debts to pay; that done, she hoped to leave England and take herself and Fanny to Italy or Switzerland. So once more she was acting as literary assistant to Mr Johnson, reviewing new books, writing articles for the *Analytical Review* and working at a novel, *The Wrongs of Woman, or Maria*. She frequented the hospitable upper room and met again the radical circle, among them Holcroft, Blake, Tooke, and the artist John Opie. The last of these was much to her liking and they became good friends; he occasionally accompanied her to the theatre; a few months later he was to paint the portrait by which she is known to posterity. It is a charming picture, reproducing the quality of her spirit, by subtle colouring and line and a visionary look in the eyes. He must have studied her well during these months of friendship.

One day when she was out walking she saw Imlay on horseback advancing towards her. To her surprise the shock to her nerves was not overwhelming. He dismounted and they talked together for a short while. No passion touched the banal words they exchanged. She probably astonished herself as much as him. It was not only that she had lost all esteem for him and with it all desire, but her association with Godwin had affected all her values. Imlay weighed little now, either as a lover, once passionately adored, or as father of Fanny. Later Godwin managed to secure from Imlay a written settlement on the child, but neither the capital nor interest was ever paid. In fact there was little to be said for this man for whom Mary had tried to cast away her life. Here, could she but digest the bitter fruit of her experience, was food for wise reflection. Beneath her outer calm and industry she could at times still bleed from old wounds, but now the hurt was generalized. It was the state of the world, the incurable injustices and sorrows of defenceless people, that darkened her spirit. In this she was with Godwin on equal ground. With him she had come to think that personal suffering was of no importance except that it led to deepened understanding of others' sorrows. Some viewers of Opie's portrait of her remarked on the expression of compassion on her face and the lack of any asperity. This was her best triumph.

Godwin became increasingly attracted by her. As he explained in his *Memoirs*, their love 'grew with equal advances in the mind of each. It would have been impossible for the most minute observer to have said who was before, and who was after. One sex did not take the priority which long-established custom has awarded it, nor the other overstep that delicacy which is so severely imposed'.

True as this was, without overstepping the bounds of delicacy it was she who made the position clear. 'You are the man,' she frankly acknowledged in a letter. Her meeting with Godwin marked the end of the misery of deception and loneliness. This time she had made the right choice, in spite of certain physical and non-physical traits which at first she found somewhat unattractive. But he had what she most needed, an affectionate and faithful heart. He listened to her admonitions without offence; where she was concerned he had little vanity, which counted much in his favour. In truth, it was not so much Godwin who was becoming bewitched as Mary herself. Lately at Johnson's she had met Fuseli and remembered with astonishment the power he had once exercised over her. And then of course there was Imlay, but she could not yet analyse her feelings for him or even dwell upon them without hurt. Time would eventually restore her defences; but time could not banish from little Fanny's features the reminders of her mother's enslavement and her folly of self-destruction. Again and again, even when happiness was the ascendant star, Mary felt a familiar wave of black misery approach. Now, however, she could make a quick recovery.

She began to reconsider her plan to leave England for the Continent; here in London she had friends, work and social intercourse of a high order. She was accepted as an equal by men of considerable literary worth, and by outstanding women: Amelia Alderson, Mrs Sarah Siddons, the tragic muse, Mrs Reveley, Mary Hays, Mrs Barbauld, and Mrs Inchbald—the two bald women, as Lamb called them. In truth, Mary Hays and Mrs Inchbald were more Godwin's friends than hers; and she and Godwin had made a pact not to go out in society together but to keep their circles separate. They did not wish to be considered as a couple but as separate writers with their own followers and admirers. This theory did not work as well as they had hoped, and in the case of Mrs Inchbald it went badly wrong.

None the less, Mary and Godwin were drawn ever more closely together. He felt tenderly towards the fatherless Fanny, which strengthened the bonds with the child's mother. They took to writing little notes to each other every day and exchanging books. She sent him *La Nouvelle Héloïse*, informing him that she did not give him credit for as much philosophy as Rousseau. They were becoming very necessary to each other, and when in July Godwin decided to visit his mother in Norfolk he found it was a wrench to have to leave Mary behind in London. He realized how much he depended on her for a certain quality of spiritual and moral support; although, as later transpired, he was even then experimenting with the possibility of deriving something of this from the beautiful Mrs Inchbald whose successful novel, *A Simple Story*, he had lately read. Mary was aware that the man she was beginning to love and the woman who was a literary and social rival were engaged in rather stately flirting. She dubbed her rival 'Mrs Perfection' and wisely decided not to take the matter too seriously.

While Godwin was away in Norfolk Mary moved from Cummings Street to No. 16 Judd Place, W., on the outskirts of Somers Town, near to Godwin's place. She arranged her new lodgings to make a cheerful home for Fanny. The attractions of life on the Continent had faded, and she was thinking of the possibility of a permanent residence for herself and Fanny. Too long they had wandered from one dreary set of rooms to another, and little Fanny was becoming bewildered. She longed for some stability and made an intuitive childish bid for it when she christened Godwin 'Man'. 'Mamma, perhaps Man come today?' she queried to dispel her own and her mother's sad mood. From Norwich Godwin wrote in July a long letter to Mary:

'Now I take all my Gods to witness—do you know how many they are—but I obtest & obsecrate them all—that your company infinitely delights me, that I love your imagination, your delicate epicurism, the malicious leer of your eye, in short everything that constitutes the bewitching tout ensemble of the celebrated Mary. But to write! Alas, I have no talent, for I have no subject. Shall I write a love letter? May Lucifer fly away with me, if I do! No, when I make love, it shall be with the eloquent tones of my voice, with dying accents, with speaking glances (through the glass of my spectacles), with all the witching of that irresistible, universal passion. Curse on the mechanical, icy medium of pen & paper. When I make love, it shall be in a storm, as Jupiter made love to Semele, & turned her at once to a cinder. Do not these menaces terrify you? Well, then, what shall be my subject? Shall I send you an eulogium of your beauty, your talents & your virtues? Ah! that is an old subject: beside, if I were to begin, instead of a sheet of paper, I should want a ream.

'Shall I write to citizenness Wollstonecraft a congratulatory epistle upon the victories of Buonaparte? That I may rejoice the cockles of her heart, shall I cause once more to pass in review before her the Saint Jerome, the Santa Cecilia, & the other inestimable treasures, of which that ferocious freebooter has robbed the classical & delicious cities of Italy?'[1]

This letter did indeed rejoice the cockles of her heart. When Godwin called on her on his return from Norfolk he found her installed in her new lodgings, which were much more convenient for their frequent visits to each other. Mary had no false shame in inviting him:

'I suppose you mean to drink tea with me *one* of these day[s].—
How can you find in your heart to let me pass so many evenings
alone?—you may saucily ask, why I do not send for Mr Twiss—
but I shall reply with dignity—No, there will be more dignity
in silence—so mum.'[2]

When he was dining with Mrs Inchbald or Miss Alderson, as
happened quite frequently, she certainly felt the pangs of jealousy.
'I did not wish to see you this evening, because you have been
dining, I suppose, with Mrs Perfection, and comparison[s] are odious.'
Or when she knew he was about to call on Miss Alderson she warned
him: 'Miss Alderson was wondering this morning whether you *ever*
kissed a maiden fair. As you do not like to solve problems, *on paper*,
TELL her *before* you part—She will tell *me* next—year.' On the
envelope she had written, 'Not to be opened until the Philosopher
has been an hour at least in Miss Alderson's company, cheek by
jowl.'

This was putting a brave face on a situation which was giving
Mary ignoble feelings. How could she in her capacity of Female
Philosopher, one who claimed equality with detached self-sufficient
man, allow the torment of possessiveness to grip her vitals? Yet
that was exactly what was happening. She spent an evening with
Amelia Alderson and wrote to Godwin: '—you, I am told, were
ready to devour her—in your little parlour. Elle est très jolie, n'est-ce
pas?' On another occasion, when he was in the company of the
more seductive of the two 'bald ladies', Mrs Inchbald, she warned
him: 'As you are to dine with Mrs Perfection today it would be
dangerous, not to remind you of my existence—perhaps—a word
then in your ear—should you forget, for a moment, a possible
accident with the most delightful woman in the world, your fealty,
take care not to look over your left shoulder—I shall be there—'

Her attitude towards Godwin was undergoing a change. It was a
revelation to her that he was found desirable by other gifted and
beautiful women; certainly she had been taking him too much for
granted. Godwin in his *Memoirs* has described their feelings towards
each other as 'friendship melting into love'. Perhaps with Mary
the sublimating process had unexpectedly quickened, for with a

shock she became aware she had put herself in danger once more.

They became lovers a few weeks after Godwin's return from visiting his mother. According to him there was 'no period of throes and resolute explanation'. With Mary it was otherwise. That night she began to examine her own behaviour and blamed herself. 'I perceive that I shall be a child to the end of the chapter.' Then she examined his words and also found fault there.

> 'Struggling as I have been a long time to attain peace of mind (or apathy) I am afraid to trace emotions to their source which border on agony. Is it not sufficient to tell you that I am thoroughly out of humour with myself? Mortified and humbled, I scarcely know why—still, despising false delicacy I almost fear that I have lost sight of the true. . . . My imagination is for ever betraying me into fresh misery. . . . You talk of the roses which grow profusely in every path of life—I catch at them; but only encounter the thorns.
>
> 'I would not be unjust for the world—I can only say that you appear to me to have acted injudiciously; and that full of your own feelings, little as I comprehend them, you forgot mine—or do not understand my character. It is my turn to have a fever today—I am not well—I am hurt—But I mean not to hurt you. Consider what has passed as a fever of your imagination; one of the slight mortal shakes to which you are liable—and I —will become again a *Solitary Walker*. Adieu, I was going to add God bless you!'[3]

It was a painful letter for her to have to write. She was, as she said, mortified and humbled; she had fallen short of her own estimation of herself and could not resist the temptation to put much of the blame on him. But reading between the lines it is possible to detect her deepened affection and dependency on him. He replied that same night in a letter, which was unique in his writing, not only for its deep sincerity but also for the effort it made to enter into the feelings of someone who was in so many ways the antithesis of himself. The letter revealed Godwin at his best, generous and full of understanding. It was obvious he was afraid of her swaying moods, her tendency to plunge into despair, driven by a

mind that never ceased its activity, whether to probe its own weaknesses or those of others who were dear to her. He could not forget
how quickly and with what desperate logic she could drive herself
into fatal action. He exhorted her to be a philosopher because he
guessed that she could mistake a torrent of ideas rushing through
the brain for guidance from an infallible source. In truth Mary had
little of the philosopher in her; but she had the instincts of a profoundly humane being, and it was these that Godwin called upon
to save herself and succour him.

His letter, 'his talk on paper', presented him with such difficulties
that he almost renounced writing it, yet it was very necessary to
withdraw without delay the thorns that had pierced her hand when
she stretched it out to gather roses.

'How shall I answer you? . . . I had rather at this moment talk
to you on paper than in any other mode. I should feel ashamed
in seeing you. You do not know how honest I am. I swear to you
that I told you nothing but the strict & literal truth, when
I described to you the manner in which you set my imagination
on fire on Saturday. For six & thirty hours I could think of
nothing else. I longed inexpressibly to have you in my arms.
Why did not I come to you? I am a fool. I feared still that
I might be deceiving myself as to your feelings, & that I was
feeding my mind with groundless presumptions. I determined
to suffer the point to arrive at its own denouement. I was not
aware that the fervour of my imagination was exhausting itself.
Yet this I believe is no uncommon case.

'Like any other man, I can speak only of what I know. But
this I can boldly affirm, that nothing that I have seen in you
would in the slightest degree authorise the opinion that, *in
despising the false delicacy, you have lost sight of the true.* I see
nothing in you but what I respect & adore. I know the acute-
ness of your feelings, and there is perhaps nothing upon earth
that would give me so pungent a remorse, as to add to your
unhappiness. Do not hate me. Indeed I do not deserve it. Do
not cast me off. Do not become again a *solitary walker.* Be just
to me, & then, though you will discover in me much that is

foolish and censurable, yet a woman of your understanding will still regard me with some partiality. Upon consideration I find in you one fault, and but one. You have the feelings of nature, & you have the honesty to avow them. In all this you do well. I am sure you do. But do not let them tyrannise over you. Estimate every thing at its just value. It is best that we should be friends in every sense of the word; but in the mean time let us be friends.

'Suffer me to see you. Let us leave every thing else to its own course. My imagination is not dead, I suppose, though it sleeps. But, be it as it will, I will torment you no more. I will be your friend, the friend of your mind, the admirer of your excellencies. All else I commit to the disposition of futurity, glad, if completely happy; passive & silent in this respect, while I am not so.

'Be happy. Resolve to be happy. You deserve to be so. Every thing that interferes with it is weakness & wandering; & a woman, like you, can, must, shall, shake it off. . . . Call up, with firmness, the energies which I am sure you so eminently possess. Send me word that I may call on you in a day or two. Do you not see, while I exhort you to be a philosopher, how painfully acute are my own feelings? I need some soothing, though I cannot ask it from you.'[3]

Mary replied in a fable about a sycamore tree that had put out its buds too soon and they had been nipped by the frost. This brought forth a surprising protest:

'Your fable of today puts an end to all my hopes. I needed soothing, & you threaten me. . . . For every pain I have undesignedly given you, I am most sincerely grieved; for the good qualities I discern in you, you shall live for ever embalmed in my memory.'[4]

As a consequence of his pleading she fell into a mood of self-abasement.

'I am sometimes painfully humble—Write me, but a line, just to assure me, that you have been thinking of me with affection, now and then—Since we parted—'

This roused him to violent protest.

'Humble—for heaven's sake be proud, be arrogant! You are—but I cannot tell what you are. I cannot yet find the circumstance about you that allies you to the frailty of our nature. I will hunt it out.'[5]

All this time Mary had been continuing her work on her novel *The Wrongs of Woman, or Maria,* and now she was anxious to have Godwin's opinion of it. Godwin was also at work, on a dramatization of his novel *Caleb Williams,* called *The Iron Chest.* They met in the evenings to compare the fruits of their labours. Godwin was aware of his superiority over her in mastery of words and in the unravelling of a plot. His works would sell more easily, and he tried to make this clear to her without hurt to her pride as an author, and as a woman dependent on no one for her maintenance. He knew she was in debt, in fact that this was quite a usual condition with her, and he thought it would help her towards solvency if she could improve the quality of her output. He tried his best to be tactful but apparently was not very successful. To the end of her days, Mary found criticism hard to accept.

'I do not intend to let you extend your skepticism to me,' she wrote, 'or you will fright away a poor weary bird who, taking refuge in your bosom, hoped to nestle there to the end of the chapter. The day is dreary. The Iron Chest must wait—Will you read your piece at your fire side or mine? And I will tell you in what aspect I think you a *little* unjust.'[6]

There followed a cool interlude between them, broken by Mary a few days later when she felt the full force of some of his criticism.

'Labouring all the morning, in vain, to overcome an oppression of spirits, which some things you uttered yesterday produced; I will try if I can shake it off by describing to you the nature of the feelings you excited. I allude to what you remarked, relative to my manner of writing—that there was a radical defect in it—a worm in the bud. ... What is to be done, I must either disregard your opinion, think it unjust, or throw down my pen in despair; and that would be tantamount to resigning existence; for at fifteen I resolved never to marry for interested motives, or to endure a life of dependence. You know not how painfully my sensibility, call it false if you will, has been wounded by some of the steps I have been obliged to take for others. I have even now plans at heart, which depend on my exertions; and my entire confidence in Mr Imlay plunged me into some difficulties, since we parted, that I could scarcely away with. I know that many of my cares have been the natural consequence of what, nine out of ten would [have] termed folly—yet I cannot coincide in the opinion, without feeling a contempt for mankind. In short, I must reckon on doing some good, and getting the money I want, by my writings, or go to sleep for ever. I shall not be content merely to keep body and soul together. . . . I am compelled to think that there is some thing in my writings, more valuable than in the productions of some people on whom you bestow warm eulogiums—I mean more mind—denominate it as you will—more of the observation of my own senses, more of the combining of my own imagination— the effusions of my own feelings and passions than the cold workings of the brain on the materials procured by the senses and imagination of other writers.'⁷

The rift was healed, and a walk taken in company with Godwin and Mrs Inchbald seemed to put the stamp on Mary's good resolutions. 'If I do not admire her more I love her better—She is a charming woman,'⁸ she wrote to Godwin. None the less, Mrs Perfection still gave Mary some anxiety. Now that she and Godwin were united it was not easy to have this beautiful and talented woman, who did not know the true position, frequently in their company. This was something Mary had to teach herself to endure and keep her temper sweet. At times she was oppressed by the effort she was obliged to make over her own natural reactions. 'I do not like to see you when I am not half alive,' she wrote. 'I want to see you— and *soon*. Pray come to your

Mary.'⁹

Fanny, now three years old, was playing her part in this rebuilding of her mother's happiness. Godwin was much attached to the little girl, who had never known the affection of a father, and Fanny was quick to track down this source of love which her discerning little soul had detected. 'Go this way, Mama,' she would plead when they were out walking together, 'me wants to see Man.' There could be no stronger advocate in Godwin's favour with Mary than this spontaneous cry of her child. She softened towards him and re-proached herself for 'idle complaints'.

> 'I wanted to tell you,' she wrote, 'that I felt as if I had not done justice to your essay, for it interested me extremely—and has been running in my head while other recollections were all alive in my heart—You are a tender considerate creature; but, entre nous, do not make too many philosophical experi-ments, for when a philosopher is put on his metal, to use your own phrase, there is no knowing where he will stop—and I have not reckoned on having a wild-goose chase after a wise man.'[10]

Mary wrote more frequently than Godwin, because it was less easy for her to get out and visit friends, and her pen was always ready on her desk. Still, the autumn was particularly lovely that year: suggesting a day in the country she wrote, 'The return of the fine weather has led me to form a vague wish that we might *vagabondize* one day in the country—before the summer is clear gone. I love the country and like to leave certain associations in my memory, which seem, as it were, the landmarks of affection.'[11] She sent him a message almost daily, or at least Fanny to wish good-morning. Without one or the other, he 'augured nothing good', and she wrote reassuringly: '. . . you are not only in my heart, but my veins, this morning. I turn from you half abashed —yet you haunt me, and some look, word or touch thrills through my whole frame—yes, at the very moment when I am labouring to think of something, if not somebody, else. Get ye gone Intruder! though I am forced to add dear—which is a call back. When the heart and reason accord there is no flying from voluptuous sensa-tions, I find, do what a woman can—Can a philosopher do more?'[12]

Godwin took seriously Mary's outrages on syntax and grammar and offered to give her lessons, which she now accepted in good part.

'I shall not be very angry if you sweeten grammatical disquisitions after the Miltonic mode—Fancy, at this moment, has turned a conjunction into a kiss; and the sensation steals o'er my senses. . . . You have led me to discover that I write worse than I thought I did, there is no stopping short—I must improve, or be dissatisfied with myself.'[13]

In the meanwhile 'poor Fannikin' caught chickenpox and was 'tearing herself to pieces', and Mary's nights were bereft of sleep, which made her querulous. 'Say only that we are friends,' she scribbled on a piece of paper, and sent it to him. 'Friends, why not?' he answered, 'if I thought otherwise, I should be miserable.'

At times, to vary the correspondence, they broke into French, which had an undeniable British flavour.

'I shall be with you at five, to receive what you promised to give me, *en passant—Mais, à notre retour, rien que philosophie. Mon cher ami. Êtes-vous bien fâché, Mon Bien-aimé—Moi aussi, cependant la semaine approchant*—do you understand me— . . .' and he: '*Admirable maîtresse, J'espère que vous êtes plus gai ce matin. Prenez garde à vous.*'[14]

Although they were living so near to each other they found it necessary to write almost every day.

'What say you'—asked Mary in one of her notes—'may I come to your house about eight—to philosophize? You once talked of giving me one of your keys, I then could admit myself without tying you down to an hour. . . .

'You do not know how much I admired your self-government, last night, when your voice betrayed the struggle it cost you— I am glad that you force me to love you more and more, in spite of my fear of being pierced to the heart by every one on whom I rest my mighty stock of affection. Your tenderness was considerate, as well as kind. Miss Hays entering in the midst of the last sentence, I hastily laid my letter aside without finishing, and have lost the remain—Is it sunk in the quicksand of Love?'[15]

It was Mary herself who was in danger of getting sunk in this quicksand, as had already happened twice in her life. This time both protagonists were in like danger, although Godwin expressed less anguish and had greater control over himself. It was Mary's changeability of mood that tormented him and herself, although it was superficial in character; beneath it the growth of a deep relationship continued. '—you know not how much tenderness for you may escape in a voluptuous sigh . . .' she wrote. 'Voluptuous is often expressive of a meaning I do not now intend to give. I would describe one of those moments, when the senses are exactly tuned by the rising tenderness of the heart, and according reason entices you to live in the present moment, regardless of the past or the future.'[16]

Godwin at times felt the strain of matching her in attacks of gaiety and of sadness, in quick rising and fall of the spirit. 'I believe this boy-pupil,' he wrote of himself, 'turns mole-hills into mountains.'

'Can you solve this problem?' she asked. 'I was endeavouring to discover last night, in bed, what it is in me, of which you are afraid. I was hurt at perceiving that you were—but no more of this—mine is a sick heart; and in a life, like this, the fortitude of patience is the most difficult to acquire.'[17]

Godwin feared the harm she might do herself rather than him when she sank into despondency. There was, however, an infallible way to mend any hurt he might have inflicted on her, and that was to read one of her works which hitherto he did not know.

'I think as an *amende honorable*,' she told him, 'you ought to read my answer to Mr Burke [*A Vindication of the Rights of Men*]. Fanny writes to ask Man's pardon—she won't cry any more.[18] Like Fanny, her mother could not be happy unless "Man" was well disposed towards her.'

'Till we meet joy be with thee,'[19] she wrote in a moment of gratitude for all the good he had brought into her life; the sense of belonging, of purpose, of consolation for the mistakes she had made, since all ended in his appreciative love. She could not have nurtured so deep an affection for him had she not suffered horribly from misplaced trust. She knew the value of the treasure she had discovered. It would put her varied experience into proper perspective; take away some of the reproach that she had blundered repeatedly into the same errors. He, and he alone, understood the motives behind her acts, which appeared like senseless gestures. He knew better. At times her heart overflowed in gratitude.

> 'There is such a magic in affection that I have been more gratified by your clasping your hands round my arm, in company, than I could have been by all the admiration of the world, tho' I am a woman—and to mount a step higher in the scale of vanity, an author.' [20]

In this way she sums up the position of a woman who has won esteem in literary circles and who is yet so fixed in her feminine nature that no degree of such success can still her heart. She was cast in an unbreakable mould. All the traditional services of a woman for the man she loves came naturally to her; she would care for his clothes, mend his household linen and be concerned for his health. It was borne in on her that she was acting a role for which she had professed no admiration. 'I am not sure that I did not feel a sensation of pleasure at thus acting the part of a wife, though you have so little respect for the character.' The idea of marriage had now taken root in her mind, and to a lesser degree in his. Hitherto he had been outspoken in his condemnation of it. 'It is,' he had written, 'a question of property, the worst of all ... the most odious of all monopolies.' [21] Yet here he was in a position to perpetuate this folly, 'to engross one woman to myself and to prohibit my neighbour from proving his superior deserts and reaping the fruits of it.'

For a moment they both put the question out of their minds, and they fell into disagreement on a subject of lesser import. He was failing her, she said, in little marks of affection. He did not observe what she was wearing, he took her too seriously when she was testing his sense of humour; he was too much the 'profound grammarian'. He met her complaints by a little note: 'Yes, I am alive. Perhaps I am better. I am glad to hear how enchanting & divine you will appear this evening,—you spoil little attentions by anticipating them.'

It was very necessary, she told herself, to guard against falsely interpreting his words, for he seemed unable to distinguish between jest and what was earnest. His literal-mindedness was creating a prison: she must always be explaining herself.

'Allow me a little more tether than is necessary for the purpose of feeding, to keep soul and body together,' she wrote. 'Let me, I pray thee! have a sort of *comparative* freedom, as you are a profound Grammarian, to run round as good, better, best; cheerful, gay, playful; any even frolicksome, once a year— or so, when the whim seizes me of skipping out of bounds. Send me a *bill of rights*—to this purport under your hand and seal, with a *Bulletin* of health.'

He replied with waning patience:

'I can send you a bill of rights & a bill of health; the former *carte blanche*, the latter Much better. . . . But to fulfil the terms of your note, you must send me a bill of understanding. How can I always distinguish between your jest & earnest, & know when your satire means too much & when it means nothing? But I will try.'[22]

Mary's health began to deteriorate. She caught a cold that persisted; her head ached and she became fretful, not sure whether she did or did not long for his company. One day she was writing 'our *sober* evening was very delicious—I do believe you love me better than you imagined you should'; and on another,

'I am sorry I kept you with me last night—and insist on your going without me this evening. . . . I was a little displeased with you for mentioning, when I was seriously indisposed, your inclination to go—and was angry with myself for not permitting you to follow your inclination.'

A week later she felt better but was still inclined to complain: 'You tell me that "I spoil little attentions by anticipation". Yet to have attention, I find, that it is necessary to demand it. My faults are very inveterate—for I *did* expect you last night. . . .'[23] She got better, felt she needed to relax and hoped Godwin would understand this and offer to accompany her to the theatre, but he could not because he had already arranged to take Mrs Inchbald; however, he supplied two tickets for her to go with a friend. She found it humiliating to have to seek a companion, but this she did. Alas, the seats were not good.

'I want to scold you for not having secured me a better place. We were thrust into a corner, in the third row, quite as bad as the Gallery. . . . I am determined to return to my former habits and go by [my]self and shift for myself. . . . You and Mrs I[nchbald] were at your ease enjoying yourselves—while, poor I! I was a fool not to ask Opie to go with me. . . .'[24]

Her spirits sank again: something was wrong, but she was not sure what.

'I thought, after you left me, last night, that it was a *pity* we were obliged to part—just then. . . . There is a manner of leaving a person free to follow their own will that looks so like indifference, I do not like it. Your *tone* would have decided me —But to tell you the truth I thought by your voice and manner that you wished to remain in society. . . . I mean to be with you, as soon as I can, this evening. . . . But do not stay at home on that account, unless you intend it, though I do not intend to *peck* you.'[25]

In fact she had been 'pecking' altogether too much and Godwin was becoming irritated by the discomfort, and decided to peck back a little.

'I like the note before me better than six preceding ones,' he wrote. 'I own I had the premeditated malice of making you part with me last night unwillingly. I feared Cupid had taken his final farewell.'[26]

This sounded an alarming note, the more so for his not calling with the same regularity. 'Perhaps Man come today?' Fanny comforted her mother. In truth, he did call, and Mary told him her suspicions of the reason why lately she had become so difficult to please. She feared she was pregnant. He did not disappoint her by the way he received the news.

'Was not yesterday a very pleasant evening?' she asked. 'There was a tenderness in your manner, as you seemed to be opening your heart, to a new-born affection, that rendered you very dear to me. There are other pleasures in the world, you perceive, beside those know[n] to your philosophy.'[27]

Unfortunately the clearing of the clouds did not hold. 'I am not well today,' she complained. 'A lowness of spirits, which I cannot conquer, leaves me at the mercy of my imagination, and only painful recollections and expectations assail me. . . . I dare say you are out of patience with me.'[28]

The painful recollections probably arose from her memory of what she had experienced the first time that maternity was a near prospect. Was she again to bring into the world a child who could acknowledge no father? She knew, although probably Godwin did not, that Fanny was conscious of a lack in her family background. 'Man' was not permanently at her mother's side, and what was worse, he was always vanishing, then reappearing. Other fathers did not act like this. And why was her mother so anxious, so quickly gay and then so quickly sad again? It was all very confusing, and 'Mamma' did not explain things satisfactorily.

Mary tried to detach her thoughts by reading some of Godwin's essays and criticizing them anew, for she was already familiar with most of his work. 'The one I most earnestly wished you to alter, from the most perfect conviction, was that on public and private education. I wanted you to recommend *Day* Schools, it would obviate the evil, of being left with servants, and enable children to converse with children without clashing with the exercise of domestic affections, the foundation of virtue.'[29]

Mary's 'most perfect conviction' on public affairs was apt to blind her to private matters, such as her attitude towards the man she loved, who was intellectually her superior. It was not only her grammar that at times hampered the expression of her thought. She could not rival him in clear-mindedness, in the mastery of subject-matter. Her ideas were apt to become clouded by waves of strong feeling which befogged the issue. In her private life the same sort of waves risked destroying her love for Godwin. 'You treated me last night with extreme unkindness: the more so, because it was calm, melancholy, equable unkindness,' he wrote. 'You wished we had never met; you wished you could cancel all that had passed between us. Is this,—ask your own heart,—Is this compatible with the passion of love? Or, is it not the language of frigid, unalterable indifference? You wished all the kind things you had ever written me destroyed.' [30]

These reproaches were too much for her to take. They were written on the last day of the year 1796 and were the worse for seeming to sum up a period barren of profit. Was this to be the final outcome? If so, how far had she contributed to her own undoing? At first she thought very little. 'This does not appear to me just the moment to have written me such a note as I have been perusing. I am, however, prepared for any thing. I can abide by the consequences of my own conduct, and do not wish to involve any one in my difficulties.' [31]

One of the causes of the strained relations between Mary and her lover was the financial situation. She was careless about money and he feared that in the end he would be made responsible for her insolvency, at this time when she could not herself redeem her debts. He thought of applying to his friend Wedgwood for a loan of fifty pounds, but hated the idea as much as Mary did.

'I cannot bear that you should do violence to your feelings by writing to Mr Wedgewood. No, you shall not write—I will think of some way of extricating myself. You must have patience with me, for I am sick at heart. Dissatisfied with every body and every thing.' [32]

A few days later the breach had been healed and Mary wrote that she was better and would expect to see Godwin that day.

18

Marriage with Godwin

Mary's views on marriage were bound up with those she held on the whole position of women in society. Her plea for equality in civil, economic and political rights was not so much aimed at society's assumptions of what constituted a woman's duty to her husband, but in support of women's participation in the natural rights of mankind. In the *Vindication* she had complained that except in criminal cases women had no civil existence. Since they were deprived of all political privileges, it was not surprising they took little interest in the community as a whole. 'Speaking of women at large,' she wrote, 'their first duty is to themselves as rational creatures, and the next, in point of importance, as citizens, is that of a mother.'

She emphasized the vital connection of women's economic position with her claims upon man's respect. Here was the crux of the question. In her last book, *The Wrongs of Woman*, based on her sister Eliza's unhappy experiences of matrimony, she recalled Eliza's despair when she left her husband with an empty purse and an empty heart. 'Yet women as well as men ought to have the common appetites and passions of their nature.' Eliza's deprivations had driven home a wife's extreme vulnerability. Marriage was held to be a protection for women, yet it could prove a prison and make women worse off than bond servants. As the heroine of her last book exclaimed:

'Marriage had bestilled me for life. I discovered in myself a capacity for the enjoyment of the various pleasures existence affords; yet fettered by the partial laws of society, this globe was to me a universal blank.'

At this point in her life Mary undoubtedly desired the status of a married woman. She had not relished her previous position of an unmarried mother, although it was fully consistent with her published ideas. She knew her child was growing increasingly aware of an irregularity in her background. She had called herself Mrs Imlay and her friends had refrained from examining her claims to the title. Hitherto the pretence had served its purpose, but now that she was expecting a child and Imlay and she had long been separated, there must be an admission of the truth.

Godwin's views on marriage were not, like Mary's, based on first-hand witness of its working. His approach was intellectual, without the support of flesh and blood experience. It concerned man's liberty of action, his freedom of heart, his progress in society, his ability to act as an individual, all of which depended upon his being free from interference by State or Church. But the idea of promiscuity was repellent to him, however much he rejected the institution of marriage. He foresaw no difficulties arising out of the abolition of that institution. Man's vices were, in his opinion, wholly due to the restraining influences of the law. Relieve man of this heavy hand upon him and natural goodness would triumph. But man's actions should not be wholly egotistical. No individual should push his own ends to the detriment of the greatest happiness of the greatest number. Altruistic benevolence based on truth must underlie social reform.

From these very different approaches the two authors and lovers contemplated the legal solution of their problem. Both continued to hold the views outlined in their respective books, but Mary was counting upon Godwin's 'good humour, kindness and benevolence'. How could she do otherwise? Her debts, her child, her unfinished book, her fear of repetition of previous history, all pressed her to make a decision which she knew would expose her, and also Godwin, to much malicious comment. Yet they must accept that.

On 29th March 1797 they were married at Old St Pancras Church, an event recorded in Godwin's diary under that date: 'Panc. Leroux called. Call on Northcote.' That one abbreviation, 'Panc.', stood for a decision he had arrived at painfully. It was the avowal of a defeat, an invitation to the mockery of his friends and the abuse of his enemies. Yet he also had reason to congratulate himself, for he had gained a wife of high quality, Southey, writing to his brother, said: 'She is a first-rate woman, sensible of her own worth but without arrogance or affectation.' And, as the portrait Opie was making of her would reveal, a woman of much attraction, with her rich auburn hair, expressive eyes and feminine appeal of soft flesh. She was not a beauty like Mrs Inchbald, but she had acquired much wisdom by bitter experience; also her ability in the field of social philosophy was unrivalled by any other woman in England. For achievement of this order she had arrived at the top, entirely by her own efforts.

However, Godwin was embarrassed by his capitulation and felt it necessary to explain, when he wrote to his friend Wedgwood, from whom he had recently borrowed fifty pounds.*

'Some persons have found an inconsistency between my practice in this instance and my doctrine. But I cannot see it. The doctrine of my *Political Justice* is that an attachment in some degree permanent between two persons of opposite sexes is right, but that marriage as practised in European countries is wrong. I still adhere to that opinion. Nothing but a regard for the happiness of the individual, which I have no right to injure, could have induced me to submit to an institution which I wish to see abolished, and which I recommend to my fellow-men never to practise, but with the greatest caution.'

He also wrote to two women with whom he had been on warm, friendly terms. The first, Mary Hays, presented no embarrassment, for she was entirely devoted to the other Mary.

'My fair neighbour,' he wrote her, 'desires me to announce to you a piece of news, which it is consonant to the regard that she

* See p. 221 above.

and I entertain for you, you should rather learn from us than from any other quarter. She bids me remind you of the earnest way in which you pressed me to prevail upon her to change her name, and she directs me to add that it has happened to me, like many other disputants, to be entrapped in my own toils; in short, that we found there was no way so obvious for her to drop the name of Imlay, as to assume the name of Godwin. Mrs Godwin—who the devil is that?—will be glad to see you at No. 29, Polygon, Somers Town, whenever you are inclined to favour her with a call.'[1]

But his task in informing the beautiful and haughty Mrs Inchbald, in whose company he had passed many an enjoyable evening, was more exacting. He had not been quite open with her about his relationship with Mary; it was a shock to all his women friends who had been accustomed to call upon him to be their squire. Most of them took the news in good part, but Mrs Inchbald sent a sub-acid note which wounded his feelings and was an indirect slur on Mary.

'I most sincerely wish you and Mrs Godwin joy. But, assured that your joyfulness would obliterate from your memory every trifling engagement, I have entreated another person to supply your place, and perform your office, in securing a box on Reynold's night. If I have done wrong, when you next marry, I will act differently.'

One who shared her mocking tone was Fuseli, whom Mary still saw occasionally. Recently she had demanded the return of her letters but so far he had not complied. He now professed himself much amused by the recent events; it gave him the opportunity to turn a witty phrase for which he was grateful. 'Have you heard,' he wrote, 'that the assertrix of female rights has given her hand to the *balancier* of political justice?'[2] Another comment of similar order came from Joseph Ritson, a friend only in name.

'You have heard by the way that Godwin is lately married to Mary (alias Mistress Wollstonecraft) according to the rites and ceremonies of the Church of England, which he was supposed to hold in the utmost contempt and detestation. His *cara sposa*

225

it seems had been deceived by trusting in the honour of philosophy of one hackney author already.'

Mrs Inchbald, who had taken the author of *Political Justice au
pied de la lettre*, now expressed the shock to her sensibilities on dis-
covering that Mary, known as Mrs Imlay, had no claim to be so
called. Obviously there was nothing to be done now but break off
the friendship. Mrs Siddons took a similar decision. She had been
deceived and resented it. Since becoming a respectable married
woman Mary was no longer acceptable in good society, because her
present respectability revealed past dishonour, all the worse for
having been concealed. Such was the moral code of the times. Mrs
Barbauld, sweeter in spirit than her 'bald' sister, observed in a
letter to Mrs Beecroft:

> 'I suppose you have seen it in the papers the marriage of Mr
> Godwin and Mrs Imlay, alias Miss Wollstonecraft. A very suit-
> able match, but numberless are the squibs that are thrown out at
> Mr Godwin on this occasion.' [3]

Wise Amelia Alderson showed herself worthy of a philosopher's
esteem:

> 'Heigho,' she wrote, 'what charming things would sublime
> theories be, if one could make one's practice keep up with them;
> but I am convinced it is impossible and am resolved to make
> the best of everyday nature.'

She was to marry the artist Opie, who when asked by a man
whose portrait he was painting with what he mixed his paint, replied
'with brains'. Amelia's friendship with Mary survived thanks to the
same recipe.

But there was one person who wrote the sort of congratulation
they had hoped to receive in greater numbers. Thomas Holcroft,
Godwin's dearest friend, appealed strongly to Mary and she was in
danger of breaking the pact between herself and Godwin to keep
their friends each for themselves. His letter compensated for what
was lacking in others.

> 'From my very heart and soul I give you joy,' he wrote. 'I

think you the most extraordinary married pair in existence. May your happiness be as pure as I firmly persuade myself it must be.'[4]

A letter from Godwin's mother must have brought a wry smile to his lips, so precisely did it express her forthright personality.

'Your broken resolution in regard to matrimony encourages me to hope that you will ere long embrace the Gospel, that sure word of promise to all believers, and not only you, but your other half, whose souls should be both one. . . . You might have been so good as told me a few more particulars about your conjugal state, as when you were married. . . you are certainly transformed in a moral sense, why is it impossible in a spiritual sense, which last will make you shine with the radiance of the sun for ever.'[5]

Morally he and Mary were influencing each other for good; both were deeper in understanding for having met each other. In this sense they certainly had made progress. He had only to look back upon himself and her as they were less than a year earlier to appreciate as much. But spiritually speaking they did not shine with the brilliance of the sun. It is true Mary was no atheist; she had settled for a kind of pantheistic Deism. 'Nature itself,' she wrote, 'would be no better than a vast blank if the mind of the observer did not supply it with an animating soul.' When she walked in the country-side, enjoying its beauty, she felt she was in converse with God. But Godwin did not share her mystical gift: too much philosophy and too many material cares came between him and such intimations of the eternal. But he did nothing to deprive Mary of this source of comfort and strength. He had become an admirable partner. As Coleridge later observed to Southey, 'Godwin is no great thing in intellect, but in heart and manner all the better for having been the husband of Mary Wollstonecraft.'

They decided to share a house, and No. 29 the Polygon became their joint home, but Godwin rented rooms for himself about twenty paces away. Usually he worked here until dinner time, when he joined Mary for the rest of the day. Much the same sort of company as had gathered in Johnson's home (with the exception of Blake, who did not care for Godwin) now met in a room in the Polygon, where Opie's portrait of Mary dominated the scene. It seemed to inspire the talk as much as the original of the portrait, who was always present, seeing to the comfort of her guests. They gave a dinner-party, at which Fuseli, Horne Tooke and Opie were present. Fuseli considered himself the lion on this occasion, but was not sufficiently supported in his belief and left in a huff. Mary was not upset. It seemed hardly possible to her now that at one time the opinion of this vain, talented man could make heaven or hell for her. She was beginning to feel for the first time in her life the inner peace of security, and became indifferent to human malice as her confidence in the future grew. One or two of her women friends might still make spiteful comments, but sister souls such as Mary Hays and Mary Robinson, one-time mistress of the Prince of Wales, now a novelist and playwright, and Maria Reveley, wife of the architect who had drawn the plans of an ideal prison and who was a disciple of Godwin, and Eliza Fenwick, another novelist, could be counted on as people who cared nothing about a mere change of name. They all met at each other's houses, and their children played together in the hayfields about Somers Town.

Mary, it seemed, was fitting all too well into the role of a good middle-class housewife. But it was not advisable to take the part so wholeheartedly, for Godwin was to write in his novel *St Leon*:

'Few women of regular and reputable lives have that ease of manners, that flow of fancy and that graceful intrepidity of thinking and expressing themselves that is sometimes to be found among those who have discharged themselves from the tyranny of custom. . . . A judicious and limited voluptuousness is necessary to the education of the mind, to the polishing of the understanding.'

Mary still belonged to the intellectual left. She had not forgotten she had been a friend of Madame Roland and of Brissot and Tom Paine. She had no need of 'a limited voluptuousness' to educate her mind, which had been formed by more stern, varied and dangerous experience. But to ensure the inner peace which at that moment was necessary to her she became a trusted companion to liberal-minded women who perhaps would never have risked their respectability as Mary had.

Scarcity of ready money was one of their constant trials. As Mary explained to Godwin,

> 'Mr Johnson, or somebody, has always taken the disagreeable business of settling with tradespeople off my hands. I am perhaps as unfit as yourself to do it—and my time appears to me as valuable as that of other persons accustomed to employ themselves. Things of this kind are easily settled with money, I know; but I am tormented by the want of money—and feel, to say the truth, as if I was not treated with respect, owing to your desire not to be disturbed.' 6

A short while before their marriage Mary and Godwin had received a visit from Everina, who had given up her position as a governess in Ireland and was on her way to take up a situation with the Josiah Wedgwoods at Etruria. Her arrival had interfered with the pleasant daily coming and going between her sister and future brother-in-law.

> 'You must excuse this seeming neglect,' Mary wrote to Godwin. ... 'I would call on you this morning but I cannot say when. ... The evenings with her silent I find very wearisome and embarrassing. ... I am going out with Montagu to-day, and shall be glad by a new train of thoughts to drive my present out of my head.'

When Everina was on the point of departure she caught cold and, to Mary's distress, postponed leaving. She was very tired of her sister yet insisted upon Godwin paying her due respect. 'I suppose you will call this morning to say adieu! to Everina. Do not knock loud, for a child is born.' At last Everina left and the pleasant social life she had interrupted was resumed.

> 'You are to dine with me on Monday—remember the salt-beef awaits your pleasure,' Mary wrote. 'I must dine with Mrs Christie. ... Do not give Fanny a cake today. I am afraid she

staid too long with you yesterday.' 'And so, you goose, you lost your supper—and deserved to lose it, for not desiring Mary to give you some beef. . . . There is a good boy, write me a review of *Vaurien*. I remember there is an absurd attack on a methodist Preacher, because he denied the Eternity of future punishments.'

The problem of ready money continued to disturb their peace and quiet, and now even more mundane worries arose, for the sink had gone wrong and the landlord must be approached. But Godwin did not relish such tasks; neither did Mary, and her spirit became harassed.

'Do you know you plague me a little by not speaking more determinedly to the landlord of whom I have a mean opinion. He tires me by the pitiful way of doing things.'

These trifles were mounting up and an explosion was imminent.

'I am pained,' Godwin wrote, 'by the recollection of our conversation last night. The sole principle of conduct of which I am conscious in my behaviour to you, has been in everything to study your happiness. I found a wounded heart, &, as that heart cast itself upon me, it was my ambition to heal it. Do not let me be wholly disappointed. Let me have the relief of seeing you this morning. If I do not call before you go out, call on me.'[7]

The dissension was intensified by the fact that Mrs Inchbald had accompanied Godwin and Mary to the theatre recently and the event had not been a success. It was the first time she had met them since their marriage and she relieved her feelings in words that were 'base, cruel and insulting'. Doubtless Mary had become doubly touchy owing to her pregnancy.

'I am sorry,' she wrote to Godwin, 'we entered on an altercation this morning, which probably has led us both to justify ourselves at the expence of the other. Perfect confidence, and sincerity of action is, I am persuaded, incompatible with the present state of reason. I am sorry for the bitterness of your expressions when you denominated, what I think a just contempt of a false principle of action, *savage resentment, and the worst of vices,* not because I winced under the lash, but as it led me to infer that the coquetish [*sic*] candour of vanity was a much less generous motive. . . . The cruelest [*sic*] experience will not eradicate the foolish tendency I have to cherish, and expect to meet with, romantic tenderness. . . . Montagu called me this morning, that is, breakfasted with me, and invited me to go with him and the Wedgwoods into the country tomorrow, and return next day. As I love the country and think with a poor mad woman I knew, that there is a God, or something very consolatory in the air, I should, without hesitation, have accepted of the invitation; but for my engagement with your sister.'[8]

Mary had indeed winced under the lash, but the hurt did not last long because she felt that Godwin was the best of men as far as she was concerned and that her craving for 'romantic tenderness' was a weakness she should have corrected long since. Far more important than Godwin's difficulties in expressing such sentiments was his kindness towards her little Fanny, his truly parental feelings, which were much to his honour and revealed his fundamental decency. Mary's quality as a conscientious mother promised well for Godwin's first child, his son, as he hoped. He would be a second William, who would accomplish that for which Godwin had drawn only the blue-print. The second William was constantly in their thoughts. The future might prove difficult, since both parents were putting in a proprietary claim to the child's mind. 'I still mean to be independent,' Mary confided to Amelia Alderson, 'even to the cultivating sentiments and principles in my children's minds, (should I have more,) which he disavows.'[9] This was an unwise admission, surprising in one who should by now have outgrown sublime theories, but she was an incurable romantic by nature. Education was important, good laws were important, ideas were important, understanding was important, but above all these was liberty to express the feelings of the heart which could not be falsified. In *The Wrongs of Woman* she tried to express her deep conviction on matters of relationship, but she found the writing of this novel more difficult than her masterpiece the *Vindication*. Certain passages she wrote and rewrote, and still she could not quite express in words the sentiments and principles which did not owe their power to reason. Reason was great, but greater still was sensibility; there were feelings for which it is 'not necessary coldly to ransack the understanding or memory, till the laborious efforts of judgment exclude present sensation and damp the fire of enthusiasm'.

Godwin fortunately knew nothing of Mary's desires for the child's future development in a romantic rather than a rational vein, and if he had he would not in all probability have opposed her, for her judgment had even greater driving power than his own. It is true that under her influence he was changing inwardly and losing some of his clockwork precision. She had an invincible sense of what was right and what was wrong. 'For soundness of understanding and sensibility of heart she was perhaps never equalled,' he wrote of her. And it was this sort of strength which conquered him. In the meanwhile both indulged their hopes about little 'William', who became the symbol of their private aspirations.

All was well. Mary had entered on a period of happiness unrivalled in her experience. Godwin, whatever his faults, was intrinsically good, not only in his private life but also in his genuine concern for the future happiness of man.

> 'I love to contemplate the yet unexpanded powers and capabilities of our nature, and to believe that they will one day be unfolded to the infinite advantage of the happiness of the inhabitants of the globe,' he wrote.

There was some naïveté in his outlook. As his daughter was to remark,

> 'It may seem strange that anyone should in the sincerity of his heart believe that no vice could exist with perfect freedom, but my father did. It was the very basis of his system, the keystone of the arch of justice.'

This single-mindedness shining through all his theories had bound Mary to him. In a note she sent asking him to call on Johnson, she added:

'But when I press anything it is always with a true *wifish* submission to your judgment and inclination.'

It is difficult to pronounce who exercised the stronger influence, Mary over Godwin, or Godwin over Mary. 'All in all we were as happy as is permitted to human beings,' said Godwin retrospectively of this time.

In the first week of June, Godwin, accompanied by his friend Basil Montagu, illegitimate son of the Earl of Sandwich, a widower seeking a new wife and desirous of making contact with one of the Miss Wedgwoods, set out in a single-horse chaise to visit Etruria, the name Josiah Wedgwood had given to the pottery works at Hanley, Staffordshire. The two friends intended making a tour of places of interest in these parts, and 'William's' first letter to his wife during the tour was sent from Hampton Lucy.

> 'I write at this moment . . . in sight of the house and park of Sir Thomas Lucy, the great benefactor of mankind, who prosecuted William Shakespeare for deer-stealing and obliged him to take refuge in the metropolis.' [10]

They were gay as larks, and nearly got themselves drowned in a brook swollen with rains. They used to rise extremely early, at four or five in the morning, and make good headway, sometimes twenty miles.

'And now, my dear love,' Godwin wrote, 'what do you think of me? Do not you find solitude infinitely superior to the company of a husband? Will you give me leave to return to you again, when I have finished my pilgrimage, & discharged the penance of absence? Take care of yourself, my love, & take care of William. Do not you be drowned, whatever I am. I remember at every moment all the accidents to which your condition subjects you, & I wish I knew of some sympathy that could inform me from moment to moment, how you do & how you feel.

'Tell Fanny something about me. Ask her where she thinks I am. Say I am a great way off, & going further & further, but that I shall turn round & come back again some day. Tell her

I have not forgotten her little mug & that I shall chuse a very
pretty one. Montagu said this morning about eight o'clock
upon the road, "Just now little Fanny is going to plungity
plunge." Was he right?'[11]

Godwin remembering little Fanny in her bath enjoying 'plungity
plunge' was a different being from the writer who combined ignorance of man's everyday nature with fanatical devotion to logic. His
intelligence and his emotions were usually at war with each other,
but in these letters which he wrote to his wife there is a release
from the restraint of the intellect. His faith in man's great potentialities was for the time being overborne by trifles such as 'plungity
plunge', a child's merriment, and happy companionship with a
friend. Here was a genial Godwin who could melt the frozen areas
round Mary's heart as she wrote:

'Men are spoilt by frankness. . . . I will add what will gratify
your benevolence, if not your heart, that on the whole I may
be termed happy. You are a tender, affectionate creature; and
I feel it thrilling through my frame giving and promising
pleasure. . . . I find you can write the kind of letter a friend
ought to write, and give an account of your movements. I
hailed the sunshine and moonlight and travelled with you
scenting the fragrant gale—Enable me still to be your company, and I will allow you to peep over my shoulder, and see
me under the shade of my green blind, thinking of you, and all
I am to hear, and feel when you return—you may read my
heart—if you will. . . . I am not fatigued with solitude—yet
I have not relished my solitary dinner. A husband is a convenient
part of the furniture of a house, unless he be a clumsy fixture. I
wish you, from my soul, to be rivetted in my heart; but I do not
desire to have you always at my elbow—though at this moment
I did not care if you were. Yours truly and tenderly, Mary.'[12]

The two travellers on their way to Etruria met Dr Samuel Parr,
the distinguished educationist and author and friend of Godwin,
whom they intended visiting; but he dissuaded them. His daughter
had eloped with one of the Doctor's pupils, a Mr Wynn, a young

man of eighteen. The couple were by now at Gretna Green and the Doctor was overwhelmed by the event.

Godwin and his companion pursued the road to Etruria, continuing to keep the exhausting time-table they had imposed upon themselves. 'Every night we have ceased to travel at eleven; every morning we have risen at four.' . . . They reached Birmingham and saw the remains of Joseph Priestley's house, which had been burned down along with the Unitarian church during the anti-Jacobin riots of 1791, and reached Etruria a little after eight. Their reception appeared to be cordial, although Mr Wedgwood had written a letter to prevent their coming. However, they had not received it and here they were, as Godwin sent news to Fanny, in 'the land of mugs'. Mary's tender letter had rejoiced him. 'You cannot imagine how happy your letter made me,' he wrote back.

'No creature expresses, because no creature feels, the tender affections, so perfectly as you do; &, after all one's philosophy, it must be confessed that the knowledge that there is some one that takes an interest in our happiness, something like that which each man feels in his own, is extremely gratifying. We love, as it were, to multiply our consciousness . . . even at the hazard of what Montagu described so pathetically one night upon the New Road, of opening avenues for pain & misery to attack us.'[13]

Small clouds blew up, due largely to Godwin's inability to express himself with light affection. So quickly he fell into the role of philosopher.

'One of the pleasures I promised myself in my excursion, was to increase my value in your estimation, & I am not disappointed. What we possess without intermission, we inevitably hold light; it is a refinement in voluptuousness, to submit to voluntary privations. Separation is the image of death; but it is Death stripped of all that is most tremendous, & his dart purged of its deadly venom. I always thought St. Paul's rule, that we should die daily, an exquisite Epicurean maxim. The practice of it, would give to life a double relish.'[14]

Sometimes letters got delayed, which caused Godwin the sort of anxiety and foreboding that usually Mary indulged in.

'What am I to think?' he wrote. 'The least I can think is, that you recollect me with less tenderness & impatience than I reflect on you. There is a general sadness in the sky; the clouds are shutting round me, & seem depressed with moisture; every thing tunes the soul to melancholy.'[15]

This was new language for him to employ. Perhaps he had caught the tone from her, particularly just now when they were separated and could not always account for the delay in receiving letters. Then the episode of Miss Pinkerton added tension. Miss Pinkerton, a previous acquaintance of Godwin, had become strongly attracted to him and now made similar proposals to those made by Mary herself in the past to Mr and Mrs Fuseli. There was no real danger to Mary's marriage, yet the possibilities of another desertion were more than she could contemplate.

What right had Miss Pinkerton to intrude on this marriage, which was still in its early stages, still fragile and beset by theories that had not yet been proved in action? Would Godwin's 'icy philosophy' withstand this unexpected attack on his defences? Mary was frightened. Miss Pinkerton was writing to Godwin, trying to persuade him to make an appointment with her. In Mary's estimation it was outrageous. But how much responsibility in all this was Godwin's? 'You judge not in your own case as in that of another,' she reproached him.

'You give a softer name to folly and immorality when it flatters—yes, I must say it—your vanity. ... You treat with a mildness calculated to foster it a romantic selfishness and pamper conceit, which will even lead the object to—I was going to say misery—but I believe her incapable of feeling it. ... Yet you, at the very moment, commenced a correspondence with her whom you had previously almost neglected—you brought me a letter without a conclusion—and you changed countenance at the reply. My old wounds bleed afresh.'[16]

Poor Mary! There was no doubt that the affair caused her acute misery. The more she thought of Miss Pinkerton the deeper she sank into the familiar slough of jealousy and despondency. 'Sooner than endure the hundred[th] part of what I have suffer[ed] I could wish my poor Fanny and self asleep at the bottom of the sea.'[17] These words in view of Mary's recent history frightened Godwin and he made haste to calm her. Unfortunately Miss Pinkerton intended to visit Mary, to whom the idea was most unpleasant. She wrote to the lady, first sending the note to Godwin for his approval.

'Miss Pinkerton, I forbear to make any comments on your strange behaviour, but unless you can determine to behave with propriety, you must excuse me for expressing a wish not to see you at our house.' Godwin replied to Mary asking her to defer sending the note until one or two o'clock. He also crossed out 'strange behaviour' and substituted 'incomprehensible conduct'—'The delay,' he assured her, 'can be of no consequence, & I like to have a thing lay a little time on my mind before I judge.'[18]

Mary had succeeded in putting Miss Pinkerton to flight without hurt to her personal philosophy. There was some inconsistency in her possessive attitude but there was much common sense and the justification of a lesson learned with bitter suffering. Godwin could not match her in depth of experience. Nothing in his life could parallel those terrible moments when she drew the filthy water of the Thames into her lungs and, pressing her sodden clothes to her body, made ready to sink to the bottom. She had tasted death then and knew the piercing loneliness of the moment of passing. Not for a mere Miss Pinkerton would she risk another such experience, and if Godwin's vanity was hurt it was a wound that would quickly heal.

The note to Miss Pinkerton terminated the affair; but for a repentant reply: 'At length I am sensible of the impropriety of my conduct. Tears and communication afford me relief.'

Mary was victorious and her reflections would find outlet in the book she was writing. Even so there was much left over to feed a sad philosophical mood, but she sought relief in contemplating nature. Everina was not overjoyed to meet her brother-in-law at Etruria and avoided the first meal at which he appeared in Wedgwood's house. It lasted from three o'clock until eleven and was a test of endurance which any young woman might hope to avoid. But when next day a visit to the manufactory was organized she made one of the party and consented to talk to Godwin. The event proved most interesting for all. She was in high spirits and helped choose the mug for little Fanny.

'Tell Fanny,' Godwin wrote to Mary, 'we have chosen a mug for her & another for Lucas [a neighbour's little son]. . . . With respect to their beauty, you will set it forth with such eloquence as your imagination will supply. . . . Your William (do you know me by that name?) affectionately salutes the trio, M., F., & last & least (in stature at least) little W.'

Mary at home was getting impatient. She could go out little and her writing was not giving her much satisfaction. Fanny kept her company and babbled about 'Man'. Mrs Reveley came one evening to drink tea and they spent a day together. Even so time passed slowly.

'Pray tell me the precise time, I mean when it is fixed,' she wrote to Godwin. 'I do believe I shall be glad to see you!—if you return—and I will keep a good look out. William is all alive and my appearance is no longer doubtful—you, I dare say, will perceive the difference. What a fine thing it is to be a man! You were very good to write such a long letter. Adieu. Take care of yourself—now I have ventured on you, I should not like to lose you.' [19]

The travellers, on the eve of leaving Etruria, spent a last festive evening at the theatre at Stoke-on-Trent. Their company numbered nine and this made up one half of the whole audience, excluding the gallery. Godwin did not enjoy the event; he thought the actors would have done better to stick to the potter's wheel. Next morning they visited Hardcastle Tunnel, travelling in a small boat drawn by a horse, and in parts where the light did not penetrate and they had to depend on candles, pushing their way along with boat-staves applied to the tunnel walls. Montagu had proposed to Sarah Wedgwood and been accepted; at least the young lovers appreciated the adventure. Godwin was anxious because few letters from Mary were arriving.

They left Etruria at five o'clock the next morning en route for Derby where they intended visiting Dr Erasmus Darwin—the grandfather of Charles Darwin—and Dr Parr. On their arrival at Derby they learned that Dr Darwin had gone to Shrewsbury for a few days and they decided they could not wait for his return. 'So extraordinary a man, so truly a phenomenon as we should probably have found him,' wrote Godwin to Mary, 'I think we ought not to have scrupled the sacrifice of thirty-six hours.' Having failed to see Darwin they visited his friend of forty years, Mr Bage, philanthropist and author.

'We spent a most delightful day in his company. When we met him, I had taken no breakfast, &, though we had set off from Burton that morning at six, & I spent the whole morning in riding & walking, I felt no inconvenience in waiting for food until our dinner-time, at two.'

Eventually they arrived at the house of Dr Parr and found there the Gretna Green couple, Mr and Mrs Wynn.

'You cannot imagine anything like Mr Wynn and his wife,' Godwin wrote two days later. 'He is a raw, country booby of eighteen, his hair about his ears and a beard that has never deigned to submit to the stroke of the razor. . . . Poor Sarah . . . has an uncommon understanding, & an exquisite sensibility, which glows in her complexion, & flashes from her eyes. Yet she is silly enough to imagine that she shall be happy in love & a cottage, with John Wynn.'

They proceeded to Warwick and from there walked to Kenilworth Castle, the former seat of Simon de Montfort, Earl of Leicester, founder of the House of Commons. From Warwickshire they went to Cambridge, still fifty-three miles from home, where Mary was beginning to lose both patience and temper, and when Monday passed without sight of them her patience snapped, and she gave vent to her ill feeling.

'I wrote to you to Dr Parr's—you take no notice of my letter—
Previous to your departure I requested you not to torment me
by leaving the day of your return undecided. But whatever
tenderness you took away with you seems to have evaporated
on the journey, and new objects—and the homage of vulgar
minds—restored you to your icy Philosophy. . . . Your being
so late to-night, and the chance of your not coming, shews so
little consideration, that unless you suppose me a stick or a
stone, you must have forgot to think—as well as to feel, since
you have been on the wing. I am afraid to add what I feel.'[20]

This was a harsh letter; fortunately the travellers arrived without
much further delay and were forgiven, and Mary's good temper was
restored. She continued with the writing of her novel; in addition
to which she was composing a series of essays called *Fragments of
Letters on the Management of Infants*. She remembered the 'petty
cares' which had obscured the morning of her own life: 'continual
restraints on the most trivial matters, unconditional submission to
orders'. At least her own daughter had escaped those miseries and
she hoped by her new book to make life more pleasant for other
young children. Little Fanny, with her 'strong well-formed limbs
and florid complexion', was an example to follow, and the coming
infant would further illustrate her ideas on bringing up children.
In this matter as in many others Mary was full of confidence.

These were the last days of her pregnancy, and it was a happy
period. She felt well, she visited her friends as usual, and her relations with Godwin were maturing with a rich promise of future
happiness. In one of her recent letters she confessed: 'I must tell
you that I love you better than I supposed I did when I promised
to love you for ever.'

19

Birth of a Second Daughter and Death of Mary

Mary was in excellent spirits; her husband was at home again and their satisfactory partnership could be resumed. She was, as Godwin wrote in his *Memoirs*, a worshipper of domestic life,

'she loved to observe the growth of affection between me and her daughter, then three years of age, as well as my anxiety respecting the child not yet born. . . . The serenity of her countenance, the increasing sweetness of her manners, and that consciousness of enjoyment that seemed ambitious that every one she saw should be happy as well as herself, were matters of general observation to all her acquaintance. She had always possessed, in an unparalleled degree, the art of communicating happiness.'

It is true she had been wounded by the disapproval of Mrs Siddons and Mrs Inchbald, and others holding their views, who since her marriage had never come near her. This was indeed a disappointment, the more severe because she had never attempted to conceal the truth about her relationship with Imlay, even going so far as to explain the facts to persons totally indifferent to her. But her marriage had revealed the truth to all, or rather it revealed what some people, who knew the truth, had not wished to see.

She had insisted upon having a woman midwife, a Mrs Blenkinsop of the Westminster Lying-in Hospital, wishing to show her confidence in her own sex, but she engaged no nurse. She had visited Mrs Blenkinsop at the Hospital several times and in addition she had been examined by her old acquaintance, Dr George Fordyce. Anthony Carlisle, surgeon and close friend of Godwin, was keeping in touch. It seemed every precaution had been taken and Mary, cheerful and optimistic, had no qualms when on Wednesday, 30th August, at five o'clock in the morning labour pains set in. There was no cause for alarm and Godwin went off to his study. Mary dressed and had breakfast. Soon after she wrote to Godwin:

'I have no doubt of seeing the animal today, but must wait for Mrs Blenkinsop to guess at the hour—I have sent for her—Pray send me the newspaper—I wish I had a novel, or some book of sheer amusement, to excite curiosity, and while away the time—Have you any thing of the kind?'[1]

She had belittled childbirth. It was, she maintained, over-dramatized, and women would be well advised to treat it as a normal occurrence. After Fanny's birth she had been up and about within the week, so Godwin could expect her at the dinner-table in a day or two after the event. Following upon her first note to him came another:

'Mrs Blenkinsop tells me that everything is in a fair way, and that there is no fear of the event being put off till another day—Still, *at present*, she thinks, I shall not immediately be freed from my load—I am very well—Call me before dinner time, unless you receive another message from me.'[2]

He was not due home to dinner that day, for he had been invited to dine with Mr and Mrs Reveley. At three o'clock, an hour after she had retired to her room, Mary sent another note: 'Mrs Blenkinsop tells me that I am in the most natural state, and can promise me a safe delivery—But I must have a little patience.' There was a hint in this that she was having difficulties, and in fact the delivery was not entirely normal. Godwin returned home in the early evening but Mary did not wish him to be present at the birth. He waited in the parlour downstairs and at half past eleven he was informed that a girl had been born. The 'William' they had both talked into being was not to be theirs, but the little girl, Mary, would make good the loss. Not that they had much time to dwell on such a small disappointment, for all was not well with the mother. Mary had had an agonizing delivery and was having fainting fits. Mrs Blenkinsop became deeply alarmed; it seemed the placenta had not been discharged and the patient was in acute pain.

Godwin on being informed of this rushed off to the Westminster Hospital and brought back with him Dr Poignand, physician and obstetrician. He started at once to remove the placenta and thought he had succeeded. Unfortunately it broke and he had to deal with the pieces, but, as it transpired, some remained in place. During this process Mary suffered such excruciating pain that later on she told Godwin that nothing she had experienced before had equalled it. Only the determination not to leave him kept her alive.

She wished to see her old friend, Dr George Fordyce, but Dr Poignand was opposed to this, as Dr Fordyce was not an obstetrician. Mary insisted and Dr Poignand left her and said in the circumstances he would not return, a fatal mistake. Fordyce came that afternoon and took an optimistic view of the case. Mary, he pronounced, was now out of danger, a verdict that so encouraged Godwin, who had spent the whole day in the sick-room, that he felt he could attend to some urgent business away from home. He was absent the whole day, and when he returned Mary seemed better, but she was alarmingly weak. Anthony Carlisle came on Saturday evening and did not report anything alarming. Yet it is surprising that Godwin was so far relieved of his anxiety that he passed Sunday morning making a round of social calls in company with Basil Montagu.

'Sunday, the third of September,' Godwin wrote in his *Memoirs*, 'I now regard as the day, that finally decided on the fate of the object dearest to my heart that the universe contained. Encouraged by what I considered as the progress of her recovery, I did not return till dinner-time. On my return I found a degree of anxiety in every face. She had had a sort of shivering-fit and had expressed some anxiety at the length of my absence

... I felt a pang at having been so long and so unreasonably absent, and determined that I would not repeat the fault.'

During her shivering-fit every muscle of the body trembled, her teeth chattered and the bed shook under her. This continued for five minutes. Later, she told Godwin that it had been a struggle between life and death and that she had been more than once on the point of expiring.

Godwin, in agony of mind, rushed out between two and three in the morning to get Dr Poignand. It seems that the piece of the placenta that Dr Poignand had not succeeded in removing was poisoning her system. Godwin also sent for Dr Fordyce, and because of this Dr Poignand eventually declined to pay any further visits. Dr Fordyce, when he called on Tuesday, brought with him Mr Clarke, surgeon of New Burlington Street.

'I pertinaciously persisted in viewing the fair side of things,' Godwin wrote in his *Memoirs*, 'and therefore the interval between Sunday and Tuesday evening, did not pass without some mixture of cheerfulness.... Dr Fordyce forbad the child's having the breast, and we therefore procured puppies to draw off the milk.... Nothing could exceed the equanimity, the patience and affectionateness of the poor sufferer. I intreated her to recover; I dwelt with trembling fondness on every favourable circumstance.... Her smiles and kind speeches rewarded my affection.'

Fordyce had ordered that she should be supplied freely with wine, and on Wednesday afternoon Godwin began to hold the wineglass to her lips.

'I knew neither what was too much, nor what was too little,' he wrote. 'Having begun, I felt compelled, under every dis-advantage to go on. This lasted for three hours. Towards the end of that time I happened foolishly to ask the servant ... what she thought of her mistress. She replied that in her judgment she was going as fast as possible.'

Godwin in great anxiety entreated Basil Montagu to fetch Mr

Carlisle, who was four miles out of town. They returned together that Wednesday evening, after which Carlisle never left the patient until she died. But he could do nothing, and when next day Mr Clarke, the surgeon, came he too was powerless, for the patient was too weak for an operation. She was surrounded by doctors and male and female friends, all combining in the battle for her life. At times she seemed to rally.

'I retired to bed for a few hours on Wednesday night,' Godwin wrote. 'Towards morning he [Carlisle] came into my room with an account that the patient was surprisingly better. . . . The greatest anguish I have any conception of, consists in that crushing of a new-born hope which I had already two or three times experienced. . . . Till now it does not appear that she had any serious thoughts of dying; but on Friday and Saturday . . . she occasionally spoke as if she expected it. . . . Her faculties were in too decayed a state, to be able to follow any train of ideas with force. . . . Her religion . . . was not calculated to be the torment of a sick bed; and in fact, during her whole illness, not one word of a religious cast fell from her lips.'

But the patient was not in truth any better, and she knew it. When Godwin, with the utmost tact, talked to her about the children, trying to discover what were her plans for them, she said: 'I know what you are thinking of,' but added that she had nothing to say on the subject. She was affectionate and compliant to the last, he wrote. Her husband's constant presence at the bedside was her greatest comfort. When he gave her a pain-relieving drug, she exclaimed: 'Oh Godwin, I am in heaven!' And he, true to character, replied: 'You mean, my dear, that your physical sensations are somewhat easier.' She did mean that, and much more. She thought of the past, when she had to fight alone against mental pain, almost as acute as the physical agony she was now enduring, but now she had a partner who shared everything with her. 'He is the kindest, best man in the world,'[3] she whispered. They were almost her last words.

For two days she had no shivering fits but was so weak that Mr Carlisle said her continuance was almost miraculous. On Saturday night Godwin, worn out by anxiety and sorrow, retired to bed, but at six o'clock in the morning of Sunday, 10th September, Mr Carlisle called him to come to his wife. She died with him beside her at twenty minutes before eight.

Godwin, on this day, recorded in his diary: '20 minutes before eight. . . .' He was left alone with his grief while his friends Marshall and Basil Montagu arranged the funeral, and Mary Hays and Mrs Reveley attended to the children. He had retreated to Marshall's lodging, where he sat writing letters. To write was his only solace. He found it impossible to attend the funeral, which began at ten o'clock on 15th September.

His first note had been to Holcroft:

'My wife is now dead. She died this morning at eight o'clock. She grew worse before your letter arrived. Nobody has a greater call to reproach himself except for want of kindness and attention in which I hope I have not been very deficient. . . . But reproach will answer no good purpose, and I will not harbour it. I firmly believe that there does not exist her equal in the world. I know from experience we were formed to make each other happy. I have not the least expectation that I can now ever know happiness again.'[4]

On the day of her funeral he sent a note to Anthony Carlisle, who had been so whole-heartedly devoted.

'My mind is extremely sunk and languid,' he wrote, 'but I husband my thoughts, and shall do very well. I have been but once since you saw me in a train of thought that gave me alarm. One of my wife's books now lies near me but I avoid opening it. I took up a book on the education of children, but that impressed me too forcibly with my forlorn and disabled state with respect to the two poor animals left under my protection, and I threw it aside. If you have any . . . consolation in store for me, be at pains to bestow . . . it. But above all be severely sincere. I ought to be acquainted with my own defects and to trace their nature in the effects they produce.'[5]

Godwin's grief had torn the veil from before his eyes; he contemplated himself, not as an 'icy philosopher' but as the husband of a woman of genius who had not yet fulfilled the promise of her first output. She was only thirty-eight years of age at the time of her death and was still educating herself. Her last book, *The Wrongs of Woman*, slowly written, was never completed because she was now far more conscious of the niceties of composition and balanced structure. Also, with maturity she lost her excess of assurance in her own values. Had she lived undoubtedly she would have experienced the same need for self-appraisal which now assailed him.

In his *Memoirs* he analyses both his own and Mary's inner nature.

'I have been stimulated ... by an ambition for intellectual distinction but ... I have been discouraged when I have endeavoured to cast the sum of my intellectual value, by finding that I did not possess, in the degree of some other man, an intuitive perception of intellectual beauty. I have perhaps a strong and lively sense of the pleasures of the imagination; but I have seldom been right in assigning to them their proportionate value, but by dint of persevering examination. ... What I wanted in this respect, Mary possessed, in a degree superior to any other person I ever knew. The strength of her mind lay in intuition. She was often right, by this means only, in matters of mere speculation. Her religion, her philosophy ... were the pure result of feeling and taste. She adopted one opinion, and rejected another, spontaneously, by a sort of tact, and the force of a cultivated imagination; and yet, though perhaps, in the strict sense of the term, she reasoned little, it is surprising what a degree of soundness is to be found in her determinations. But, if this quality was of use to her in topics that seem the proper province of reasoning, it was much more so in matters directly appealing to the intellectual taste. In a robust and unwavering judgment of this sort, there is a kind of witchcraft; when it decides justly, it produces a responsive vibration in every ingenuous mind. In this sense, my oscillation and scepticism were fixed by her boldness. When a true opinion emanated in this way from another mind, the conviction produced in my own assumed a similar character, instantaneous and firm. This species of intellect probably differs from the other, chiefly in the relation of earlier and later. What the one perceives instantaneously . . . the other receives only by degrees. What it wants, seems to be nothing more than a minute attention to first impressions, and a just appreciation of them; habits that are never so effectually generated, as by the daily recurrence of a striking example. This light was lent to me for a very short period, and is now extinguished for ever!'

Godwin, who thought it was wrong to indulge long in depression and mourning, now roused himself. The children had come home.

'The poor children! I am myself totally unfitted to educate them', he wrote to Mrs Cotton. 'The scepticism which perhaps sometimes leads me right in matters of speculation is torment to me when I would attempt to direct the infant mind. I am the most unfit person for this office; she was the best qualified in the world.'[6]

He was equally unfitted to organize his household. A Miss Louisa Jones took charge for the time being, with the aid of a nurse for the children. Pitiful small sufferers; theirs was to be a sad and melancholy childhood. Later, one day when Coleridge had been to dine he wrote to Southey: 'The cadaverous silence of Godwin's children is to me quite catacombish.'[7] It was not surprising. There was no permanent substitute mother. Miss Jones left after a short time; the place was too gloomy, since Godwin insisted on deep quiet in order not to be disturbed at his work. She would have liked to replace Mary in his affection but failed to rouse him. On her departure Godwin's sister Hannah came for a while, then others took a turn. Eventually, in 1801, Godwin remarried. The little girls must have found it hard to adapt to these changes. For Fanny, a beloved mother had vanished. In view of her sad life subsequently it may be surmised she never recovered from the loss.

Godwin was engaged in writing his *Memoirs* which when published were for the most part extremely unfavourably reviewed and resulted in much posthumous abuse of Mary. He had been over-frank in his account and had revealed the humiliating story of her liaison with

Imlay. It was not a wise thing to have done, and Mary's sisters indignantly broke off relations with him. But Godwin, determined that all should be known about this remarkable woman who had been his wife, had applied to her friends, in particular to Johnson the publisher, for details. She had lived with a man without being married to him, she had had an illegitimate child, she had twice tried to commit suicide. It was a disquieting record; it was not really surprising that the *Memoirs* were received with coolness and condemned as 'the most hurtful book of the year 1798'. In a second edition the memoirs were drastically cut, but the damage had been done.

20

'An Undaunted and Masculine Spirit'

Mary can be called a child of the French Revolution. Its philosophy inspired her and was the foundation of her hopes for the future. Although she was in Paris during the worst period of the Terror and on one occasion had her feet spattered with blood, like Tom Paine, no temporary excesses or abuses could quite destroy her confidence in the final outcome of the great movement. As Robespierre stated, the purpose of the Revolution was to put into laws the moral truths culled from the philosophers. The most influential of the latter was Rousseau, who had always exercised a powerful influence over Mary, and many of his ideas are echoed in her *Vindication*. In truth, her mind was so dominated by the thought of the enslavement of both men and women by outworn codes of behaviour that she considered the Revolution both inevitable and justified. But for her, rights of men must necessarily include rights of women, and when the Assemblée Nationale treated with contumely the suggestion that women should share political power, at least two of its leading figures, Talleyrand and Condorcet, upheld this view.

The Revolution soon lost what little attraction it had ever had for most English people, even for many with moderately progressive views. Its early idealism was forgotten as more and more was known of the brutal acts that marked its course. Along with this disillusionment went mistrust and dislike of the few English

'Jacobins', who still proclaimed their faith in the final outcome of the struggle. For them a new world would come into being; progress was ensured once men turned their thoughts to 'the grand pursuits that exalt the human race and promote general happiness' as Mary had averred in the *Vindication*. But this was not the general opinion; 'progress' has many facets and those given it by the philosophers were not particularly acceptable to the common run of people.

On Mary's death the press announced the event by a number of obituary notices, and when a little later Godwin put his *Memoirs* into print further notices appeared, few of them favourable. Mary Hays in the *Gentleman's Magazine* composed the most appreciative account of her old friend; together with that published by the *Analytical Review*, for which Mary had written so many articles and literary reviews, they were the only ones that did any justice to her.

'Mary Wollstonecraft was a woman of uncommon talent and considerable knowledge, well-known throughout Europe by her literary work,' wrote Mary Hays. 'For soundness of understanding and sensibility of heart, she was perhaps rarely equalled. Her practical skill in education was even superior to her speculations upon that subject.'

On the publication of Godwin's *Memoirs* the *Analytical Review* attempted to counter some of the less kind obituary notices.

'It is obvious that Mrs Godwin entertained singular opinions, and reduced them to practice. This circumstance will invite many to criticise and some to censure her character. We think it was due to Mrs Godwin to have stated *how* these opinions were formed and the *reasons* by which she supported them. . . . The narrative gives no correct history of the formation of Mrs Godwin's mind. . . . First Mrs Godwin's notions and practice respecting marriage will meet violent objections.'

The *Monthly Mirror* gave grudging praise.

'Upon the whole the life of Mrs Godwin leaves no very considerable impression upon our feelings: had it pleased heaven to prolong her days and extend her labours, the world by and by might possibly have been in possession of facts which would have redounded more to the celebrity of her name. ....'

The *European Magazine*, April 1798, was adverse:

'The Lady ... appears to have possessed good qualities ... but with an overweening conceit of herself, much obstinacy and self-will and a disposition to run counter to established practices and opinions. The latter part of her life was blemished with actions which must consign her name to posterity as one whose example if followed would be attended by the most pernicious consequences to society, a philosophical wanton, breaking down the bars intended to restrain licentiousness. A female unrestrained by the obligations of religion, is soon ripe for licentious indecorums. Such was the catastrophe of a female philosopher of the new order; such the events of her life; and such the apology of her conduct. It will be read with disgust by every female who has any pretentions to delicacy. ....'

The *Critical Review* redeemed to some extent the offensiveness of these opinions by a forthright statement:

'Mrs Godwin was not only possessed of great genius ... but had also an undaunted and masculine spirit. ... Her sentiments however in some respects are too much at variance with those which have been generally adopted. We are not afraid to express our opinion that the doctrines upon which she has principally insisted are unfriendly to human happiness, and if practically followed might injure the sex they are intended to vindicate and protect.'

The *Anti-Jacobin* continued for no less than three years to publish attacks on Mary and her husband, seeking both in their private lives and their works evidence of corruption. 'Her *Rights of Woman* which the superficial imagine to be profound and the profound know to be superficial—had little title to the character of ingenuity.' Richard Polwhele published a poem in 1799.

'An Undaunted and Masculine Spirit'

'See Wollstonecraft, whom no decorum checks,
Arise, the intrepid champion of her sex:
O'er humbled men assert the sovereign claim,
And slight the timid blush of maiden shame.'

The Reverend gentleman, not finding poetry adequate for his strong feelings, made an analysis in prose of Mary's life.

'I cannot but think,' he wrote, 'that the hand of Providence is visible in her life, in her death, and in the *Memoirs* themselves. ... As she had died a death that strongly marked the distinction of the sexes, by pointing out the destiny of women and the diseases to which they were peculiarly liable, so her husband was permitted in writing the *Memoirs* to labour under a temporary infatuation, so that every incident might be seen without a gloss and every fact exposed without an apology.'

In the index of this magazine, under the heading 'Prostitution' the words 'See Mary Wollstonecraft' had been inserted. [1]

Her stay with the Kingsborough family in Ireland was recalled. The tragedy of Mary Elizabeth King, Mary's former pupil, who had eloped with her cousin, which led to his being shot by Lord Kingsborough, was attributed to the influence of the governess.

Mary was vulnerable on two scores. First she was one of the hated English 'Jacobins', considered agents of the satanic Robespierre—a group which was, by the time of her death, highly unpopular—and secondly, she dealt with long-established prejudices in matters of sex and the legal expropriation of women's property. The law was a scandal, for it worked wholly in the interests of one sex, and was so crushingly unfair that men feared lest any wide exposure of its workings might lead to reform. Mary had assailed the stronghold of masculine greed and tyranny; for such a rebel there could be no mercy, no appreciation of her struggle against flagrant injustice, no understanding of her difficult life with its overtones of passion and revolt.

It was some time before Mary's influence on the customs and laws of her country began to work, not only directly through her own output but also indirectly through her impact on other writers.

There were four editions of the *Vindication* between 1833 and 1856, and then no more until 1890. But the leaven was beginning to take effect; she was the first woman to cry out against and call attention to the incredibly unfair position of women in the legal sphere, and in the social sphere where she had only her beauty to fend for her. When in 1838 the Chartist Movement made known its principles, women's suffrage was one of them.

It is not known whether John Stuart Mill ever read the *Vindication*, yet there was no more eloquent propagator of Mary's ideas than he. In his book *The Subjection of Women* he wrote:

'All the moralities tell them that it is the duty of woman . . . to live for others . . . to have no life but in their affections. . . . When we put together three things—first, the natural attraction between opposite sexes; secondly, the wife's entire dependence on the husband, every privilege or pleasure . . . depending entirely on his will; and lastly, that the principal object of human pursuit, consideration and all objects of social ambition, can . . . be obtained by her only through him, it would be a miracle if the object of being attractive to men had not become the polar star of feminine education. . . . The disabilities to which women are subject from the mere fact of their birth, are the solitary examples of the kind in modern legislation. In no instance except this, which comprehends half the human race, are the higher social functions closed against anyone by a fatality of birth.'[2]

Mill was elected a Member of Parliament in 1865 and the women's movement was then given its first real impetus. Highly qualified members such as Mrs Garrett Anderson, physician and the first female mayor of England, and Emily Davies, one of the founders of Girton College, and Mrs Belloc, organized a petition to Parliament, and women's suffrage societies came into existence all over England. After years of discussion, meetings in drawing-rooms, halls, schools, chapels, on street corners and village greens, and long processions of women through the streets of London, the suffragettes were still opposed by Parliament, for the Prime Minister, Herbert Asquith, was determined not to give in to them. In 1913, under the leadership of Christabel Pankhurst, the movement became militant and caused an uproar throughout the country, Finally, in June 1917, when women's activity during the First World War had convinced men that women were capable of doing work equally with men, work of the greatest importance, and in other ways were eligible for electoral franchise, the Bill for the enfranchisement was carried in the House of Commons.

It was not until the Education Act of 1870 that education was made compulsory for girls as well as boys. Three years later Girton College was founded at Hitchin, then it was moved to Cambridge, and in 1876 Newnham, also at Cambridge.

The Married Women's Property Act of 1882 redressed one of the most outstanding injustices to women when the law established that they were capable of acquiring, holding and disposing of by will any real or personal property in the same manner as if they were single, without the intervention of any trustee. Legal equality between the sexes politically, professionally and educationally was arrived at approximately by 1929. But the battle for economic equality has still to be won; however, in 1970 it was a woman Cabinet Minister, Barbara Castle, who steered through the Commons a Bill on equal pay which brought economic equality between the sexes significantly nearer.

During this crucial period in the struggle for women's rights Mary's name has rarely been mentioned. Along with others who participated in the Reform Movement, Tom Paine, Godwin, Dr Price, she has been largely forgotten, yet she was the pioneer of the reform of women's place in society. Many of her ideas have been adopted, but a great number still remain to be fulfilled. Her name is certainly prominent in the records of the women's movement, although later figures such as Christabel Pankhurst and Millicent Fawcett have tended to eclipse that of the original advocate.

Godwin's *Memoirs* were translated into French and German; the book was widely read, and later reviews of it became far less censorious. Most of the blame laid on Godwin was for revealing so much that in the opinion of the general public was not in Mary's favour. Few lives could stand up to such complete candour in the relating. Slowly too the true quality of Mary's life and works triumphed over preconceived notions. It was realized how faithfully she had held to her ideals, how much travelled and experienced she was, how deeply she had suffered, and how disinterested had been her acts. In fact there were not many women who could compare with her, and her rare quality, her charm, her impulsive sympathy, and her courage slowly became acknowledged. Her portrait by Opie, now in the National Portrait Gallery, revealed the whole truth about her. The womanly beauty, the look of compassion and intelligence in the eyes, the wide generous mouth, the feeling of victory over suffering and general serenity make it unforgettable. It is not surprising that Godwin worked for over thirty years with this portrait above his desk. He desired to be buried with her, and when the moment came this was done.

In 1814, the child whose birth cost her mother her life, Mary Wollstonecraft Godwin, now seventeen years old, attracted the notice of the poet Shelley. Her mother's name was one that resounded down the years and was revered by idealists and social reformers. Shelley and the young Mary met at the grave of the author of the *Vindication of the Rights of Woman* and lingered there to talk about her and their love for each other. They returned often, until in July 1814 they eloped, left the country, and were eventually married. Shelley was then composing *The Revolt of Islam* and he dedicated it to the daughter of the Mary who 'had left the earth'. That Mary was 'one whose life was like a setting planet mild'—words that express the rare quality of the portrait and do justice to its subject.

Reference Notes

The letters between Mary Wollstonecraft and her sisters, and from Mary to Fanny and George Blood, are in the possession of Lord Abinger; they were made available to Mr R. M. Wardle for his *Mary Wollstonecraft, A Critical Biography*. Extracts from this correspondence are referred to below as 'Letters'.

Chapter 1

    1. Wollstonecraft, Mary, *Mary, a Fiction*, 1788, pp. 12 and 13.

Chapter 2

    1, 2. Letters.
      3. *Letters to Imlay*, XXXII.
    4–7. Letters.

Chapter 3

    1. Wollstonecraft, Mary, *Thoughts on the Education of Daughters*, p. 79.
    2.   ,,   ,,   ,, ,, ,,   ,,   ,,   ,,   p. 74.
  3–11. Letters.
    12. Rousseau, *Émile*.

Chapter 4

    1. Quoted in Thompson, E. P., *The Making of the English Working Class*, p. 91.
    2. Wardle, *Mary Wollstonecraft; A Critical Biography*, p. 80.
  3, 4. Letters.

Chapter 5

    1. Wardle, *Mary Wollstonecraft*, p. 112.

    2. Burke, *Reflections on the Revolution in France.*

    3. *A Vindication of the Rights of Men*, p. 152.

  4, 5. Letters.

Chapter 6

    1. Ford, B. (ed.), *From Blake to Byron.*

    2. Mason, E., *The Mind of Henry Fuseli.*

    3. Jaloux, E., *J. H. Füssli*, p. 54.

    4. Letter to a writer apologizing for Rousseau. Wardle, *Mary Wollstonecraft*, p. 131.

    5. Wardle, *Mary Wollstonecraft*, p. 286.

    6. Godwin, W., *Political Justice.*

    7. Wollstonecraft, Mary, *Posthumous Works*, vol. i, p. 34.

  8, 9. Wardle, *Mary Wollstonecraft*, p. 140.

10, 11. *A Vindication of the Rights of Woman*, Chapter V.

Chapter 7

1 to 21 inclusive, *A Vindication of the Rights of Woman*, Chapter V.

22 to 25 inclusive, *A Vindication of the Rights of Woman*, Chapter XII.

Chapter 8

  1, 2. Wardle, *Mary Wollstonecraft*, p. 174.

    3.   „   „   „   p. 181.

    4. Wollstonecraft, Mary, *Posthumous Works*, vol. i, pp. 43–5.

Chapter 9

    1. Pope-Hennessy, Una, *Madame Roland*, p. 309.

    2.   „   „   „   „   p. 400.

    3.   „   „   „   „   p. 403.

    4.   „   „   „   „   p. 405.

    5.   „   „   „   „   p. 411.

  6, 7.   „   „   „   „   p. 457.

    8. *Letters to Imlay*, II.

    9. „   „   „   IV.

  10. „   „   „   V.

Chapter 10

    1. Pope-Hennessy, Una, *Madame Roland*, p. 491.

    2.   „   „   „   „   p. 496.

3. Pope-Hennessy, Una, *Madame Roland*, p. 530.
4. *Letters to Imlay*, X.
5.   „   „   „   XI.
6.   „   „   „   XII.
7.   „   „   „   XVI.
8.   „   „   „   XVII.
9. Wardle, *Mary Wollstonecraft*, p. 200.
10. Letters.
11. Pope-Hennessy, Una, *Madame Roland*, p. 536.
12.   „   „   „   „   P. 535.
13. *Letters to Imlay*, XVIII.
14. Wardle, *Mary Wollstonecraft*, p. 202.
15, 16. *Letters to Imlay*, XX.
17.   „   „   „   XXI.
18.   „   „   „   XXII.

Chapter 11

1. *Letters to Imlay*, XXI.
2.   „   „   „   XXII.
3.   „   „   „   XXIII.
4.   „   „   „   XXIV.
5.   „   „   „   XXVI.
6, 7.   „   „   „   XXVII.
8.   „   „   „   XXVIII.
9, 10.   „   „   „   XXIX.
11.   „   „   „   XXXI.
12.   „   „   „   XXXV.
13, 14.   „   „   „   XXXVI.
15, 16. *Supplement to Memoirs*, p. 247.
17. *Letters to Imlay*, XXXVI.
18. Wardle, *Mary Wollstonecraft*, p. 221.
19. *Letters to Imlay*, XXXVII.

Chapter 12

1. *A Vindication of the Rights of Woman*, Chapter I.
2. *Letters to Imlay*, XXXVIII.
3.   „   „   „   XXXIX.
4–7.   „   „   „   XL.

8, 9. Letters.

Chapter 13

1. *Letters to Imlay*, XLIV.
2.   „   „   „   XLII.
3.   „   „   „   XLIX.
4.   „   „   „   LI.

Chapter 14

1–3. *Letters written during a short residence in Sweden, Norway and Denmark*, I.
4.   „   „   „ „ „   „   „   „   „   „ III.
5.   „   „   „ „ „   „   „   „   „   „ IV.
6.   „   „   „ „ „   „   „   „   „   „ V.
7. *Letters to Imlay*, LV.
8.   „   „   „   LVI.
9.   „   „   „   LX.
10.   „   „   „   LXI.

11, 12. *Letters written during a short residence in Sweden, Norway and Denmark*, VIII.
13.   „   „   „ „ „   „   „   „   „   „ IX.

Chapter 15

1, 2. *Letters written during a short residence in Sweden, Norway and Denmark*, XII.
3, 4.   „   „   „ „ „   „   „   „   „   „ XIII.
5, 6.   „   „   „ „ „   „   „   „   „   „ XVI.
7, 8.   „   „   „ „ „   „   „   „   „   „ XVII.
9.   „   „   „ „ „   „   „   „   „   „ XVIII.
10, 11.   „   „   „ „ „   „   „   „   „   „ XIX.
12, 13.   „   „   „ „ „   „   „   „   „   „ XX.
14.   „   „   „ „ „   „   „   „   „   „ XXI.
15. *Letters to Imlay*, LXIV.
16.   „   „   „   LXV.

17–19. *Letters written during a short residence in Sweden, Norway and Denmark*, XXIII.
20. *Letters to Imlay*, LXVIII.

Chapter 16

1, 2. *Letters to Imlay*, LXVIII.

3, 4. *Letters to Imlay*, LXIX.
  5.   „   „   „   LXX.
  6.   „   „   „   LXXIV.
  7.   „   „   „   LXXV.
8, 9.   „   „   „   LXXVI.
 10.   „   „   „   LXXVII.
 11.   „   „   „   LXX.
 12. *Letters written during a short residence in Sweden, Norway and Denmark*;
     Wardle, *Mary Wollstonecraft*, p. 253.
 13. Wardle, *Mary Wollstonecraft*, p. 286.
 14. *Political Justice*, vol. III.
 15. Wardle, *Mary Wollstonecraft*, p. 259.

Chapter 17
  1. Wardle, *Godwin and Mary*, July 13 1796.
  2.   „   „   „   „   Aug. 2 „
3, 4.   „   „   „   „   „ 17 „
  5.   „   „   „   „   „ 22 „
  6.   „   „   „   „   „ 31 „
7, 8.   „   „   „   „   Sept. 4 „
  9.   „   „   „   „   „ 8 „
10, 11.   „   „   „   „   „ 10 „
 12.   „   „   „   „   „ 13 „
 13.   „   „   „   „   „ 15 „
 14.   „   „   „   „   „ 29 „
 15.   „   „   „   „   „ 30 „
 16.   „   „   „   „   Oct. 4 „
 17.   „   „   „   „   „ 7 „
 18.   „   „   „   „   „ 26 „
 19.   „   „   „   „   Nov. 3 „
 20.   „   „   „   „   „ 10 „
 21. Glynn, Rosalie, *William Godwin and his World*, p. 41.
 22. Wardle, *Godwin and Mary*, undated.
 23.   „   „   „   „   Nov. 28 1796.
 24.   „   „   „   „   Dec. 7 „
 25.   „   „   „   „   „ 13 „
26, 27.   „   „   „   „   „ 23 „

28. Wardle, *Godwin and Mary*, Dec. 28 1796.
29–31.   „   „   „   „   „ 31 „
32.   „   „   „   „   Jan. 1 1797.

Chapter 18

1. Wardle, *Mary Wollstonecraft*, p. 287.
2, 3.   „   „   „   p. 289.
4, 5.   „   „   „   p. 288.
6.   „   „   „   p. 290.
7. Wardle, *Godwin and Mary*, Apr. 20 1797.
8.   „   „   „   „ May 21 „
9. Wardle, *Mary Wollstonecraft*, p. 289.
10, 11. Wardle, *Godwin and Mary*, June 5 1797.
12.   „   „   „   „   „ 6 „
13, 14.   „   „   „   „   „ 10 „
15.   „   „   „   „   „ 12 „
16, 17.   „   „   „   „ July 4 „
18.   „   „   „   „ Aug. 9 „
19.   „   „   „   „ June 10 „
20.   „   „   „   „   „ 19 „

Chapter 19

1, 2. Wardle, *Godwin and Mary*, Aug. 30 1797.
3. Wardle, *Mary Wollstonecraft*, p. 306.
4, 5.   „   „   „   p. 307.
6.   „   „   „   p. 311.
7.   „   „   „   p. 324.

Chapter 20

1. Polwhele, R., *The Unsex'd Females*, 1798.
2. Mill, J. S., *On the Subjection of Women*, 1869.

Bibliography

BIRLEY, Robert, *The English Jacobins: from 1789 to 1802*, O.U.P., 1924.

BRAILSFORD, H. N., *Shelley, Godwin and their Circle*, London, 1913.

BROWN, F. K., *The Life of William Godwin*, Dent, London, 1926.

BURKE, Edmund, *Reflections on the Revolution in France*, London, 1790.

CARLYLE, Thomas, *The French Revolution. A History*, 3 vols., London, 1837.

FORD, Boris (editor), *From Blake to Byron*, Penguin.

GODWIN, William, *Things as They Are: or, The Adventures of Caleb Williams*, 3 vols., London, 1794; *An Enquiry concerning the Principles of Political Justice, and its Influence on General Virtue and Happiness*, 2nd edition, 2 vols., London, 1796; *Memoirs of the Author of the Vindication of the Rights of Woman*, Johnson, London, 1798; edited (with additional material) by W. Clark Durrant, Constable, London, 1927; Ed. *The Posthumous Works of the Author of 'A Vindication of the Rights of Woman'*, Johnson, London, 1798.

GRYLLS, G. R., *William Godwin and his World*, Odhams Press, London, 1953.

HARRIS, R. W., *England in the Eighteenth Century*, Blandford, London, 1963.

HOBSBAWM, E. J., *The Age of Revolution, 1789–1848*, Weidenfeld and Nicolson, London, 1962.

INCHBALD, Elizabeth, *A Simple Story*, 4 vols., London, 1791; edited by G. L. Strachey, London, 1908.

LIOTARD, J., *Johann Füssli, 1741–1825*, Musée de L'Orangerie, Paris, 1948.

LOOMIS, S., *Paris in the Terror*, Cape, London, 1965.

MASON, E. C., *The Mind of Henry Fuseli*, Routledge & Kegan Paul, London, 1951.

MILL, J. S., *On the Subjection of Women*, Oxford, 1869.

Bibliography

PAINE, Thomas, *Rights of Man: Being an Answer to Mr. Burke's Attack on the French Revolution*, 2 parts, London, 1791–2; edited by H. P. Bonner, 1907; *The Age of Reason: Being an investigation of true and fabulous Theology*, London, 1795.

POLWHELE, Richard, *The Unsex'd Females*, London, 1798.

POPE-HENNESSY, Una, *Madame Roland*, Nisbet, London, 1947.

ROUSSEAU, Jean-Jacques, *Œuvres complètes*, Bibliothèque de la Pléiade, Gallimard, Paris, 1959.

RUDÉ, George, *Revolutionary Europe 1783–1815*, Collins, London, 1964.

STORR, M. S., *Mary Wollstonecraft et le mouvement feministe dans la littérature anglaise*, Paris, 1931.

THOMPSON, E. R., *The Making of the English Working Class*, Penguin, 1960.

WARDLE, R. M., *Mary Wollstonecraft: A Critical Biography*, Richards Press, London, 1952; *Godwin and Mary*, Constable, London, 1967.

WATSON, J. S., *The Reign of George III*, O.U.P., 1959.

WILLEY, Basil, *The Eighteenth Century Background*, Chatto & Windus, London, 1946.

WOLLSTONECRAFT, Mary, *Thoughts on the Education of Daughters*, London, 1787; *Mary, a Fiction*, London, 1788; *A Vindication of the Rights of Men*, London, 1790; *An Historical and Moral View of the Origin and Progress of the French Revolution* (uncompleted), 1794; *Original Stories from Real Life*, with illustrations by William Blake, London, 1796; *A Vindication of the Rights of Woman*, London, 1792; *The Wrongs of Woman, or Maria* (vols. i–iii of Posthumous Works), 1798; *Letters Written during a short residence in Sweden, Norway and Denmark*, London, 1796; *Letters to Imlay*, Kegan Paul, 1879.

WOODCOCK, G., *William Godwin*, Penguin, 1946.

WOODWARD, W. E., *Tom Paine: America's Godfather*, London, 1947.

Index

Index